Eat Up Slim Down!

Annual Recipes ✳ 2011

200 Simply Delicious Recipes for Permanent Weight Loss

From the Editors of *Prevention*®

RODALE

Interior photography credits appear on page 358.
Book design by Barbara Reyes.

ISBN-13   978–1–60529–172–7

ISBN-10   1–60529–172–2

2 4 6 8 10 9 7 5 3 1   hardcover

SPECIAL THANKS

In grateful appreciation to all the contestants in the many *Prevention* recipe contests, we would like to thank all the readers of *Prevention* magazine and Prevention.com who were kind enough to share their delicious recipes, clever tips, and inspiring stories of weight loss. We salute you and wish you continued success.

And sincere, heartfelt thanks to the five weight-loss winners who shared their stories with us in personal profiles: Priscilla Bartlett, Sheri Harkness, Tanzy Kilcrease, Debra Lambert, and Sarah Montague.

A very special thank-you to everyone who had a hand in creating *Eat Up Slim Down Annual Recipes 2011*, especially Andrea Au Levitt, Carol Angstadt, JoAnn Brader, Hope Clarke, Anne Egan, Paige Hicks, Laurie Knoop, Christine Langfeld, Mitch Mandel, Marielle Messing, Stacy Petrokovitch, Sean Sabo, Kimberly Schmick, and Troy Schnyder.

Contents

Contributors

This book includes many of the delicious and creative recipes sent to us by weight-loss and health winners from across North America. All of the recipes have been prepared in the Rodale test kitchen, ensuring each one is delicious and easy to prepare. Here are this year's recipe contributors. We salute their innovative efforts in the kitchen and hope you'll enjoy using their recipes to reach your own weight-loss goals.

NAME AND RESIDENCE	RECIPE	PAGE
Amy Albani, Oceanside, California	Tuna-Stuffed Peppers	219
Virginia Anthony, Blowing Rock, North Carolina	Pasta-Ratatouille Casserole	224
Nicole Ayrey, Bronx, New York	Mousse-Filled Cannoli	314
Margaret Barclay, Niagara Falls, New York	Sweet Popcorn Treat	167
	Pumpkin Pie in a Cup	170
Linda Brockinton, Alexander, Arkansas	Heavenly Strawberry Cake	259
Mary Ellen Brown, Chicago, Illinois	Apple Delight	261
Kathy Burr, Plano, Texas	Chocolate Chip Cookies	159
Marla Clark, Moriarty, New Mexico	Falafel Burgers with Tzatziki Sauce	106
	Taste of Summer Steak and Spinach Salad	186
Mary Collins, Mt. Rest, South Carolina	Ms. Effie's Salmon Patties	117
Emily Cornwell, Wayne, West Virginia	Light Strawberry Trifle	311
Cynthia Davis, Glendale, Arizona	Mushroom-Spinach Lasagna	227
Jay Davis, Knoxville, Tennessee	Grilled Chicken with Zippy Bar-B-Q Sauce	198
Marcia Leigh Dier, Estacada, Oregon	Glazed Pumpkin-Date Bread	92
Vicky Dillingham, Plymouth, Florida	Apple-Walnut Pie	281
Ashley Domes, Bliss, New York	Chocolate Cream Pie	273
Marie Farrington, Dixmont, Maine	Blueberry Treat	168
Greg Fontenot, The Woodlands, Texas	Grilled Zucchini Sandwiches	120

Introduction

Food is your friend. When you're dieting, it's easy to think that food is the enemy. Not true, insist the weight-loss winners featured in *Eat Up Slim Down 2011*. In this edition, you'll find delicious recipes these winners ate to get trim and stay that way. You'll also find favorites culled from the pages of *Prevention* magazine, giving you over 200 satisfying recipes. We've counted the calories, carbs, fats, and protein so all you have to do is cook and eat. Your family will never know they are eating "diet" food, as each mouthwatering dish is sure to please even the pickiest eater.

The first five chapters are jam-packed with weight-loss solutions. Lose Weight after 40 offers essential tips for determining calorie needs to lose weight based on your activity level. Decipher your hunger levels and the optimum time to eat. Did you know that adults take in 15 percent more calories on the weekends? Follow the advice on page 18 to splurge smarter on weekends. Learn which foods support your efforts while supplying the most overall nutrition and the healthiest cooking tips. Not ready for a full-scale diet? Then discover how even small changes can give you big results.

Hungry yet? Flip to Chapter 6, where the recipes begin. Each one went through the paces in our test kitchen, ensuring great results in your kitchen. Whip up a batch of Granola Pancakes with Fruit Sauce, Strawberry-Banana–Topped French Toast, or Zucchini and Dill Frittata for a hearty start. Fill up at lunch with a choice of burgers, pizzas, sandwiches, salads, and more. Dinner becomes a breeze with quick, healthful "take-out" dishes like Hoisin Pork Stir-Fry or Orange Chicken and Broccoli. Or choose the classic Chicken Salad Casserole, bursting with great taste minus the traditional fat and calories. Finally, turn out one of 58 scrumptious desserts, including Chocolate Hazelnut Fondue and Four-Berry Pie.

Peppered throughout the recipes are "Quick Tips." You'll also find "Nutrition News to Use," offering the latest weight-loss breakthroughs and research. For example, studies have found that chewing your food more—25 chews versus 10—makes you feel fuller and more satisfied. Look for "Health Hearsay" to get expert answers to common health concerns like "Does fat really make me fat?" Want to know now? Turn to page 110.

Looking for more inspiration? Check out the weight-loss stories in "It Worked for Me," complete with before and after photos, and read how five *Prevention* readers changed their eating habits to achieve their weight-loss goals. Over 500 pounds was lost among them! Their top tips offer nuggets of motivation. Take Priscilla Bartlett, who lost 85 pounds without deprivation: "When I started dieting, I incorporated chocolate—my weakness—into my new plan."

We hope we've whetted your appetite—and sparked your interest to read more. As Tanzy Kilcrease, who's maintained a 72-pound weight loss, says, "Losing weight and staying healthy is a lifelong journey." Turn the page to start yours.

Lose Weight after 40

Fat makes you fat. No, wait, carbs are the enemy. The truth is, when it comes to losing weight, it's all about calories: You have to burn off more than you take in to shed pounds. But that message has gotten lost over the years, which may be partially to blame for our increased calorie consumption. Women now eat 22 percent more calories than they did in 1971, for an average of 1,877 per day. That may sound low, but only 19 percent of adults are highly active. This means that few women burn enough calories to warrant the amount they eat. The lowdown: Every pound of body weight burns through 10 calories daily if you're inactive but up to 15 if you exercise 30 to 60 minutes most days. When guessing how many calories you can eat, being off by just 100 calories a day can keep you 6 to 10 pounds overweight. Experts say this is precisely why women in their forties are 25 pounds heavier now, compared with 1960—and why getting calories right is the only way to reach your ideal weight. The following guide will show you how.

STEP 1: FIND OUT HOW MANY CALORIES YOU EAT

Many people often underestimate how much they really eat, so follow these suggestions.

Track, Don't Count

You don't need to become a human calculator, but you should get a baseline idea of how many calories you're consuming every day. (A survey of more than 1,000 people found that only 13 percent knew how many calories they eat a day.) The best way is to record each morsel you take in for a day or two. (Use the free journal at prevention.com/healthtrackers to keep track of your diet.) Getting a grasp on exactly what you're eating can help you find out where the bulk of your calories comes from. Then you can make simple substitutions that shave off calories without sacrificing taste or satisfaction. For example, trading a handful of pretzels for 3 cups of air-popped popcorn sprinkled with 1 tablespoon of grated Parmesan cheese saves about 115 calories and has loads more flavor while tripling your portion size.

Read Labels Right

The Nutrition Facts info on a package lists the calorie count in 1 serving. But don't forget to compare that with the amount you actually eat or drink; many packages contain 2 servings or more. For example, a 20-ounce bottle of organic lemonade contains 110 calories per serving and 2½ servings per bottle. Drink the whole thing and you rack up 275 calories; that's nearly 20 percent of the calorie needs per day for most women.

Look for Total Calories, Not Type

Surveys show that women look at grams of fat and sugar before calories, a habit that can mislead you into eating more than you should—especially when it comes to reduced-fat or low-sugar foods. For example, three regular Oreo cookies provide 160 calories. Four of the reduced-fat version have 200. And "sugar free" doesn't mean "calorie free." Five tiny Hershey's sugar-free dark chocolate candies provide 190 calories, and 1 cup of Edy's no-sugar-added Fudge Tracks ice cream contains 220.

STEP 2: DETERMINE HOW MANY CALORIES YOU NEED

Knowing your ideal goal weight prevents weight gain—and helps you lose.

Use this simple equation to find your daily calorie needs.

Your Weight Goal

Multiply your goal weight:

$\times 10$ if you don't exercise at all

$\times 13$ if you rarely exercise or only play the occasional weekend golf or tennis game

$\times 15$ if you regularly exercise (swim, walk, or jog) for 30 to 60 minutes most days of the week

.... **Total daily calories**

Aim for this number every day to reach and maintain your weight goal.

To up your daily calorie allotment, move more. Going from being inactive to walking your dog every other day means you can multiply your weight goal by 13 rather than 10. For a 150-pound woman, that's an increase of 450 calories per day: So you could add a slice of whole wheat toast, 1 tablespoon of almond butter, 1 cup of grapes, and ¼ cup of semisweet chocolate chips to your daily diet without gaining.

✳ TEST YOUR CALORIE IQ

Q: Which type of calorie turns into fat faster?

A. Sugar	B. Protein	C. Carbs	D. Fat

Answer: None of them! It doesn't matter where calories come from—if you eat too many, they get converted to fat at the same rate. Focus on total calorie intake to get slim.

STEP 3: MAKE SMART CHOICES ALL DAY

It's easier than you think. Just remember a few key tips around this sample menu. The meals total 1,600 calories, the number most moderately active women need per day to support a healthy weight.

BREAKFAST

8 ounces fat-free latte

1 large tangerine

Egg sandwich

    1 whole wheat English muffin

    1 egg scrambled in 1 teaspoon canola oil

    1 slice reduced-fat Cheddar cheese

    ¼ avocado, sliced

    4 cherry tomatoes, halved

Total calories: 498

LUNCH

6 ounces fat-free strawberry yogurt

Garden salad with chickpeas

    1 cup salad greens

    ¼ cup shredded red cabbage

    10 baby carrots

    5 yellow cherry tomatoes, halved

    ½ cup chickpeas (or 3 ounces grilled boneless, skinless chicken breast)

    2 tablespoons chopped walnuts

    2 tablespoons reduced-fat Italian dressing

Total calories: 479

DINNER

½ cup steamed edamame

¾ cup brown rice

Shrimp stir-fry

    15 large shrimp and

    1½ cups broccoli stir-fried in

    2 teaspoons peanut oil with

    1 teaspoon low-sodium soy sauce

    1 teaspoon minced garlic

    1 teaspoon minced ginger

Total calories: 493

SNACK

1 cup green and red grapes

Total calories: 104

✳ "HARMLESS" HABITS THAT ADD POUNDS

> **Listening to music.** Soft, appealing sounds encourage you to dine longer and order more food. Loud, fast music speeds eating, meaning you scarf what's on your plate before you realize that you're full.
INSTEAD Turn off the music at home and focus on the pleasure you get from each bite. Or fill up on good conversation instead of dessert during restaurant meals.

> **Standing.** Those who eat out of plastic containers at a kitchen counter consume up to 50 percent more the next time they eat than those who sit at a table and eat off a plate. Standing makes the meal feel more like a snack, which people consider less satisfying, researchers say.
INSTEAD Eat at a proper place setting, even if you're only munching on hummus and carrot sticks, to help make it feel like a meal.

> **Eating a little of everything.** People given 24 flavors of jelly beans ate twice as many as those given only six flavors, according to the *Journal of Consumer Research*. A larger assortment appears more interesting and encourages you to sample extra.
INSTEAD Survey the food at a party or buffet and decide what you want before filling a plate.

Include only one high-fat food (such as full-fat dressing, nuts, croutons, or cheese) per meal. High-fat foods pack more calories into a smaller serving, which add up quickly.

Choose bread with holes in it. There's more air (and fewer calories!).

Snack on a baseball-size portion of fresh fruit. It provides about 50 to 100 calories, the amount in only three pretzel twists.

Pick "slippery" salad dressings such as oil and vinegar or reduced-fat vinaigrette. They coat your salad more easily than thick ones like blue cheese or Russian, so you can use less.

Always measure these foods: rice, cereal, peanut butter, and oil. They're hard to eyeball, and they're calorie dense. A heaping cup of rice has 25 percent more calories than a level one.

Make veggies half of the bulk of your meals. Fresh produce contains a lot of water, which makes it naturally low in calories.

Opt for whole fruit over juice. One cup of orange juice has more than 2½ times the calories of the tangerine. Plus, it's totally portion controlled.

✳ MAKE FRIENDS WITH YOUR SCALE

For years, many experts recommended tossing your scale—good advice when you consider the emotional whiplash that weighing yourself can cause. As the number goes down, your confidence goes up, but a gain of even a pound can easily ruin your day.

It's time to end the love-hate relationship with your scale. A review of a dozen studies tracking more than 16,000 dieters provides indisputable evidence that the bathroom scale is one of the most effective tools for losing weight and preventing pounds from creeping on. A whopping 75 percent of members of the National Weight Control Registry—men and women who have lost at least 30 pounds and kept it off—weigh themselves at least once a week.

Here are five surprising facts that will help you make peace with your scale—and use it to your weight-loss advantage.

SURPRISE No. 1

The more you weigh yourself, the more you lose.

Out of sight, out of mind simply doesn't work. In one study, daily weighers dropped twice as many pounds as weekly weighers—12 pounds versus 6, possibly because it was a regular reminder to stay on track. Meanwhile, dieters who avoided the scale altogether gained 4 pounds. And despite the common belief that focusing on weight makes women feel bad about themselves, scientists have found that tracking your weight can actually improve your mood by giving you a sense of control.

TIP Weigh yourself daily. (More than that isn't really helpful. See "The Scale Diary" on page 8.)

SURPRISE No. 2

A cheaper model is better.

You can spend hundreds on a high-tech scale that also estimates your body-fat percentage and more through a series of mathematical algorithms, but you're just getting another number to worry about that's possibly less accurate than your weight. "I avoid scales that measure body fat because there are so many inaccuracies based on fluctuations in how much water you drink," says exercise physiologist Kara Mohr, PhD, who's done extensive scientific research on weight loss.

TIP Buy a basic digital scale that displays weight to the nearest ½ or ²⁄₁₀ pound to minimize fluctuations.

SURPRISE No. 3
Weight can fluctuate 5 pounds in 24 hours.

The biggest culprit is water (and water in the food you eat). The calories in a liter of soda would add about ¹⁄₁₀ pound if you didn't burn them off, but step on the scale immediately after drinking it and you'll be up more than 2 pounds; go to the bathroom and you'll likely drop 1 to 1½ pounds. You even lose water weight—about 2 pounds a day— just by breathing and sweating. Day-to-day fluctuations can be the result of a high-sodium meal or your level of hydration, while your menstrual cycle can cause changes all month long. "It's important to keep the bigger picture in mind," Mohr says. No one meal or single splurge will move the scale's

needle in a lasting way unless it becomes a habit. A difference of 100 calories at every meal, however, could add up to more than 30 pounds in a year—in either direction.

TIP Weigh yourself at the same time each day, first thing in the morning after using the bathroom and removing your pajamas, to avoid factors like water weight and clothing. Track your results, and focus on the pattern over time. The number may go up and down from one day to the next, but the overall direction from month to month should be down if you're trying to lose weight. If you see an upward trend, it's time to take action.

SURPRISE No. 4
You can lose inches without weighing less.

In a recent study from the University of California, Berkeley, women in their mid-fifties followed a 12-week cycling routine while eating a diet designed to maintain their weight. The result: One 56-year-old lost just 1 pound but dropped two sizes, thanks to a 7 percent decrease in body fat. She replaced about 4 pounds of fat with 4 pounds of muscle—pound for pound, muscle is firmer and denser, and it takes up about one-third of the space of fat. But don't assume your scale is stuck due to new muscle. On average, it takes about a month of strength training to add a single pound of muscle, according to Wayne

Westcott, PhD, author of *Get Stronger, Feel Younger.*

TIP Track other markers such as the size of your waist and thighs (using a tape measure), how your clothes fit, or how much energy you have—and celebrate those successes.

SURPRISE No. 5
Where you put your scale matters.

In most cases, your bathroom floor will work just fine, but if the floor is textured or the grout creates an uneven surface, the readout might be off. Bath mats or carpet of any thickness can absorb some of your weight, throwing off the scale's sensors and decreasing your weight by 20 pounds or more, explains Keith Erickson, company spokesperson for Tanita scales. Some higher-end scales come with carpet feet to accommodate the inconsistencies, but our tester still found a several-pound discrepancy.

TIP Weigh yourself in the same spot every day. Even if it's off by a few pounds, you'll still be able to see changes over time. For the most accurate reading, place your scale on a bare floor that's hard, flat, and level. You can test the scale's accuracy by weighing an object whose weight you know— like a dumbbell.

✳ THE SCALE DIARY

Don't let the number determine your self-worth! An anonymous forty-something reader shared how her weight fluctuated over 24 hours.

7:15 a.m.	133.8 lb	Right before hopping in the shower
8:30 a.m.	137.5 lb	Wow, my clothes weigh 3.7 lb
9:15 a.m.	138.7 lb	Gained 1.2 lb from breakfast
10:30 a.m.	137.9 lb	Bathroom break, lost 0.8 lb
1:00 p.m.	135.8 lb	Lost 2.1 lb, thanks to a sweaty cardio workout
1:30 p.m.	137.4 lb	Up 1.6 lb from lunch
4:00 p.m.	138.6 lb	Gained 1.2 lb, probably from all the water I was drinking
5:30 p.m.	137.5 lb	Bathroom break, lost 1.1 lb
11:00 p.m.	140.8 lb	Yikes! Gained 3.3 lb—probably the pasta I ate and the wine!
11:30 p.m.	137.1 lb	Undressed—huh, gained 3.3 lb since this morning
7:15 a.m.	135.4 lb	Lost 1.7 lb while sleeping

EAT TO LIVE LONGER

What we eat is linked to how long we live, suggests more and more research. Extra weight can take a dramatic toll on our bodies—and subtract years from our lives. The good news: "What works best for weight loss helps slow the aging process as well," says Cheryl Forberg, RD, nutritionist for NBC's *The Biggest Loser*. Following are her top science-based tips to turn back the clock.

Get a Daily Dose of Omega-3s

"I like to call them the anti-aging fat," Forberg says. Getting the recommended amount of these healthy fats can help lower cholesterol, keep cells functioning properly, and combat inflammation, which reduces your risk of cancer, stroke, and heart attack. Flaxseed, walnuts, and some leafy greens contain omega-3s, but seafood is the best source. Research published in the *Journal of Nutrition* found that DHA, an omega-3 found in cold-water, fatty fish, helps keep aging brains healthy.

TRY THIS Eat two 3-ounce servings of salmon, herring, lake trout, or other fatty fish each week, plus a daily serving of ground flaxseed, walnuts, soybean oil, spinach, or kale.

Eat Antioxidants Every 4 Hours

These nutrients slow the aging process by protecting our cells from harmful free radicals. But some, such as vitamin C, are water soluble. "That means they remain in our body for only 4 to 6 hours, so you have to replenish regularly," Forberg explains. Vibrantly colored fruits and vegetables are loaded with these disease-fighting substances.

TRY THIS Have a fruit or vegetable at every meal and snack. Aim for three to five colors a day.

Double Your Fiber

It may help protect against cancer and can keep blood sugar levels steady and promote heart health. In fact, according to research published in the *American Journal of Clinical Nutrition,* every 10 grams of dietary fiber you consume daily reduces your risk of death from coronary heart disease by 17 percent. The daily recommendation is 25 to 35 grams per day, but most Americans eat half or less.

TRY THIS Boost your intake with star sources: cooked lentils (8 grams per ½ cup), cooked chickpeas (6 grams per ½ cup), barley (16 grams per ½ cup), apples (4 grams in one medium), and raspberries (8 grams per cup).

Get 25 percent of Calories from Healthy Fats

The good-for-you variety—like monounsaturated fatty acids—can lower bad LDL cholesterol, raise cardio-protective HDL cholesterol, and decrease your risk of atherosclerosis. Plus, studies suggest that a higher intake of these fats may contribute to longer life expectancy. For a 1,600-calorie diet, that's about 44 grams per day.

TRY THIS Healthy fats include ¼ cup of pistachios (7 grams), ¼ cup of almonds (11 grams), 1 tablespoon of olive oil (10 grams), or ¼ cup of avocado (3.5 grams).

Stop When You're 80 Percent Full

Centenarians in Okinawa, Japan, practice this eating rule; they also consistently consume a lower-calorie diet, which researchers hypothesize is a key component to longevity. Eating more slowly can automatically help you control calories: A recent study found that women who ate at slower rates felt fuller and ate fewer calories than those who ate more quickly.

TRY THIS The key is to stop when you are satisfied, not stuffed, Forberg says. A reminder: "You shouldn't have to unbutton or unzip anything." Slow your eating pace by taking smaller bites and chewing thoroughly.

Pack Protein into Every Meal and Snack

Protein provides essential building blocks for the daily repair of nearly every single cell in your body. Getting enough is critical to your health and vitality, especially as you get older, when cellular damage can become more frequent. Aim to get 30 percent of your daily calories (or 120 grams based on a 1,600-calorie diet) from lean protein.

TRY THIS Good sources include skinless white meat from chicken, pork, or turkey (about 21 grams per 3 ounces), fat-free milk (8 grams per cup), egg whites (7 grams for two), and beans (about 8 grams per ½ cup).

Listen
and
Lose

Humans have an instinctual (even good) fear of getting hungry. Take the film *Into the Wild*: When the main character can't find food, his hunger drives him to a screaming, shake-his-fist-at-the-heavens rage, a stark example of the primal nature of our need for nourishment.

Today, most of us know where our next meal is coming from, yet our reaction to hunger has not evolved with our convenience-centered world. This is why even the thought of being hungry may send you running to the mini-mart for sustenance. If you want to lose weight, however, you must tune in to your body's signals. "Hunger is a physical cue that you need energy," says Dawn Jackson Blatner, RD. It can be your best diet ally: If you listen to your body, you'll instinctively feed it the right amount. But fall out of touch, and hunger becomes diet enemy number one. You might eat more than you need or get too hungry and stoke out-of-control cravings. The following six tips teach you to spot hunger and eat to stay satisfied—so you control calories and shed pounds without "dieting."

LEARN TO IDENTIFY YOUR SPOT ON THE HUNGER SCALE

Do you really know what hunger feels like? Before you can rein it in, you must learn to recognize the physical cues that signal a true need for nourishment. Prior to eating, use this hunger scale to help figure out your true food needs.

Starving. An uncomfortable, empty feeling that may also be accompanied by light-headedness or jitteriness caused by low blood sugar levels from lack of food. Binge risk: high.

Hungry. Your next meal is on your mind. If you don't eat within the hour, you enter dangerous "starving" territory.

Moderately hungry. Your stomach may be growling, and you're planning how you'll put an end to that nagging feeling. This is optimal eating time.

Satisfied. You're satiated—not full but not hungry either. You're relaxed and comfortable and can wait to nosh.

Full. If you're still eating, it's more out of momentum than actual hunger. Your belly feels slightly bloated, and the food does not taste as good as it did in the first few bites.

Stuffed. You feel uncomfortable and might even have mild heartburn from stomach acids creeping back up into your esophagus.

To Slim Down

The best time to eat is when you are "moderately hungry" or "hungry." When you hit either of these stages, you've used most of the energy from your last meal or snack, but you haven't yet hit the point where you will be driven to binge.

✳ 5 WAYS TO CONQUER OVEREATING

1 You eat a muffin at break-fast but are starving only a short time later.

Solution: Try a bowl of oatmeal microwaved with reduced-fat milk. The fiber in the oats will fill you up longer.

2 It's late afternoon and you're low on energy. The office vending machine is calling your name.

Solution: Stash single-serving packages of nuts and dried fruit in your desk drawer.

3 It's not quitting time yet, but you're so hungry that you can't wait for dinner.

Solution: Have a 150- to 200-calorie snack, such as a serving of yogurt with some fruit or celery.

4 You're ready for lunch but stuck in traffic.

Solution: Keep a high-fiber, protein-packed bar in your purse or glove compartment to snack on; later, eat a light lunch to compensate for the extra calories.

5 It's well past your normal bedtime, and now your stomach is growling.

Solution: Eat a fiber-filled piece of low-calorie fruit instead of, or at least before, diving into the cookie jar.

REFUEL EVERY 4 HOURS

Still can't tell what true hunger feels like? Set your watch. Moderate to full-fledged hunger (our ideal window for eating) will usually hit 4 to 5 hours after a balanced meal. Waiting too long to eat can send you on an emergency hunt for energy—and the willpower to make healthful choices plummets. When researchers in the United Kingdom asked workers to choose a snack just after lunch, 70 percent picked foods like candy bars and potato chips; the percentage shot up to 92 percent when workers chose snacks in the late afternoon. "Regular eating keeps blood sugar and energy stable, which prevents you from feeling an extreme need for fuel," says Kate Geagan, RD, based in Park City, Utah.

To Slim Down

If you're hungry between meals, a snack of 150 calories should help hold you over. Here are a couple of ideas.

1 Munch on whole foods such as fruit and unsalted nuts—they tend to contain more fiber and water, so you'll fill up on fewer calories. Bonus: They're loaded with disease-fighting nutrients.

2 Avoid temptation by packing healthful, portable snacks such as string cheese and dried fruit in your purse before heading out for the day.

EAT BREAKFAST WITHOUT FAIL

A study published in the *British Journal of Nutrition* tracked the diets of nearly 900 adults and found that when people ate more fat, protein, and carbohydrates in the morning, they stayed satisfied and ate less during the day than those who ate their bigger meals later on. Unfortunately, many Americans fall short of this goal. In one survey, consumers reported that even when they eat in the morning, the meal is a full breakfast only about one-third of the time.

To Slim Down

If you're hungry before noon, your morning meal is probably too small. Aim for at least 250 calories, and make it a habit.

✳ BEST SNACK PAIRS FOR WEIGHT LOSS

If cravings kill your diet, munch on these hunger-busting snacks, suggests Tanya Zuckerbrot, RD. In a 4-week survey, she found that women who snack on a combination of protein, fiber, and healthy fats feel more satisfied and have less of an urge to overeat. Fiber increases satiety, and protein and fats digest slowly, delaying hunger. Here are Zuckerbrot's top three combos— only 150 calories each.

✳ 2 cups popcorn + 2 tablespoons trail mix

✳ ½ cup fiber-rich cereal + 1 serving fat-free Greek yogurt

✳ 1 ounce baked potato chips + 2 tablespoons bean dip

✳ POP QUIZ: HOW DISEASE-PROOF IS YOUR DIET?

Similar foods can contain drastically different nutrient levels. Are your picks protecting your health as well as they could? Test yourself.

Which is the best food:

1 To Lower Cholesterol?

 Red bell pepper **OR** Green bell pepper

2 To Prevent Dementia?

 Almonds **OR** Peanuts

3 To Ward Off Hearing Loss?

 Broccoli **OR** Spinach

4 To Maintain Healthy Blood Pressure?

 Low-fat yogurt **OR** Cottage cheese

Answers

1 **Red bell pepper** for a double dose of heart-healthy vitamin C. A recent study found that 500 milligrams daily can significantly reduce LDL (bad) cholesterol and triglycerides.

2 **Almonds** for three times the vitamin E. Getting about 8 milligrams daily can help lower your risk of Alzheimer's disease by 67 percent.

3 **Spinach** for twice as much folate. A study of 26,273 men found that a high intake can reduce your risk of hearing loss by 20 percent.

4 **Low-fat yogurt** for three times the calcium. Getting 1,000 to 1,200 milligrams daily can help reduce blood pressure by up to 40 percent, according to researchers.

1 Prepare breakfast before bed; for example, cut fruit and portion out some yogurt.

2 Stash single-serving boxes of whole grain cereal or packets of instant oatmeal and shelf-stable fat-free milk or soy milk at work to eat when you arrive.

3 If you can't handle eating a big breakfast (or anything at all) early in the morning, save your meal for a later time. "Don't force anything," says John de Castro, PhD, a behavioral researcher and dean of the College of Humanities and Social Sciences at Sam Houston State University. "Just wait a while and eat at 9:00, 10:00, or even 11:00 a.m. It will help you stay in control later in the day."

BUILD LOW-CAL, HIGH-VOLUME MEALS

There's a reason that your parents always told you to eat your vegetables. Solid foods that have a high fluid content can help you suppress hunger. "When we eat foods with a high water content like fruits and vegetables versus low-water-content foods like crackers and pretzels, we get bigger portions for less calories," says Barbara Rolls, PhD, author of *The Volumetrics Eating Plan* and a professor of nutritional sciences at Pennsylvania State University.

Bottom line: You consume more food but cut calories at the same time. Rolls has found a similar effect in foods that have a lot of air. In a recent study, people ate 21 percent fewer calories of an air-puffed cheese snack, compared with a denser snack.

To Slim Down

Eat fewer calories by eating more food.

1 Start dinner with a salad, or make a large salad your meal (be sure to include protein such as lean meat or beans).

2 Choose fresh fruit over dried. For around the same number of calories, you can have a whole cup of grapes or a measly 3 tablespoons of raisins.

3 Boost the volume of a low-calorie frozen dinner by adding veggies such as steamed broccoli or cauliflower, freshly chopped tomatoes, and bagged baby spinach.

MUNCH FIBER ALL DAY LONG

Fiber can help you feel full faster and for longer. Because the body processes a fiber-rich meal more slowly, it may help you stay satisfied long after eating. Fiber-packed foods are also higher in volume, which means they can fill you up so that you eat fewer calories. One review recently published in the *Journal of the American Dietetic Association* linked a high intake of cereal fiber with lower body mass index—and reduced risk of type 2 diabetes and heart disease.

To Slim Down
Aim to get at least 25 grams of fiber every day with these tips.

1 Include produce such as apples and carrots—naturally high in fiber—in each meal and snack.

2 Try replacing some or all of your regular bread, pasta, and rice with whole grain versions.

INCLUDE AT LEAST ONE HEALTHY PROTEIN AT EACH MEAL

When researchers at Purdue University asked 46 dieting women to get either 30 percent or 18 percent of their calories from protein, the high-protein eaters felt more satisfied and less hungry. Plus, over the course of 12 weeks, these women preserved more lean body mass, which includes calorie-burning muscle.

To Slim Down
Boost your protein intake with these ideas.

1 Have a serving of lean protein such as egg whites, chunk light tuna, or boneless, skinless chicken at each meal. A serving of meat is about the size of a deck of cards or the palm of your hand—not including your fingers.

2 Build beans into your meals. Black beans, chickpeas, and edamame (whole soybeans) are low in fat, high in fiber, and packed with protein.

SHRINK BELLY BLOAT WITH FOOD

If belly bulge is sapping your summer-body confidence, don't despair. The reason for your puffy midsection may well be bloat, not fat. That's because one of the worst culprits for this problem—a slow digestive system—is common among women over age 40. However, exciting research suggests you can get your digestion moving and beat bloat with a few easy menu and lifestyle tweaks. Put all of these ideas into effect right now, and you should be flatter and sexier and fitting comfortably into your clothes in less than a week.

EAT THESE!
Add: Two kinds of fiber
Why it beats bloat: Constipation distends your belly, and one easy way to get rid of it is by starting each morning with a breakfast cereal that guarantees your body a daily dose of fiber. This gets the digestive system moving within a day or so and keeps it that way. Based on a recent study of breakfast cereals, University of Toronto researchers say that consuming two kinds of fiber at once is most effective. The scientists found that participants had an easier time staying regular with a cereal that contained both insoluble fiber (from bran) and gel-like soluble fiber (from psyllium). The two types work together to pull water into your colon and speed up elimination, explains Joanne Slavin, PhD, a professor of food science and nutrition at the University of Minnesota. The result? You look and feel lighter.
Good Food Fix: ⅓ cup Kellogg's All-Bran Bran Buds every day

Add: Potassium-Rich Foods
Why they beat bloat: Foods such as bananas and potatoes help your body get rid of excess water weight, minimizing your middle. The extra fluid is typically present because the two main minerals that control the amount of water in your body—potassium and sodium—have gotten out of balance. When your sodium level is too high, your tissues hold on to fluid. You can restore your sodium-potassium equilibrium by increasing your potassium intake to an optimum 4,700 milligrams per day. To do this, you need to eat about 4½ cups of produce daily, including the especially rich sources mentioned below. As you rebalance your system, you'll flush out the extra sodium along with the water. Presto! Less puffiness.

Watch out, though. Food is a safe source of potassium, but supplements are not. They can cause potassium to build up in your body and potentially lead to abnormal heart rhythms and even heart attack, especially in people with kidney or heart problems, says Leslie Bonci, RD, MPH, director of sports medicine nutrition for the Center for Sports Medicine at the University of Pittsburgh Medical Center.

Good Food Fixes: 1 medium baked potato with skin, 1 medium banana, 1 medium papaya, ½ cup steamed edamame, ½ cup tomato sauce, ½ cup cooked spinach, 1 medium orange

Add: Yogurt with Probiotics

Why it beats bloat: Research published in *Alimentary Pharmacology & Therapeutics* reveals that an imbalance of bacteria in your gut can cause your digestive system to slow down and your belly to puff up. However, yogurts that contain live bacteria, otherwise known as probiotics, can help. Though researchers don't fully understand the mechanism, a study in the *Journal of the American Dietetic Association* found that the bacteria seem to tame tummy bloat by causing an improvement in intestinal mobility, thereby relieving constipation.

Good Food Fix: a daily 4-ounce container of low-fat or fat-free yogurt containing live, active cultures

Add: More Fluids

Why they beat bloat: Drinking enough liquid supports the other ways you're trying to flatten your tummy, Bonci says. For example, she explains, when there's enough fluid present in your system, the dual-fiber cereal you have eaten is better able to pull liquid into your lower intestine and ease constipation. "Women who don't drink sufficient fluids can get that blown-up belly feeling, despite all their other efforts to get rid of it," Bonci warns.

How much fluid do you need? Getting rid of bloat means being well hydrated, so aim for at least 8 glasses of liquid each day, plus plenty of fluid-rich foods, such as fruits and vegetables. You can meet your quota with any liquid, including water, milk, juice, coffee, and tea—though not soda or alcohol, which has a dehydrating effect on your system.

Good Fluid Fix: Tap water is an excellent option because it has no calories, salt, sugar, or additives. And it's free!

DON'T EAT THESE!

Subtract: Sodium

Why it causes bloat: Sodium makes you retain water, puffing up your belly. Most of us eat more than twice as much sodium as we should—topping 3,400 milligrams a day, rather than the recommended 1,500, according to the Centers for Disease Control and Prevention (CDC).

Good Strategies: Stop salting your food at the table, and check for sodium on the labels of packaged foods, which usually provide about three-quarters of the daily intake for most women.

Subtract: Candy, Soda, and Gum

Why they cause bloat: Once air from any source reaches your digestive system, you experience it as gas and a distended belly. Eating or drinking quickly, sipping through a straw, sucking on hard candy, and chewing gum can make you swallow air.

Good Strategies: "When eating, chew slowly with your mouth closed," Bonci says. Trade carbonated drinks for flat ones, such as juice or water, and lose the gum and candies.

Subtract: Sugar Alcohols

Why they cause bloat: We don't completely digest these low-cal sweeteners (found in flavored waters and low-carb, diabetic, and sugar-free foods). Bacteria in the large intestine ferment them, causing gas and even diarrhea.

Good Strategy: Check food labels to help avoid sugar alcohols; common ones are sorbitol, mannitol, xylitol, and lacitol.

Subtract: Raw Produce

Why it causes bloat: Fresh fruits and vegetables are healthy, but they're also high-volume foods that take up room in your stomach, distending it.

Good Strategies: Spread fresh produce consumption over the day, so that you're not eating more than one-third of the recommended daily total of 4½ cups at any one sitting. You can also shrink produce by cooking it, creating a more compact serving, Bonci says.

✳ SPLURGE SMARTER ON WEEKENDS

There's something about weekends that sends caution—and calories—to the wind. Even if your workweek is all about smart snacks and sensible dinners, for many of us, all bets are off come 5:00 p.m. Friday, says clinical psychologist Robert Maurer, PhD, author of *One Small Step Can Change Your Life*. "It's almost like a dam bursting," he says. We're tired and feel like we've earned the right to put healthy habits on hold. A University of North Carolina at Chapel Hill study revealed that adults take in an extra 222 calories—nearly 15 percent of the number of calories an average woman needs each day—over the course of the weekend.

Of course you want to live a little on the weekend, but if you're trying to lose weight or even just keep the scale steady, you have to maintain a certain level of vigilance. Here is how to rethink your weekend habits so you'll lose weight all week.

Weekend Think
This week was tough; I deserve to splurge
Healthier Strategy: **Splurge with savvy**

The need for some kind of reward is just human nature, says Stephen Gullo, PhD, author of *The Thin Commandments Diet*. And for many, that "something special" is food. You can't change what makes you happy, but you can try to minimize the diet damage. Choose one portion-controlled item that requires you to leave the house, such as a cup of lobster bisque from your favorite eatery or a small, fresh pastry from the bakery. "It's more rewarding to have a nice treat than to waste calories on regular things you can have anytime, like potato chips or cookies," Dr. Gullo

says. Doing something special works, too: Catch a movie, enjoy a massage at the spa, or buy a flattering pair of yoga pants.

Weekend Think
Eating and entertaining go hand in hand
Healthier Strategy: **Plan some activities, not meals**

Some decompressing is essential, but planting yourself on the couch for hours can lead to trouble. A long stretch of inactivity can inspire compulsive nibbling, especially if boredom is one of your overeating triggers, Dr. Gullo says. And the immobility quickly adds up: Skip your regular 1-mile walk, add those extra 222 calories

you tend to eat on weekends—and that alone can equal a gain of about 7 pounds a year! Sure, you can indulge in an afternoon of channel surfing, but not all day long. Impose a time limit; 2 hours is fine. And use that extra time to do something good for yourself, like chopping veggies for dinner that night and preparing snacks to take to work the next week. Also, don't forget to work downtime into your week so you don't feel as exhausted come the weekend.

Weekend Think
A predinner cocktail is par for the course
Healthier Strategy: **Drink it during the meal**

With fewer responsibilities and no early morning wake-up calls, even weekday teetotalers don't think twice about a cocktail before dinner—and then another while they eat. The problem: "Alcohol breaks down inhibitions, so it's harder to make healthy food choices when you do sit down," says Gary Foster, PhD, director of the Center for Obesity Research and Education at Temple University. A glass of cabernet and a few handfuls of mixed nuts while making dinner or waiting to be seated can add up to more than 600 calories—and that's even before the appetizer. Instead, have the wine with your meal, and save added calories by swapping fries for veggies or sharing the lower-cal sorbet, not the chocolate cake.

Choose high-quality drinks you'll want to savor, such as vintage wine or single-malt scotch, over high-cal fruity concoctions, and sub in one or two club sodas with lime.

Weekend Think
I'll just have one last hurrah before Monday
Healthier Strategy: **Drop that "last supper" mind-set**

Healthy eating doesn't have an on/off switch; it's a way of life, says David Grotto, RD, founder of Nutrition Housecall, a nutrition consulting firm, and author of *101 Foods That Can Save Your Life*. He encourages his clients to treat themselves during the week, maybe with a light beer one night or a child's-size ice cream cone another, so they're not feeling deprived and desperate enough to polish off a half-pint of ice cream on Friday night for 500 calories. If you blow it, don't wait until Monday to get back on track; start at your next meal or snack. Besides, giving yourself free rein on the weekend can reactivate negative eating patterns that are bound to carry over into the following week, Dr. Gullo says. A few days may not make a major difference, but keep it up and extra pounds are almost guaranteed to start sneaking their way back on.

Weekend Think
Obligations throw off my usual routine

Healthier Strategy: **Take control of your hunger, wherever and whenever you can**

Between errands, quality time with the kids, grocery shopping, and household chores, your weekends are often too packed to make time for your regular diet-and-exercise schedule. But part of developing healthy habits for life is about adapting, Dr. Foster says. It just takes a few adjustments: Toss a low-cal energy bar or apple into your purse before hitting the mall so you're not tempted by the food court; if you know you're going to be on the road all afternoon, have a later breakfast or bring a portable snack with you; if restaurant reservations aren't until late, snack on string cheese and whole grain crackers to hold you over, and then order lean fish or meat and vegetables for dinner. It's okay to shuffle around meals and snacks; just don't skip them or your hunger will overpower you, says Katherine Tallmadge, RD, author of *Diet Simple*. You may find planning these modifications hard at first, but once you start making them, they'll become second nature. And plan active family outings that aren't doable during the week, such as a tennis match with your spouse, a hike with the kids, or a long walk with the dog. You burn slightly more calories than you would at your 9-to-5 desk job, which helps even out a sensible weekend splurge.

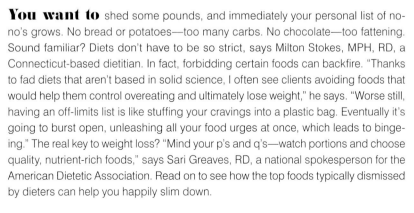

Surprising Diet-Friendly Foods

You want to shed some pounds, and immediately your personal list of no-no's grows. No bread or potatoes—too many carbs. No chocolate—too fattening. Sound familiar? Diets don't have to be so strict, says Milton Stokes, MPH, RD, a Connecticut-based dietitian. In fact, forbidding certain foods can backfire. "Thanks to fad diets that aren't based in solid science, I often see clients avoiding foods that would help them control overeating and ultimately lose weight," he says. "Worse still, having an off-limits list is like stuffing your cravings into a plastic bag. Eventually it's going to burst open, unleashing all your food urges at once, which leads to binge-ing." The real key to weight loss? "Mind your p's and q's—watch portions and choose quality, nutrient-rich foods," says Sari Greaves, RD, a national spokesperson for the American Dietetic Association. Read on to see how the top foods typically dismissed by dieters can help you happily slim down.

BREAD

Slim-Down Effect

Contains carbohydrates, which boost brain chemicals that curb overeating

Bread is an excellent source of carbs, which your brain needs to produce serotonin, a neurotransmitter that promotes feelings of comfort and satisfaction, says Nina T. Frusztajer, MD, a Boston-based physician who specializes in nutrition and is coauthor of *The Serotonin Power Diet*. "As your body digests carbohydrates, it releases insulin, which helps channel tryptophan—an amino acid—into the brain. Tryptophan then gets converted to serotonin," Dr. Frusztajer explains. When serotonin levels are optimal, you feel calm and happy and have fewer cravings; when they're low, you feel depressed and irritable, making you more likely to overeat. Breads containing whole grains are healthiest, and one serving equals one slice of bread, half an English muffin, or a small roll.

PASTA

Slim-Down Effect

A high fluid content keeps you satisfied longer

Cooked pasta and rice are about 70 percent water—and eating fluid-rich foods keeps you fuller longer, compared with dry foods, according to research from the British Nutrition Foundation. Like bread, the carbs in pasta boost serotonin to help curb overeating. The proper portion of pasta is ½ cup cooked, or about the size of a scoop of ice cream. Choose whole grain varieties for filling fiber, and add grilled chicken and lots of veggies to bulk up your dish even more.

POTATOES

Slim-Down Effect

Form resistant starch, a fiber that burns fat

These veggies may be one of our most misunderstood foods. Fried or doused in sour cream, they're not going to help you lose weight. But when boiled or baked, a potato's starch absorbs water and swells. Once chilled, portions of the starch crystallize into a form that resists digestion—resistant starch. Unlike other types of fiber, resistant starch gets fermented in the large intestine, creating fatty acids that may block the body's ability to burn carbohydrates. In their place, you burn fat. A healthy potato serving is about the size of a fist.

PEANUT BUTTER

Slim-Down Effect

Rich in healthy fats that help banish belly flab

Studies show that diets high in monounsaturated fatty acids (abundant in peanut butter and nuts) prevent accumulation of fat around the midsection, boost calorie burn, and promote weight loss. In fact, women who eat one serving of nuts or peanut butter two or more times a week gain fewer pounds than women who rarely eat them, according to recent research from the Harvard School of Public Health. One reason: A snack that includes peanut butter helps you stay full for up to

✳ HOT IDEA: EAT YOUR TEA!

How can you reap the heart and brain benefits of tea without drinking the 2 to 5 cups a day that many recent studies suggest? By infusing it into your favorite recipes. Tea can impart a unique flavor to food without adding calories, sodium, sugar, or fat and is one of the best dietary sources of age-erasing antioxidants, says chef Robert Wemischner, co-author of *Cooking with Tea*. Try one of these super-simple ways to give your family's meals a tasty health boost.

As a rub: Grind 1 teaspoon of black tea leaves in a spice mill and add to your favorite spice mixture. Rub onto uncooked chicken, beef, or fish. Let stand for 10 minutes before cooking.
TIP Use loose-leaf tea or just tear open a bag.

As a stock: Add brewed tea to broth and pour over meat or fish for braising.
TIP Use black tea where you would typically add red wine, and green tea or oolong in place of white wine.

As a marinade: Warm 1 teaspoon of black tea leaves in 1 cup of freshly squeezed orange juice. Remove from the heat and let steep for 5 minutes, then strain and discard leaves. Refrigerate scallops or shrimp in the mixture for 15 to 60 minutes before cooking.
TIP To convert into a sauce, add 1 small clove of garlic (finely minced) and 1 tablespoon of soy sauce and bring to a boil, then simmer until reduced. Spoon over seared scallops.

2½ hours, compared with 30 minutes for a carb-only snack such as a rice cake, finds research from Purdue University. (Carbohydrates satisfy a craving, while nuts keep you feeling full.) Peanut butter and nuts are high in calories, so stick with a 2-tablespoon portion—about the size of a golf ball.

CHEESE

Slim-Down Effect
Great source of calcium, which burns calories

At about 100 calories and 5 grams of fat per ounce, cheese usually tops the no-no list, but its calcium improves your ability to burn calories and fat, according to a recent research review. Not getting enough of this mineral may trigger the release of calcitriol, a hormone that causes the body to store fat. Scientists at the University of Tennessee found that people on a reduced-calorie diet who included an extra 300 to 400 milligrams of calcium a day lost significantly more weight than those who ate the same number of calories but with less calcium. Scientists aren't exactly sure why, but eating calcium-rich foods is more effective than taking calcium supplements—and cheese has about 200 milligrams per ounce. Just stick to 2-ounce portions, and choose light varieties to get health benefits for half the calories.

✳ FIVE WAYS TO SPOT A HEALTH FOOD

Food labels don't lie. But if you're one of the 60 percent of people who rely on them to make healthy choices and you don't know what to look for, they can deceive. Kathy McManus, RD, director of the department of nutrition at Brigham and Women's Hospital in Boston, offers five ways to sleuth the truth.

Nutrition Facts

Serving Size 30 g
Servings per package 1

Amount Per Serving

Calories 140 Calories from Fat 50	
	% Daily Value*
Total Fat 6 g	9%
Saturated Fat 3 g	15%
Trans Fat 0 g	
Cholesterol 20 mg	7%
Sodium 45 mg	2%
Total Carbohydrate 17 g	6%
Dietary Fiber 4 g	16%
Sugars 12 g	
Protein 4 g	8%

• **Check the servings.** If one package doesn't equal one serving, multiply the nutritional information by how many you're going to eat—especially calories: Packaged meals should contain no more than 400; snacks shouldn't exceed 150.

• **Limit bad fats.** Pick products with zero trans fat and low saturated fat. Women on a 1,600-calorie diet need no more than 13 grams of fat daily.

• **Pick low sodium.** Most people get far too much sodium, and up to 75 percent of it comes from processed foods. Full meals shouldn't exceed 500 milligrams; cap your daily intake at 2,000 milligrams.

• **Fill up on fiber.** Foods that contain 3 grams or more can help reduce appetite and cholesterol.

• **Go beyond sugar grams.** Some healthy foods are high in natural sugar. If the number of grams seems high, make sure the ingredient list doesn't contain added sweeteners.

DARK CHOCOLATE

Slim-Down Effect
Satisfies a common craving to prevent bingeing

Up to 97 percent of women experience cravings, and chocolate is the most common and "intensely" craved food, according to a recent study. Having an occasional small serving of a favorite treat is better than depriving yourself, which may lead to a binge, Greaves says. In fact, people who tried to not think about chocolate ate two-thirds more of it than people who were told to talk about it freely, according to British research. Dark varieties are more satisfying than milk chocolate, say scien-

tists at the University of Copenhagen, but measure your portion and be mindful when you eat. Slowly savoring one or two squares of a high-quality dark-chocolate bar will satisfy a craving more than wolfing down M&M's in front of the TV.

FRUIT

Slim-Down Effect
Soothes a sweet tooth naturally for few calories

Some dieters skip this low-calorie fare when they start watching the scale, thanks to once-popular diets that eliminated fruit in their most restrictive phases. But new research published in the journal *Obesity Reviews* looked at 16 different studies and found overwhelmingly that eating fruit is associated with weighing less. In one study from Brazil, women who added three small apples to their regular meals and snacks lost 2 pounds in 10 weeks without dieting. Although fruit does contain the natural sugar fructose, it doesn't raise blood sugar levels like table sugar does; plus, it's high in water and filling fiber and low in calories. Aim to have three servings of fresh fruit daily—but skip the high-calorie juice. Great picks (with average calories per cup): fresh melon (50), grapes (60), berries (70), and citrus fruits (75).

✳ WAKE UP THE HEALTH POWER OF YOUR FOOD

There's nothing more nutritious than a heaping salad of colorful raw vegetables, right? Not so fast, says new research. Scientists are finding that various methods of cooking veggies—from boiling carrots to steaming broccoli—can actually boost certain nutrients. "Some of the healthiest plant pigments in vegetables are released only when they're cooked," says Elizabeth Johnson, PhD, a scientist at the Friedman School of Nutrition Science and Policy at Tufts University. "You get more carotenoids, for example, from steamed spinach than from a spinach salad."

Raw veggies are still a great way to get vitamins and minerals, but specific cooking methods can release additional nutrients—or preserve the health benefits while making the food tastier. Next time you assemble a hearty salad or a crudités platter, toss in some of these steamed, boiled, baked, or roasted additions.

Broccoli
Steam
RAW Broccoli is high in potential cancer-fighting nutrients such as beta-carotene, lutein, and flavonols.
COOKED Steamed broccoli has higher concentrations of many carotenoids (including beta-carotene and lutein) than raw, according to a recent study in the *Journal of Agricultural and Food Chemistry*. Plus, it retains nearly 70 percent of its vitamin C and virtually all of its kaempferol, a cell-saving flavonoid.
BONUS To maximize the nutrients you get from your broccoli, wait to wash and cut it until just before steaming, suggests Ellie

Krieger, RD, author of *So Easy* and host of *Healthy Appetite* on the Food Network. Washing and cutting speeds up deterioration.

Carrots
Boil until tender
RAW Carrots are a good source of vitamin C and carotenoids, a family of antioxidants that include beta-carotene. These contribute to good eye health and may also reduce your risk of heart attack and some forms of cancer.

COOKED Boiling makes the carotenoids 14 percent more concentrated, according to a recent study in the *Journal of Agricultural and Food Chemistry*. Dietary fiber in the cell walls of carrots traps the carotenoids, but high heat releases and concentrates the compounds, making it easier for your digestive tract to access them, explains Philipp Simon, PhD, a scientist with the USDA Vegetable Crops Research Unit. The study also found that boiling increases carrots' total antioxidant capacity (their ability to attack free radicals) while only slightly diminishing vitamin C levels.
BONUS Add a drop of olive or canola oil to your cooked carrots; the fat helps your body absorb more of the beta-carotene.

Garlic
Roast cloves for no more than 3 minutes
RAW Garlic contains alliinase, an enzyme with antiplatelet properties that may help reduce blood pressure and prevent blood from

clotting, which decreases your risk of heart disease.

COOKED Roasting garlic cloves (for up to 3 minutes at no more than 390°F) helps retain nearly all of their antiplatelet properties—with less of the odoriferous side effects of raw, say researchers at the USDA and the National University of Cuyo in Argentina. Remove from the heat after 3 minutes—by 6 minutes, garlic loses about 80 percent of its clot-busting abilities; by 10 minutes, 100 percent. And don't cook in the microwave; it destroys the alliinase, says Dr. Simon.

BONUS Crush or chop cloves before cooking to release even more alliinase, even as cooking times increase.

Root Vegetables
Roast with skins on

RAW Winter veggies such as potatoes, turnips, and parsnips are high in fiber and vitamins, but many are not commonly eaten raw.

COOKED Roasting with skins intact helps retain all the nutrients. If you prefer boiling, leave the skins on (peel them after cooling, if necessary), and boil them in large chunks (preferably whole) to preserve the veggies' water-soluble nutrients, Krieger says.

BONUS Choose a colorful variety for added health benefits. Several studies show that root vegetables with darker skins (red potatoes) or flesh (purple sweet potatoes) have more cancer-fighting polyphenols than their lighter-colored cousins.

Brussels Sprouts
Steam or stir-fry

RAW Brussels sprouts contain sulforaphane, a powerful phyto-chemical that helps protect against breast cancer.

COOKED Steaming or stir-frying as quickly as possible preserves more of the cancer-fighting compounds. (Boiling Brussels sprouts causes sulforaphane to leach into the water, according to research.)

BONUS The tough cores will cook faster and more evenly if you cut an X into the bottom of each stem.

Beets
Steam gently

RAW Beets are high in betanin, a powerful plant pigment and antioxidant that can halt free-radical damage and may even stop the growth of tumor cells in the stomach, colon, lungs, and nervous system, according to several studies.

COOKED Lightly steam beets to retain more cancer-fighting powers, Dr. Johnson says. Betanin is highly sensitive to heat, so intense cooking methods like boiling or roasting destroy the benefits.

BONUS Peel and chop the beets before steaming to help liberate the betanin from the tough cell walls and allow the beets to cook faster.

Tomatoes
Roast with olive oil

RAW Tomatoes are rich in lycopene, a carotenoid that gives this fruit its red hue. Lycopene is also a powerful antioxidant that can reduce the risk of certain cancers and heart disease.

COOKED Roasting tomatoes causes cell walls to burst, releasing more lycopene. A recent German study published in the *British Journal of Nutrition* found that 77 percent of 198 people following a strict raw-food diet had plasma lycopene levels below what's considered optimal.

BONUS Splash cherry tomatoes with olive oil, then roast them in the oven until their skins rupture, Krieger suggests. Lycopene is fat soluble, so adding olive oil helps your body absorb it.

Onions
Bake for 5 minutes in foil

RAW Onions are one of the best sources of quercetin, a flavonoid with anti-inflammatory powers that may help control allergies and asthma, as well as help treat Alzheimer's and Parkinson's diseases.

COOKED Baking thick chunks wrapped in foil for 5 minutes at 390°F preserves 99.5 percent of the quercetin compounds while diminishing the bite and odor, according to a 2008 USDA/National Food Research Institute study.

BONUS Choose red or yellow onions over white; they have more flavonoids. As a general rule, the darker the color, the greater the number of antioxidants.

✳ THE VEGGIE FACTOR

Your grandma said it best: Eat your veggies. This one simple rule is the most powerful and important way to fight aging, according to research from the Jean Mayer USDA Human Nutrition Research Center on Aging at Tufts University. But to get the maximum anti-aging protection and disease prevention, you need to not only eat the right number of servings per week but also include variety—and lots of it.

That's the main message behind an often overlooked but critical recommendation within the latest USDA Dietary Guidelines report: the Ideal Veggie Schedule (opposite page). This new research reveals that eating about 14 cups of vegetables per week, from a wide range of veggie groups, raises blood levels of many protective antioxidants. In addition to their well-documented ability to fight and reduce the risk of disease, antioxidants may help preserve your long-term memory and learning capabilities, even as you get older.

Numerous studies also link a higher veggie intake to a reduced risk of stroke, cardiovascular disease, cancer, type 2 diabetes, and obesity. That's why the strongest recommendation from the USDA's report is a greater consumption of a wide variety of vegetables—advice that's mirrored by every major health organization, including the American Heart Association, American Institute for Cancer Research, and American Diabetes Association.

Convinced but still struggling to work all this produce into your real-life diet? Then follow this three-step plan, which includes a breakdown of the five essential veggie "groups," a cheat sheet for quick reference, and 7 days of actual meals. You'll be fulfilling your 14-cup quota in no time.

Easy Ways to Sneak in Veggies

✳ Swap noodle soup for bean or lentil.

✳ Serve chicken or fish over a bed of corn or wilted greens instead of rice.

✳ Use salsa or marinara sauce for dipping.

✳ Add mashed beans or chopped mushrooms to lean ground beef or turkey.

✳ Trade half of your pasta portion for chopped veggies.

The Ideal Veggie Schedule

Your goal: 14 cups per week

That might seem like a lot, but it's easier than it sounds. Researchers have divided the entire vegetable spectrum into five "groups" (yes, beans are a veggie!) and broken down your exact weekly needs.

Dark Greens

You need: 2 cups per week

Top picks: broccoli; collard, mustard, and turnip greens; mesclun; romaine; spinach

Payoff: better lung health, stronger bones, a stronger immune system, lower blood pressure, reduced inflammation, and a healthier brain

Orange Vegetables

You need: 1½ cups per week

Top picks: carrots, pumpkin, sweet potatoes, winter squash

Payoff: better vision, blood sugar control, and lung health; also high in cancer-fighting carotenoids

Beans

You need: 2½ cups per week

Top picks: black beans, chickpeas, edamame, kidney beans, lentils, pinto beans, tofu

Payoff: lower rates of heart disease, high blood pressure, breast and colon cancers, and type 2 diabetes

Starchy Vegetables

You need: 2½ cups per week

Top picks: corn, green peas, white potatoes

Payoff: nutrients ranging from vitamins A, C, B$_6$, and folate to potassium and magnesium; rich in unique antioxidants, such as cancer-fighting isoflavones in peas and blood pressure–lowering kukoamines in potatoes

Wild Card

You need: 5½ cups per week

Top picks: artichokes, asparagus, bell peppers, Brussels sprouts, cabbage, cauliflower, eggplant, green beans, mushrooms, onions, tomatoes, wax beans, zucchini

Payoff: a broad spectrum of nutrients and antioxidants that protect every system in your body, including beta-carotene in bell peppers and quercetin, a natural anti-inflammatory, in onions

Follow the cheat sheet below.

A Week at a Glance

	Monday	Tuesday	Wednesday	Thursday	Friday	Saturday	Sunday
Lunch	1 cup greens	½ cup orange veggies	1 cup greens and ½ cup beans	1 cup wild card	1 cup wild card	1 cup wild card	½ cup beans
Dinner	¾ cup starchy veggies	½ cup beans	1½ cup wild card	1 cup beans	¾ cup starchy veggies	1 cup orange veggies	1 cup starchy veggies and 1 cup wild card

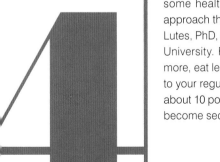

Small Changes, Big Results

If your goal is to lose weight and exercise more, forget the deprivation diet and marathon workouts. New research shows that taking baby steps—not giant leaps—is the best way to get lasting results. A study published in the *Annals of Behavioral Medicine* found that participants who made one small, potentially permanent change in their food choices and/or physical activity each week (such as drinking one fewer can of soda or walking 5 more minutes each day) lost more than twice as much belly fat, 2½ more inches off their waistlines, and about four times more weight during a 4-month program, compared with those who followed traditional calorie-restriction and physical-activity guidelines.

"When you focus on just a couple of small changes at a time, you begin to ingrain some healthy habits that last for a lifetime, rather than trying an all-or-nothing approach that more often than not fails because it's too hard to follow," says Lesley Lutes, PhD, an assistant professor in the department of psychology at East Carolina University. Following are 11 simple steps (with proven results) to help you move more, eat less, and look and feel better than ever. Add just one or two steps a week to your regular routine and you can lose nearly 3 inches from your waistline and be about 10 pounds lighter in just a few months. Even better: Once these healthy habits become second nature, they'll benefit you for a lifetime.

> **Pick Up a Pen after Every Meal** Mindlessly munch on a bag of chips and you could easily polish off the whole thing; write down how much you've eaten and you're more likely to practice portion control. Keeping a food log helps control extra calories in two ways: the combination of plain old reality check (I just ate 30 minutes ago!) and awareness that what you're putting in your mouth will soon be recorded for posterity. In a recent study, people who kept a food journal lost twice as much weight as those who didn't. When they combined it with a moderate diet-and-exercise plan, they lost an average of 13 pounds in 6 months. Journaling also gives you insight into your eating habits, Dr. Lutes says. Do you skip meals? Eat the same during the week as on the weekend? Binge when you're feeling stressed? "Knowing your routine helps you figure out what changes are right for you," she adds.

> **Skip through the Commercials** Get off your duff and move during your favorite TV shows. Skip, dance, go up and down some stairs, run in place—anything that gets your heart rate up so you feel somewhat breathless, says Geralyn Coopersmith, senior national manager at Equinox Fitness. Do it for each 2-minute break (forget the TiVo) during a typical 2-hour TV night and you'll burn an extra 270 calories a day—which can translate to a 28-pound weight loss in a year.

> **Limit High-Fat Foods to One per Week** Tag the high-fat/high-calorie foods that are typically your

✳ EASY SWAPS THAT SAVE LOADS OF CALORIES

Shaving calories from every meal, snack, or side dish is one of the easiest ways to reduce your overall intake. To lose ½ to 1 pound a week, aim to cut 250 to 500 calories a day by making two or three of these swaps.

SWAP 1 can of regular soda for 1 bottle of water
Save 100 calories

SWAP Small french fries for apple slices
Save 270 calories

SWAP 1 cup chocolate ice cream for ½ cup chocolate ice cream with ½ cup sliced strawberries
Save 115 calories

SWAP Big Mac for regular hamburger
Save 290 calories

SWAP ½ cup granola for ¾ cup high-fiber cereal
Save 110 calories

SWAP 1 tablespoon mayo for 1 teaspoon mustard on sandwich
Save 100 calories

SWAP 1 large (4½") bagel for 2 slices light whole grain bread
Save 269 calories

SWAP 1 small bag (1 ounce) pretzels for 2 cups air-popped popcorn
Save 47 calories

SWAP 2 slices pizza for 1 slice cheese pizza plus 1½ cups mixed salad with 1 tablespoon low-fat dressing
Save 229 calories

favorites (common top five: cookies, candy, ice cream, potato chips, and french fries) and gradually downshift. "If you're eating six of these foods a week, try to go down to five," says Lutes. Each week, drop another until you're at no more than one or two; at the same time, add in a good-for-you choice like baby carrots, sautéed broccoli, oranges, and other fresh fruits and veggies.

> **Sign Up for Healthy E-Newsletters** One recent study from Kaiser Permanente found that people who received weekly e-mails about diet and fitness for 16 weeks substantially increased their levels of physical activity and intake of healthy foods like fruits and vegetables while cutting back on trans and saturated fats. We can help: Go to www.prevention.com/newsletters and sign up for our weekly newsletters "Eat Up Slim Down" and "Walk Off Weight."

> **Walk 5 Minutes More Every Day** In Dr. Lutes's pilot study, increasing daily activity levels by just a few minutes at a time helped participants lose weight.

Eventually, your goal should be to do at least 30 minutes of physical activity a day (burning off about 120 extra calories daily, or 12½ pounds a year), but it doesn't have to be all at once. Some simple ways to get moving:

* Walk around the perimeter of the grocery store at least once before heading toward the items you need.

* Move in place whenever you're talking on the telephone.

* Go through or around the entire shopping mall instead of parking near the store you need.

* Take a walk around the block at lunch and after dinner.

> **Strength-Train in Mini Bursts** Basic body-weight exercises such as squats and push-ups are a simple way to build more metabolism-revving muscle in minutes, and research shows they're just as effective as hitting the gym. "Your muscles don't know the difference between working against your body's own resistance and on a fancy piece of equipment," says Wayne Westcott, fitness research director at Quincy College. "The one rule to follow is that each exercise should fatigue your muscles within 60 to 90 seconds." Try this mini workout: Do 10 reps each of knee push-ups, squats, crunches, lunges, and chair dips. Then gradually increase the number of reps it takes for your muscles to feel fully fatigued.

> **Climb Three Extra Flights of Stairs Daily** Have a choice between riding and climbing? Including 2 to 3 minutes of stair climbing per day—covering about three to five floors—can burn enough calories to eliminate the average American's annual weight gain of 1 to 2 pounds a year. It's also good for more than just your waistline: Men who climbed more than 70 flights of stairs a week had 18 percent lower mortality rates than those who climbed fewer than 20 flights a week, according to one Harvard study. Start with just a couple of flights a day; if you're already a dedicated climber, aim to add three more flights to your daily trek.

> **Take a Pedometer Wherever You Go** Just as you wouldn't leave home without your cell phone, make a pedometer a must-have accessory. Research shows pedometer users take nearly 2,500 more steps a day (over 1 mile, or about 100 calories) than nonusers. Over a year, that's enough to burn off about 10 pounds.

> **Brown-Bag It at Least Once a Week** You'll save thousands of calories (not to mention hundreds of dollars) over the course of a year. Consider this: A premade chicken Caesar wrap from a chain restaurant has 610 calories, more than 40 percent of which come from fat, as well as 1,440 milligrams of sodium (more than half the recommended daily amount). Make your own with presliced deli chicken breast on whole wheat bread with light mayo and romaine for about 230 calories. You'll cut almost 400 calories and about 520 milligrams of sodium, which leaves room for a side salad and could result in a 28-pound weight loss after a year. "When you make and eat your own food, you not only control the quality and portion sizes but also reduce the amount of sugar, salt, and fat that you're consuming, which can be significantly higher in restaurant fare," says Ashley Koff, RD, a nutrition consultant based in Los Angeles.

> **Doing Errands? Obey the 1-Mile Rule** Americans use their cars for two-thirds of all trips that are less than 1 mile and 89 percent of all trips that are 1 to 2 miles, yet each additional hour you spend driving is associated with a 6 percent increase in obesity. Burn calories instead of gas by following this rule: If your errands are less than 1 mile away, vow to walk them at a brisk pace instead of driving. Or park where you can run several errands within a mile instead of moving your car each time. Walk every day and you'll be 13 to 17 pounds lighter next year.

> **Take 10 Minutes to Eat a Treat** Try this strategy to permanently reduce cravings: Portion out one serving of your favorite treat, taking a minute to smell it, look at it, and think about it.

Take one small bite. Chew slowly, moving it around in your mouth and focusing on the texture and taste, then swallow. Ask yourself whether you want another bite or if that satisfied you. If you still want more, repeat, this time chewing the food 20 times. Continue this eating exercise for as long as you want or until you finish the serving (it should take about 10 minutes). "When you take the time to slow down and be more mindful of what something really tastes like, you'll feel more satisfied," Dr. Lutes says. "Many of our participants told us that after a while, they didn't enjoy the treat as much as they thought they would, or they were content after just a couple of bites and were better able to stop eating when they were satisfied."

✳ WEIGHT-LOSS SUPPLEMENTS WORTH A LOOK!

New research shows that the nutrients you need to stay healthy may also regulate hunger. Experts recommend getting them through food first, but because many women fall short, consider these supplements for extra insurance.

Slimming Supplement	Recommended	Health Bonus
Vitamin D People who have high vitamin D levels at the start of a diet lose more weight, suggests research presented at the Endocrine Society's annual meeting.	Get 1,000 IU through fatty fish and fortified cereal, juice, and dairy products or a D_3 supplement daily.	Vitamin D fights cancer and helps your body absorb bone-building calcium.
Prebiotics Overweight adults who took a prebiotic supplement lost an average of 2 pounds over 12 weeks, compared with those on a placebo, found Canadian researchers.	Aim for 4 to 20 g daily from foods such as garlic, onions, artichokes, and fortified yogurt or from supplements.	Prebiotics stimulate the growth of healthy bacteria (probiotics) in the gut to regulate digestion.
Calcium When women deficient in calcium took 1,200 mg of calcium daily for 15 weeks, they lost 4 times as much weight as those who took a placebo.	Get 1,000 to 1,200 mg daily from low-fat dairy and leafy green vegetables or a 500 or 600 mg calcium carbonate or citrate supplement taken twice a day.	Calcium builds and maintains strong bones to prevent injury and osteoporosis.
Multivitamin In a 15-week study, women who popped a daily multivitamin felt 45% less hungry than those who took a placebo.	Eat plenty of colorful fresh fruits and veggies, whole grains, and lean protein daily, and take a multi that provides no more than 100% of your daily value for each nutrient.	The wide range of nutrients in multivitamins plays a critical part in immune function.

✳ SEVEN WAYS TO BEAT STRESS FAT

For most of us, stress is a fact of life. Unfortunately, recent research reveals that it's also a fact of fat.

Here's what happens: Your body responds to all stress—physical or psychological—in exactly the same way. So every time you have a stressful day, your brain acts as though you're in physical danger and instructs your cells to release potent hormones. You get a burst of adrenaline, which taps stored energy so you can fight or flee. At the same time, you get a surge of cortisol, which tells your body to replenish that energy even though you haven't used very many calories in your stressed-out state. This can make you hungry . . . very hungry. And your body keeps on pumping out that cortisol as long as the stress continues.

In addition, with your adrenal glands pumping out cortisol, production of the muscle-building hormone testosterone slows down. "Over time, this drop causes a decrease in your muscle mass, so you burn fewer calories,"

explains Shawn Talbott, PhD, author of *The Cortisol Connection*. "This occurs naturally as you age, but high cortisol levels accelerate the process."

Cortisol also encourages your body to store fat—especially visceral fat, which is particularly dangerous because it surrounds vital organs and releases fatty acids into your blood, raising cholesterol and insulin levels and paving the way for heart disease and diabetes.

Obviously, getting rid of all anxiety isn't an option. But by taking these seven steps to beat stress, you can get your cortisol levels and weight under control—and improve your overall health at the same time.

1. Drop and Do 10

That's right, power out some push-ups. "Moving your muscles is an effective, instant stress reliever. It actually fools your body into thinking you're escaping the source of your stress," Dr. Talbott says. "Exercise makes your blood circulate more quickly, transport-ing the cortisol to your kidneys and flushing it out of your system." But if push-ups aren't practical, just flexing your hands or calf muscles will help move cortisol along, he says. Even taking a stroll on your lunch break is beneficial. In one study, Dr. Talbott found that 18 minutes of walking three times per week can quickly lower the hormone's levels by 15 percent.

2. Go Slowly at Meals

Under stress, we tend to scarf down even healthy food, and research has linked this behavior to bigger portions and more belly fat. But Epel hypothesizes that slowing down, savoring each bite, and paying attention to feelings of fullness may lower cortisol levels along with decreasing the amount of food you eat, thereby shifting the distribution of fat away from your belly.

3. Stop Strict Dieting

It's ironic, but research shows that constant dieting can make cortisol levels rise as much as 18 percent. In addition, when your cortisol levels spike, your blood sugar goes haywire, first rising, then plummeting. This makes you cranky and—you guessed it—ravenous. When your brain is deprived of sugar—its main fuel—self-control takes a nosedive, and your willpower doesn't stand a chance. "The only way around this is to stop rigid dieting," Dr. Peeke advises. She suggests eating three healthful meals and two snacks spaced evenly throughout the day so that your blood sugar stays level: "You won't be hungry, you won't be stressed about being hungry, and you'll still drop the extra pounds."

4. Give In to Cravings

When stress drives you toward something sweet or salty, it's okay to yield a little. "It's much better to indulge in a small way and cut off your cortisol response before it gets out of control," Dr. Epel says. "Have a piece of chocolate. You will feel better. Just stop at one." If you have trouble restraining yourself, take precautions so you won't binge. Buy a single cookie when you're out instead of keeping a box at home, or keep them in the freezer so you have to wait for one to defrost.

5. Curtail Caffeine

Next time you're under duress, choose decaf. When you combine stress with caffeine, it raises cortisol levels more than stress alone. In a University of Oklahoma study, consuming the equivalent of 2½ to 3 cups of coffee while under mild stress boosted cortisol levels by about 25 percent—and kept it up for 3 hours. When subjects took 600 milligrams of caffeine (the equivalent of 6 cups of java) throughout the day, the hormone went up by 30 percent and stayed high all day long. You'll experience these effects even if your body is accustomed to a lot of lattes. And because high cortisol levels can contribute to stress eating, you might want to consider quitting caffeine altogether.

6. De-Stress Breakfast

Deficiencies in B vitamins, vitamin C, calcium, and magnesium are stressful to your body, leading to increased cortisol levels and food cravings, Dr. Talbott says. But you can fight back by eating a breakfast that's high in these nutrients. He suggests some OJ, a grapefruit, or a large handful of strawberries to supply vitamin C; 6 to 8 ounces of low-fat yogurt, which contains calcium and magnesium; and a whole grain bagel or toast with a bit of peanut butter. Whole grains are bursting with B vitamins, while peanut butter contains fatty acids that can decrease the production of stress hormones.

7. Sleep It Off

The most effective stress-reduction strategy of all: Get enough shut-eye. "Your body perceives sleep deprivation as a major stressor," Dr. Talbott says. A University of Chicago study found that getting an average of 6½ hours of sleep each night can increase cortisol levels, appetite, and weight gain. The National Sleep Foundation recommends 7 to 9 hours. As if that weren't enough, other research shows that lack of sleep also raises levels of ghrelin, a hunger-boosting hormone. In one study, appetite—particularly for sweet and salty foods—increased by 23 percent in people who lacked sleep. The good news: A few nights of solid sleep can bring all this back into balance, and getting enough regularly helps keep it there. Says Dr. Talbott, "You'll eat less, and you'll feel better, too."

✳ SIGNS YOUR KITCHEN IS MAKING YOU FAT

The kitchen is the heart of your home, but it might also be at the heart of your unwanted weight. Everything from the size of your plates to the wattage of your bulbs has a direct effect on what and how much you eat, according to research in the *Annual Reviews of Nutrition*. Here are signs that your kitchen is sabotaging your waistline—and simple fixes to get the scale moving in the right direction.

Your Plates Are Platter-Size

"Most of us make a habit of filling our plates and finishing what's on them," says Lisa Young, PhD, RD, author of *The Portion Teller Plan*. But since the 1970s, dinner plates have grown 25 percent, to 12 inches or more in diameter. Eat off a plate about 2 inches smaller and you'll serve yourself 22 percent fewer calories per meal, which can mean a 2-pound weight loss in 1 month, says Brian Wansink, PhD, director of Cornell University's Food and Brand Lab and the author of *Mindless Eating*. **SOLUTION** Rethink your place settings. Use your salad plate to hold higher-calorie meats or pasta, and load your dinner plate with veggies, Dr. Young says. If you plan to buy new dinner plates, the best size is 10 inches in diameter, Dr. Wansink says. "Any smaller, though, and you'll go back for seconds," he adds.

You Love Bright Light

High-wattage lighting can raise stress levels, stimulating your appetite and causing you to eat faster than usual, according to research reviews. On the flip side, too dim is no better—studies show low lighting lessens inhibitions. **SOLUTION** Many modern kitchens have layers of light sources, from under-the-cabinet halogens to recessed lights around the perimeter and a decorative fixture over the table, says Joseph Rey-Barreau, a lighting designer in Lexington, Kentucky. When you're cooking, flip on as many lights as you like, but when it's time to eat, use no more than 240 total watts. That's the equivalent of four 60-watt bulbs in a four-light, over-the-table fixture, for example, or six 40-watt bulbs in six high hats; with compact fluorescent bulbs, use 75 to 100 total watts.

The Mail Is Stacked on Your Counter

"Kitchens often become dumping grounds," says Peter Walsh, a professional organizer and the author of *Does This Clutter Make*

My Butt Look Fat? A messy space makes healthy eating harder because it's a lot easier to grab a few cookies or order pizza than it is to unearth a countertop and cook. Plus, clutter leads to stress, which raises cortisol levels in the blood, increasing hunger, adds Dr. Peeke. **SOLUTION** Pick one spot for mail and newspapers, and keep large areas of counter space clear for meal prep. Also, store a few cooking tools, such as a plastic steamer or food chopper, on an easily accessible shelf. And reserve an area in the kitchen for eating only, designated by place mats, suggests Evelyn Tribole, RD, who specializes in intuitive eating. When you separate eating from other activities, you're more likely to focus on your food and listen to fullness cues. Studies show that when distracted, you'll eat 15 percent more.

Your Glasses Are Wide

People serve themselves more soda and juice when using short, wide glasses than they do with tall, skinny ones, according to recent research. That's because we focus on the height of beverages when pouring a portion. Americans drink about 350 calories a day; pour just 2 extra ounces of OJ every morning and you could gain 3 pounds in 1 year. **SOLUTION** Use skinny glasses for soda and juice, and fill wider ones with water and other calorie-free quenchers. When it comes to weight loss, what you drink has a greater impact than what you eat: Studies show that you could lose 1 pound in 6 months just by cutting out one sugar-sweetened drink serving a day.

You Have Plenty of Pantry Space

Bulk shopping can help cut food bills, but if you store groceries in their supersize packages, you're more likely to supersize your meals. Researchers found that people prepared 23 percent more food when cooking from large

containers and ate twice as many candies from big bags as from smaller ones. Having a large variety of food may cause you to overeat, too: "With four types of cookies at your fingertips, you're

more likely to try a little of each in search of satisfaction," says Domenica Rubino, MD, director of the Washington Center for Weight Management and Research in Virginia. **SOLUTION** Big packages don't have a natural stopping point, so break them down into smaller containers or single-serving portions. Also, keep only one variety of your favorite treat in the house to help curb temptation.

You Have a Clear Cookie Jar

According to a research review, just seeing tempting food makes people feel hungrier. It also causes the release of dopamine, a brain

chemical that produces a feel-good sensation and may intensify a particular craving. **SOLUTION** "Re-engineer what's within reach," Dr. Wansink says. Put trigger foods in opaque containers and stash them in an inconvenient spot. When you need a step stool to reach those cookies or have to push past veggies to get to the leftover cake in the fridge, it serves as a speed bump to help you pause and reconsider, Dr. Wansink says. You should also create a no-brainer snack bucket, Dr. Rubino adds. Load an open container with yogurt and cheese sticks, and keep it front and center in the fridge. If you chose a fruit cup instead of potato chips every day, you'd be 4 pounds slimmer in 6 months.

Your Kitchen Is Grand Central

On average, kitchens are 50 percent larger than they were 35 years ago, making them a place where lots of activities happen, such as watching TV or paying bills. According to a recent study, participants who ate while watching TV consumed more food and ate more often—about one extra meal per day. **SOLUTION** Move the TV or laptop out of the kitchen, and shift tasks like talking on the phone to the den, where food is out of sight. And between meals, keep the kitchen lights off—it's a subtle sign that says the kitchen is closed.

Give These Power Foods a Whirl!

The secret to permanent weight loss is to change your relationship with food. When you learn to eat with awareness, you empower yourself to choose healthy foods that deliver the taste you love yet fill you up for fewer calories. Including superfoods in your diet helps you not only lose weight but also fight disease and boost health. Blueberries, broccoli, and walnuts have been touted as such superfoods. But are they the best choices for your personal health goals?

Science suggests it may be time for you to branch out. A recent surge in clinical research reveals a new crop of superfoods that can help lower your risks of everything from cancer and heart disease to macular degeneration and osteoporosis. For extra motivation (because, of course, you do your best to avoid junk food, too), we've included the latest studies on surprising culprits that make these problems worse. Eat a daily dose of the right foods—and purge your diet of these health saboteurs—to get the health benefits you want most.

PROTECT YOUR HEART

Fill Up on These

> **Barley.** This grain can blast LDL ("bad" cholesterol) and triglycerides, lowering your total cholesterol an average of 13 points—without affecting your HDL ("good" cholesterol) levels, according to a 2009 research review. Barley contains beta-glucan, a type of soluble fiber that binds with cholesterol to whisk it from the body, explains David Grotto, RD, author of *101 Optimal Life Foods*. A cup and a half of cooked pearl barley contains 3 grams of soluble fiber, the daily amount recommended by the FDA.

> **Pinto beans.** Like barley, pinto beans contain cholesterol-fighting beta-glucan. In one study, participants with mild insulin resistance (a precursor to high cholesterol) who ate ½ cup of pinto beans daily dropped 19 points from their total count in 8 weeks, including a 13-point decrease in LDL.

> **Grapes.** Consuming just 1¼ cups of grapes can prevent the damaging effects of a high-fat meal that can slow circulation and increase risk of coronary heart disease, say researchers at Nationwide Children's Hospital in Columbus, Ohio. A daily dose of grapes improves blood vessel health in general, scientists believe, because the fruit contains high levels of antioxidants called polyphenols.

> **Macadamia nuts.** An Australian study published in the *Journal of Nutrition* found that when men with high cholesterol ate between 1 and 3 ounces of macadamia nuts per day for 1 month, their LDL dropped by 5.3 percent, while their HDL rose by 7.9 percent. The nuts, researchers concluded, increased the amount of healthy monounsaturated fatty acids (MUFAs) in the blood. One ounce is adequate for most people.

> **Mineral water.** The magnesium and calcium plentiful in most mineral waters (like San Pellegrino, which has 56 milligrams magnesium and 208 milligrams calcium) are both potential blood pressure reducers. In a Swedish study, 70 men and women ages 45 to 64 with borderline hypertension experienced a significant decrease in blood pressure after 4 weeks of drinking 1 liter of mineral (not seltzer) water daily.

Avoid These

> **Energy drinks.** The caffeine and guarana that are often added to energy drinks can make your blood pressure skyrocket, says John La Puma, MD, author of *Chef MD's Big Book of Culinary Medicine*.

STRENGTHEN YOUR BONES

Fill Up on These

> **Lean top sirloin.** A 4-ounce serving of this cut (grass- or grain-fed) provides more than half of the Daily Value (DV) (8 milligrams) of zinc, a bone-protecting mineral. Research shows that low levels of zinc are associated with brittle bones in middle-aged women. If you prefer seafood, an Alaskan king crab leg packs 10 milligrams.

> **Broccoli.** Broccoli is bursting with vitamin K, which helps your body transport calcium and metabolizes the mineral into your skeleton. Several studies found that vitamin K not only boosts bone mineral density in osteoporosis sufferers but also reduces fracture rates. As a result, the Institute of Medicine upped its daily recommendation to 90 micrograms for women and 120 micrograms for men (3.5 ounces of broccoli contains 141 micrograms). Other good sources include broccoli rabe and spinach.

Avoid This

> **Salt.** Excess sodium increases the amount of calcium excreted in urine. Over time, this could lead to significant bone loss, say British researchers. Grotto recommends limiting sodium intake to 2,300 milligrams daily.

PROMOTE DIGESTION

Fill Up on These

> **Blueberries.** These colorful berries aren't just good for your brain. They contain high concentrations of anthocyanins, compounds that can reduce the risk of colorectal cancer by 33 percent, according to a study of more than 6,000 people published in *Cancer Epidemiology, Biomarkers & Prevention*. Grotto recommends eating a daily cup of blueberries—or cherries, strawberries, or Concord grapes, which also contain anthocyanins.

> **Popcorn.** This popular snack is rich in insoluble fiber, which helps keep your digestive system moving. Snacking on 3 cups of air-popped (not microwaved) popcorn twice a week can reduce your risk of diverticular disease, a painful inflammation of the intestine, by 28 percent, according to a 2008 study published in the *Journal of the American Medical Association*.

> **Bananas.** Add a banana to your daily morning cereal to get a healthy dose of protease inhibitors, compounds that fight off *Helicobacter pylori*, the bacteria that researchers believe is the cause of most stomach ulcers.

Avoid These
> **Dried plums.** Although filled with healthy fiber, dried plums are also high in sorbitol, a sugar alcohol that in large quantities can cause gas, bloating, and sometimes diarrhea. Grotto suggests limiting your intake to four or five dried plums a day or substituting a sorbitol-free dried fruit, such as apricots.

SHARPEN YOUR VISION

Fill Up on These
> **Collard greens.** People who eat at least two daily servings of leafy greens, such as collard greens and spinach, are 46 percent less likely to develop macular degeneration, a leading cause of blindness in those over age 60, according to Harvard Medical School. These foods contain lutein and zeaxanthin, two powerful carotenoids that help eyes absorb short-wavelength light and protect the retina, La Puma says. Women with diets high in beta-carotene (of which collard greens are a rich source) were 39 percent less likely to develop serious cataracts, according to a Harvard Medical School study of more than 50,000 nurses. Because beta-carotene is fat soluble, cook the greens first, then add olive oil to maximize absorption.

> **Low-fat or nonfat milk.** Low- and nonfat milk have plenty of riboflavin, a B vitamin that helps prevent cataracts. Your body uses riboflavin to manufacture glutathione, which fights free radicals that can damage eye tissue. Vitamin D, found in fortified milk, might protect your eyes as well. One study showed that high blood

✳ WHEN FOOD CAUSES FATIGUE

Many naturopathic doctors think that food sensitivities sap our energy. The theory is that when you are sensitive to a particular food, your body doesn't break it down fully. These incompletely digested food molecules can enter the bloodstream through your stomach and intestinal linings. Because these molecules are larger than your body expects, your immune system sees them not as food but as foreign invaders and triggers your body's defenses just as if you had encountered a virus. You feel tired because all of your energy goes toward fighting off the invader.

If you suspect a food sensitivity is causing your fatigue, confirm it by cutting the questionable food out of your diet for 4 to 6 weeks. Even some of the "energy foods" in this book can cause problems for those with food sensitivity. Common offenders are thought to be dairy, soy, corn, couscous, and gluten, which is found in wheat, oats, rye, barley, and other grains. After more than a month of avoiding the suspected culprit, slowly reintroduce the food and see how you feel. If you eliminate more than one item, allow 3 days between adding back each food.

levels of vitamin D reduced the risk of macular degeneration by nearly 40 percent, compared with people with low levels.

> **Nuts.** The omega-3 fatty acids in nuts, especially walnuts, reduce inflammation and prevent oxidative damage to the retina, Grotto says. Just one to two weekly servings of about ¾ ounce of nuts lower your risk of developing early macular degeneration by 35 percent, according to new research published in the *Archives of Ophthalmology*.

Avoid These

> **Refined foods.** People who regularly eat white bread, cornflakes, and other foods that spike blood sugar almost double their risk of macular degeneration, according to a 10-year Tufts University study of more than 4,000 subjects. Switch to whole grain versions of bread and cereal to steady your blood sugar.

PROTECT YOUR BREASTS

Fill Up on These

> **Cauliflower.** This cruciferous vegetable contains sulforaphane, which halted the growth of breast cancer cells in test-tube studies by interfering with the cells' ability to reproduce. Cauliflower also contains a compound called indole-3-carbinol (I3C), which may lower levels of estrogens that might otherwise encourage tumors to multiply. When cooking this veggie, roast or steam but never boil it; new research says boiling causes up to 75 percent of the cancer-fighting compounds to leach into the cooking water.

> **Sweet potatoes.** One 5-inch-long sweet potato contains 11,062 micrograms of beta-carotene, a carotenoid that helps your body metabolize estrogen better, La Puma says. Women with the lowest levels of beta-carotene and other carotenoids had double the risk of breast cancer, compared with those who had the highest levels, found the New York University Women's Health Study.

> **Tomato sauce.** Research shows that lycopene, a powerful antioxidant found in tomato sauce, may protect against breast cancer by neutralizing free radicals that damage cells. Studies prove that lycopene can inhibit breast cancer cell growth in test tubes as well as suppress tumors in mice. Plus, it helps shield skin from cancer-causing sun damage. Lycopene is more easily absorbed in the body when exposed to heat, so cooked tomatoes are better than raw. Lycopene is fat-soluble, so add olive oil to help absorption.

Avoid This

> **Grapefruit.** Eating just one-quarter of a grapefruit each day or one-half every other day may increase a postmenopausal woman's chances of developing breast cancer by up to 30 percent, according to a 9-year University of Southern California study of 46,000 postmenopausal women. Although doctors aren't sure exactly why, several studies show that grapefruit interacts with estrogen and increases its potency—so much so that the FDA requires hormone-replacement medications to carry a warning label concerning grapefruit juice.

CLEAR YOUR LUNGS

Fill Up on These

> **Pears.** These fruits contain quercetin, a powerful flavonoid that may protect the lungs. A Dutch study of more than 13,000 people found that those who ate the most pears (as well as apples, which also contain quercetin) had the best lung function, while an Australian study discovered a strong association between high pear and apple consumption and lower risk of asthma.

> **Edamame.** Lung cancer victims tend to have low levels of phytoestrogens, important plant compounds, according to a study in the *Journal of the American Medical Association*. Women who ate the highest quantities of foods containing phytoestrogens, such as edamame, tofu, and lentils, slashed their lung cancer risk by 34 percent.

> **Brown rice.** This grain is high in selenium, which may help keep lung-damaging free radicals from forming. A New Zealand study found that people who got the most selenium were nearly two times less likely to develop asthma as those who got the least. You'll meet the DV of

✳ EAT A RAINBOW OF HEALTH

The healthiest (and tastiest) diet is a colorful one, but 80 percent of Americans still don't eat enough brightly hued fruits and vegetables, according to a new analysis of the National Health and Nutrition Examination surveys. Produce contains phytonutrients, plant-based compounds that researchers believe may help ward off obesity, cancer, and heart disease. Follow this color-coded breakdown of what you need more of and why. Aim for two half-cup servings from each group daily.

Eat More	They Contain	They Fight
Lettuce, spinach, zucchini, broccoli, green beans, Brussels sprouts, soybeans	Isothiocyanate, lutein, zeaxanthin, isoflavones	Alzheimer's disease, macular degeneration, lung cancer
Strawberries, tomatoes, apples, cranberries, watermelon, radishes, pomegranate	Lycopene, ellagic acid	Cell damage, breast and prostate cancer
Squash, sweet potatoes, carrots, apricots, cantaloupe, oranges, corn, pineapple, lemons	Alpha-carotene, beta-carotene, beta-cryptoxanthin, hesperidin	Heart disease, stroke, asthma, rheumatoid arthritis
Garlic, onions, pears, black-eyed peas, cauliflower	Allicin, quercetin	High blood pressure and cholesterol, bone loss
Grapes, figs, blueberries, red cabbage, black currants, eggplant, black beans, plums	Anthocyanins, resveratrol	Memory loss, premature aging, cancer, heart disease

55 micrograms with a few servings of selenium-rich foods, such as whole wheat bread, chicken, and eggs.

Avoid These
> **Soft drinks.** If you have asthma, skip soft drinks, advises La Puma. Many contain food additives sodium benzoate, MSG, and sulfites, which can exacerbate symptoms.

PAINPROOF YOUR JOINTS

Fill Up on These
> **Olive oil.** Just 2 teaspoons of olive oil (plus 3 grams of fish oil) a day may significantly improve morning stiffness, joint pain, and fatigue, according to a Brazilian study.

Research also shows that a high intake of olive oil may reduce the risk of rheumatoid arthritis by up to 61 percent.

> **Oranges.** Vitamin C activates a gene that helps cartilage synthesis, La Puma says. People who eat the most vitamin C–rich foods have 70 percent less cartilage loss than those who don't—and slow the progression of osteoarthritis by 300 percent, according to the Framingham Osteoarthritis Cohort Study.

Avoid This

> **Beer or hard liquor.** If you're prone to gout, avoid beer (just one beer daily boosts your uric acid levels by 15 percent, high levels of which can cause gout) and hard liquor (which raises it by 12 percent), according to a Harvard Medical School study of more than 14,000 people.

BOOST YOUR MEMORY

Fill Up on These

> **Apples.** Eating two or three apples a day increases levels of acetylcholine, a neurotransmitter crucial to maintaining memory that tends to decrease with age, according to research from the University of Massachusetts. Additionally, antioxidants in the fruit protect brain cells from free radical damage.

> **Chicken breast.** In a study of more than 6,000 people conducted by the Rush Institute for Healthy Aging and the Centers for Disease Control and Prevention (CDC), those who ate foods high in niacin, like chicken breast, yellowfin tuna, and Chinook salmon, had a 70 percent lower risk of mental decline and Alzheimer's. Aim for at least 14 milligrams of niacin daily, the amount in 3.5 ounces of roasted boneless, skinless chicken breast.

Give These Power
Foods a Whirl!

✱ WHAT'S YOUR "LITE" MEAL HIDING?

Diet-busting calories, that's what. Many contain an average of 18 percent more than restaurant menus claim, report Tufts University researchers who analyzed the calorie content of 29 dishes promoted as "healthy" on national sit-down and fast-food menus. If you eat out three times a week, the following could pack on a 4-pound weight gain in a year.

LARGER PORTIONS Watch for thicker cuts of meat and extra veggies—even the calories in healthy foods can add up.

DODGE 'EM If your serving looks oversize, save half of the meal before you start, or leave a few bites on your plate.

TASTE ENHANCERS Hoping to boost flavor, chefs may add more oil, butter, cream, or sugar than the recipe calls for.

DODGE 'EM Ask for sauces and dressings on the side, and use them sparingly.

FREE SIDES Oily french fries and mayo-packed pasta salads often contain more calories than the dish you ordered.

DODGE 'EM Avoid any extras listed separately on the menu.

> **Coffee.** People who drank 3 to 5 cups of filtered java a day reduced their risk of dementia and Alzheimer's by 65 percent, according to results from a Finnish-Swedish study of more than 1,400 people over 2 decades by the University of Kuopio and published in the *Journal of Alzheimer's Disease*.

Avoid This

> **Liver.** This meat—along with turnip greens and shiitake mushrooms—has large amounts of copper. A diet high in this mineral (2,750 micrograms daily) is associated with a faster rate of cognitive decline by the equivalent of 19 years, research shows, if eaten along with a diet high in saturated and trans fats.

SMOOTH YOUR SKIN

Fill Up on These

> **Canned light tuna.** This kitchen staple is packed with selenium, an antioxidant that protects skin cells against sun damage that can lead to skin cancer. People whose blood had the highest levels of selenium had a 57 percent lower rate of developing basal cell carcinoma and a 64 percent reduction in squamous cell carcinoma, compared with those with the lowest levels, according to a 2009 Australian study of almost 500 adults. Other selenium sources include turkey and fortified instant cereal. The DV for selenium is 55 micrograms, the amount found in a little less than 3 ounces of canned light tuna.

> **Dark chocolate.** New research shows that women who consumed a daily drink containing 2 tablespoons of high-flavonoid cocoa powder for 12 weeks had skin that was significantly smoother, retained more moisture, and had better circulation. Grotto says you can achieve the same effect with a daily ounce of high-flavonoid dark chocolate.

> **Black tea with citrus peel.** Longtime tea drinkers enjoy half the risk of skin cancer—especially if they sip two or more cups each day, according to a 2007 Dartmouth Medical School study. That's possibly due to tea's polyphenols, which may help protect against UV radia-tion. Brew tea with citrus peel to boost its anticancer pow-ers even more. The combined theaflavins in black tea and the d-Limonene in citrus reduced the risk of squamous cell carcinoma by 88 percent, says research from a University of Arizona College of Public Health study.

> **Carrot juice.** One cup of carrot juice (which is equal to 1 pound of carrots) contains 22 milligrams of beta-carotene, a powerful antioxidant that several studies show can help protect skin against sunburn. And the more you drink, the more protection you build up.

Avoid This

> **Alcohol.** Scientists aren't exactly sure why, but drinking more than two alcoholic beverages a day raises your risk of basal cell carcinoma by up to 30 percent, according to research at Harvard School of Public Health.

✻ FIGHT FAT WITH FOOD

You need to cut calories to lose weight. But when you eat less than you need for basic biological function (about 1,200 calories a day for most women), your body throws the brakes on your metabolism. Fuel your body with the right foods and you can lose weight and keep your metabolism humming along. Add these eight fat-burning, hunger-shattering foods to your meals and watch the pounds come off.

2. Oolong and Green Teas
Catechins found in these teas can boost the body's fat-burning fire. One study of Japanese women compared the effects of drinking oolong tea, green tea, or water on various days. Just 1 large cup of oolong tea increased calorie burning by up to 10 percent, a boost that peaked 1½ hours later. Green tea raised metabolism by 4 percent for 1½ hours. Other studies show that drinking 2 to 4 cups of either oolong or green tea daily (about 375 to 675 milligrams of catechins) may translate into an extra 50 calories burned each day—about 5 pounds' worth in a year.

1. Cinnamon
Sweeten your oatmeal or frothy coffee drinks with this flavorful spice instead of sugar (which has 16 calories per teaspoon) and you can save a couple of hundred calories a week, enough to shed 2 to 3 pounds in a year without doing anything else. You'll also be doing your heart a favor: Pakistani researchers found that ½ teaspoon of cinnamon a day could lower heart-damaging cholesterol by 18 percent and triglycerides by 30 percent.

3. Lean Protein

Gram for gram, protein has the same number of calories as carbs (and half that of fat) but takes longer to digest, so you feel full longer. It also seems to help lower levels of the hormone ghrelin, which is known to stimulate appetite. In a Danish study of 60 men and women, those following a diet that included 25 percent of calories from protein lost nearly twice as much fat after 6 months as those eating a diet with just 12 percent.

4. Flax

Flaxseed is rich in fiber and healthy fats, which help stabilize blood sugar, leaving you less likely to binge. Some research suggests flax can also help soothe symptoms of hormone swings because it's high in plant estrogens. Sprinkle ground seeds (they're easier to digest than whole seeds) over cereals, soups, and salads; add them to smoothies; or substitute 1 cup of ground flaxseed for ⅓ cup canola, corn, or other oil or shortening in muffins and cookies.

5. Walnuts

Instead of snacking on some chips, open up a bag of nuts: Walnuts are rich in omega-3 fatty acids, which may keep you feeling fuller longer. In a 1-year study of people with diabetes who were following a low-fat diet, Australian researchers discovered that those who consumed 8 to 10 walnuts a day lost more weight and body fat. The subjects also reduced their insulin levels, which helps keep fat storage in check.

6. Salmon

Just 3 ounces of salmon delivers 530 IU (more than the DV) of vitamin D and 181 milligrams of calcium, a power-packed nutritional combination that may be just what your waistline needs as you get older. In a 7-year study of more than 36,000 women ages 50 to 79, researchers at Kaiser Permanente found that those who took both calcium and vitamin D supplements gained less weight after menopause than those who took a placebo. Other research shows that without enough vitamin D, our appetite-regulating hormone leptin can't do its job.

7. Chile Pepper

If you want to burn fat, spice things up. In a study of 36 men and women, Australian researchers found that following a spicy meal, levels of insulin—the hormone that triggers body-fat storage—were lowered by as much as 32 percent. One theory: Capsaicin, the chemical that gives chiles their fire, may improve the body's ability to clear insulin from the bloodstream after you eat, so you're more likely to burn fat following a spicy meal than after one that doesn't pack heat.

8. Yogurt

Packed with filling protein, yogurt also supplies the body with much-needed calcium. "There's evidence that calcium deficiency, which is common in many women, may slow metabolism," says Tammy Lakatos, RD, co-author of *Fire Up Your Metabolism*. Another plus: Research shows that consuming calcium through low-fat or fat-free dairy foods may reduce fat absorption from other foods.

✳ THE NEW SUPERFRUITS

Though Americans are eating more fruit these days (go us!), more than half are the old standbys: bananas, apples, and oranges. Yes, they're good for you—but you're missing out. "Different fruits provide an array of disease-fighting vitamins, minerals, and antioxidants," says Joy Bauer, RD, author of *Joy Bauer's Food Cures*. In fact, broadening your horizons can measurably improve your health. Colorado State University nutritionists asked 106 women to eat 8 to 10 servings of produce daily for 8 weeks. Half of the group chose from 18 different varieties, while the others ate the same five over and over again. Two weeks later, blood tests showed that the high-variety group reduced their rates of DNA oxidation, possibly making their bodies more resilient against disease; the other group had no change.

Ready to mix it up? Here's a quickie primer on some of the smartest "exotic" picks based on their health benefits—and how to serve them in place of common favorites.

For Perfect Blood Pressure
Good: Bananas
Better: Fresh figs
Why: Six fresh figs have 891 milligrams of blood pressure-lowering potassium, nearly 20 percent of your daily need—and about double what you'd find in one large banana. In a recent 5-year study from the Netherlands, high-potassium diets were linked with lower rates of death from all causes in healthy adults age 55 and older.

You'll also get . . . a boost to your bones. Figs are one of the best fruit sources of calcium, with nearly as much per serving (six figs) as ½ cup of fat-free milk!

Shop for . . . figs that are dry on the surface and feel heavy in the hand. A perfectly ripe fig may have slight cracks that are bursting with the fruit's sweet syrup.

Serve by . . . chopping and adding to yogurt, cottage cheese, oatmeal, or green salads.

To Protect Your Heart and Fight Disease
Good: Red grapes
Better: Lychee
Why: A French study published in the *Journal of Nutrition* found that lychee has the second-highest level of heart-healthy polyphenols of all fruits tested—nearly 15 percent more than the amount found in grapes (cited by many as a polyphenol powerhouse). The compounds may also play an important role in the prevention of degenerative diseases such as cancer. "Polyphenols act like a force field, helping to repel foreign invaders from damaging your cells," Grotto says.

You'll also get . . . protection from breast cancer. A recent test-tube and animal study from Sichuan University in China found that lychee may help prevent the formation of breast cancer cells, thanks to the fruit's powerful antioxidant activity.

Shop for . . . lychee with few black marks on the rough, leathery shell, which can be anywhere from red to brown in color. Look for fruit that gives when pressed gently. Shells should be intact and the fruit attached to the stem.

Serve by . . . peeling or breaking the outer covering just below the stem; use a knife to remove the black pit.

For Beautiful Skin
Good: Orange
Better: Guava
Why: One cup of guava has nearly five times as much skin-healing vitamin C (it's a key ingredient in collagen production) as a medium orange (377 milligrams versus 83 milligrams)—that's more than five times your daily need. Women who eat a lot of vitamin C–packed

foods have fewer wrinkles than women who don't eat many, according to a recent study that tracked the diets of more than 4,000 American women ages 40 to 74.

You'll also get . . . bacteria-busting power. Guava can protect against foodborne pathogens such as listeria and staph, according to research by microbiologists in Bangladesh. Also, a cooperative study by the USDA and Thai scientists found that guava has as much antioxidant activity as some well-known superfoods such as blueberries and broccoli (though every plant contains a different mix of the healthful compounds).

Shop for . . . guava using your nose. A ripe guava has a flowery fragrance, gives a bit to the touch, and has a thin, pale green to light yellowish rind.

Serve by . . . adding to fruit cobbler recipes (the tiny seeds are edible) or simmer chunks in water as you would to make applesauce.

To Lower Cholesterol
Good: Apples
Better: Asian pears
Why: One large Asian pear has nearly 10 grams of cholesterol-lowering fiber, about 40 percent of your daily need; a large apple has about half that much. People who ate the most fiber had the lowest total and "bad" cholesterol levels, according to a recent study of Baltimore adults.

You'll also get . . . protection from creeping weight gain. The

same researchers found that people who ate the most fiber also weighed the least and had the lowest body mass index and waist circumference.

Shop for . . . pears with a firm feel; fragrant aroma; and blemish-free, yellow-brownish skin. Some pears are speckled in appearance; the markings shouldn't affect flavor.

Serve by . . . dicing into a salad of Boston lettuce, crumbled goat cheese, walnuts, and mandarin oranges.

To Fight Cancer
Good: Watermelon
Better: Papaya
Why: It is one of the top sources of beta-cryptoxanthin, which research suggests can protect against lung cancer. Like water-

melon, it is also a rich source of lycopene. "Although there is currently no recommendation for how much lycopene you should consume in a day, research shows that the nutrient may protect against several different types of cancer, including stomach, endometrial, and prostate," Grotto says.

You'll also get . . . better healing. Papayas may help speed burn recovery when used topically, thanks partly to the enzyme papain, which also aids in digestion. "Papain helps break down amino acids, the building blocks of protein," says Elisa Zied, RD, spokesperson for the American Dietetic Association.

Shop for . . . a papaya with yellow-golden skin that yields to gentle pressure.

Recipes That Slim & Satisfy

Let's get cooking! Here are more than 200 family-pleasing recipes, many from readers who have successfully lost weight and kept it off. Looking for a classic with a twist? Try the Roasted Vegetable Lasagna, Savory Turkey Stroganoff, or Apricot-Lemon Chiffon Cake. Whip up the Spicy Meatballs with Coconut Milk, Mandarin-Basil Shrimp Salad on Roasted Sweet Potatoes or Spiced Kahlua Custards when in the mood for something new and exciting. Turn the pages to find a delicious, satisfying recipe for any occasion.

breakfasts

Frittata with Rosemary Potatoes, Tomatoes, and Feta

2 tablespoons olive oil

½ bag (16 ounces) refrigerated rosemary and roasted-garlic diced red potatoes

1 can (14 ounces) diced tomatoes, drained

6 eggs

¼ cup water

½ teaspoon ground black pepper

½ cup crumbled feta cheese

HEAT the oil in a large nonstick skillet over medium-high heat. Add the potatoes and tomatoes. Cook, stirring occasionally, for 3 minutes, or until heated through and all the liquid evaporates.

BEAT the eggs, water, and pepper in a medium bowl. Pour into the skillet. Cook for 1 minute, or until the edges start to set. With a spatula, carefully lift up the edge to let the uncooked egg run underneath. Sprinkle with the cheese. Cover and reduce the heat to low. Cook for 2 minutes, or until the eggs are cooked through.

Total time: 15 minutes　✳　Makes 6 servings

Per serving: 247 calories, 10 g protein, 20 g carbohydrates, 14 g fat, 5 g saturated fat, 544 mg sodium, 4 g fiber

A frittata is an Italian version of an omelet. Often baked to finish the cooking, this superfast frittata is cooked with a lid on to finish the cooking while still on the stove.

HEALTH HEARSAY

Q: Can eating too much sugar cause type 2 diabetes?

A: Not in the same smoking-gun way that cigarettes cause cancer, but research shows that sugar may play a part, and it's smart to limit your intake. First, consuming too much sugar can lead to weight gain, and being overweight does increase your risk of developing type 2 diabetes. Emerging research also suggests that excess sugar intake can increase diabetes risk regardless of weight. A landmark study in the *Journal of the American Medical Association (JAMA)* found that women nearly doubled their diabetes risk when they increased the number of sweetened drinks they had from one or fewer a week to one or more per day over an 8-year period. Rapidly absorbed sugars—like those in colas—may damage the pancreas cells that secrete insulin, says study author Frank B. Hu, MD, PhD, a professor of nutrition and epidemiology at the Harvard School of Public Health.

Zucchini and Dill Frittata

2 teaspoons butter

1 medium zucchini, finely chopped

2 large scallions, thinly sliced

6 egg whites

4 eggs

1 tablespoon water

2 tablespoons chopped fresh dill

¼ teaspoon ground black pepper

3 tablespoons grated Parmesan cheese

PREHEAT the broiler.

MELT the butter in a large nonstick skillet over medium heat. Cook the zucchini for 5 minutes, stirring occasionally. Stir in the scallions and cook for 3 minutes, or until the zucchini is just tender.

MEANWHILE, whisk together the egg whites, eggs, water, dill, pepper, and 2 tablespoons of the cheese in a medium bowl. Add to the skillet and cook for 5 minutes, occasionally lifting the edges of the egg mixture with a spatula and tilting the pan, allowing the uncooked mixture to flow underneath. (The eggs will be set on the bottom but still moist on the top.) Remove from the heat and sprinkle with the remaining 1 tablespoon cheese.

BROIL 4" from the heat for 2 minutes, or until the eggs are set on the top. Cut into quarters to serve.

Total time: 24 minutes ✳ Makes 4 servings

Per serving: 143 calories, 14 g protein, 4 g carbohydrates, 8 g fat, 3 g saturated fat, 231 mg sodium, 1 g fiber

If you don't have an ovenproof skillet, wrap the skillet handle with a double thickness of foil to prevent burning.

Broccoli and Sun-Dried Tomato Quiche

- 1 deep-dish frozen 9" pie shell, thawed
- 5 ounces (2 cups) bagged broccoli florets, coarsely chopped
- ½ cup chopped onion
- 3 tablespoons olive oil
- ½ teaspoon salt
- ½ teaspoon ground black pepper
- ½ teaspoon ground paprika
- 1 cup half-and-half
- ¼ cup chopped oil-packed sun-dried tomatoes
- 1 cup (4 ounces) shredded Parmesan-Romano-Asiago cheese blend
- 3 eggs

PREHEAT the oven to 400°F. Bake the pie shell for 8 minutes, occasionally pricking with a fork to deflate any air bubbles, or until lightly colored. Remove to a rack. Reduce the oven temperature to 350°F.

MEANWHILE, combine the broccoli, onion, oil, salt, pepper, and paprika in an 8" × 8" microwaveable baking dish. Cover with plastic wrap, leaving a small corner vent. Microwave on high, stirring once, for 3 minutes, or until sizzling. Remove.

ADD the half-and-half, tomatoes, and ¾ cup of the cheese. Add the eggs one at a time, beating with a fork after each addition. Pour the filling into the pie shell. Sprinkle with the remaining ¼ cup cheese. Bake for about 35 minutes, or until a knife inserted in the center comes out clean. Let stand for 15 minutes.

Total time: 1 hour 10 minutes ✳ Makes 6 servings

Per serving: 276 calories, 9 g protein, 12 g carbohydrates, 20 g fat, 8 g saturated fat, 502 mg sodium, 1 g fiber

NUTRITION NEWS TO USE

A new study from McMaster University in Ontario finds that the average woman consumes 550 calories when eating solo but up to 800 when eating with three female friends. Dining in groups encourages lingering over a meal and extra eating, says lead study author Meredith Young, PhD. To keep calories in check, pay closer attention to portions when eating in groups, or dine with your favorite person: According to Young's research, you'll eat about the same amount as you would alone.

Charlie's Quiche

1 prepared 9" piecrust

1 cup egg substitute

½ cup low-fat milk

¼ teaspoon ground black pepper

6 ounces fresh spinach, rinsed and dried

1 tablespoon water

1 can (15 ounces) great Northern beans, rinsed and drained

¼ cup shredded reduced-fat Swiss cheese

PREHEAT the oven to 350°F. Bake the piecrust for 10 minutes. Remove to a rack.

MEANWHILE, beat the egg substitute, milk, and pepper in a medium bowl. Set aside.

COOK the spinach in a skillet with the water over medium heat, stirring, for 2 minutes, or just until wilted. Squeeze dry. Place the spinach on the bottom of the crust. Top with the beans. Pour the egg mixture over the beans. Sprinkle with the cheese.

BAKE for 30 to 40 minutes, or until a knife inserted in the center comes out clean. Let stand for 15 minutes.

Total time: 1 hour ✳ Makes 6 servings

Per serving: 261 calories, 11 g protein, 27 g carbohydrates, 13 g fat, 5 g saturated fat, 550 sodium, 4 g fiber

I'm a stay-at-home mom who recently decided to take control of eating and felt that including my 7-year-old son, Charlie, in healthy cooking and eating habits would be a good idea. One night I told him that we were going to make a quiche, and I asked him what he would like to put in it. He said greens and beans! I thought it was a wonderful idea, and it really does taste quite nice! **—Donna**

Mexican Eggs

1 can (15 ounces) vegetarian refried beans

¾ cup refrigerated or jarred salsa

4 eggs

¼ cup sour cream

4 whole grain tortillas (8" diameter), warmed

COAT a large nonstick skillet with cooking spray. Cook the beans and ½ cup of the salsa over medium-high heat for 2 minutes, or until the mixture is bubbling hot.

USE the back of a spoon to make 4 indentations in the beans. Working one at a time, break each egg into a custard cup and pour into each indentation. Cover and cook for about 8 minutes, or until the eggs are cooked to the desired doneness.

SCOOP each portion of egg-topped bean mixture onto 4 plates. Top each serving with 1 tablespoon of the reserved salsa and 1 tablespoon of the sour cream. Serve with the warmed tortillas.

Total time: 15 minutes ✳ Makes 4 servings

Per serving: 273 calories; 16 g protein; 39 g carbohydrates; 9 g fat; 3 g saturated fat; 1,040 mg sodium; 8 g fiber

Make these eggs your way—go for spicy beans and salsa to start the day with a kick or opt for mild salsa and plain beans for a hearty and mildly flavorful meal.

Poached Eggs on Tomatoes and Eggplant

1½ tablespoons distilled white vinegar

1 small eggplant, peeled and cut into 8 rounds (each ¼" thick)

1 tablespoon olive oil

¼ teaspoon salt

¼ teaspoon ground black pepper

2 tomatoes, each cut into 4 slices

¼ teaspoon garlic powder (optional)

4 slices (3 ounces) ham, halved

8 eggs

3 tablespoons chopped fresh basil (optional)

PREHEAT the oven to 425°F. Fill a large, deep skillet or braising pan with hot water to within 1" from the top. Add enough of the vinegar to the water so that it tastes faintly of vinegar. Bring to a simmer over medium heat.

MEANWHILE, brush both sides of the eggplant slices with the oil and season with ⅛ teaspoon of the salt and ⅛ teaspoon of the pepper. Place on a baking sheet in a single layer. Bake for 5 to 8 minutes, or just until tender, turning once. Remove to a platter or plates.

PLACE 1 slice of tomato on top of each eggplant slice and season with the garlic powder (if using). Top each with 1 slice of ham.

BREAK the eggs one at a time into a custard cup. Slip them one at a time into the simmering water. Cook, uncovered, for 3 to 5 minutes, or until the whites are set and the yolks are almost set. Remove with a slotted spoon, drain well, and place on top of the ham. Sprinkle all with the remaining ⅛ teaspoon salt and ⅛ teaspoon pepper and the basil (if using).

Total time: 30 minutes ✱ Makes 4 servings

Per serving: 260 calories, 21 g protein, 11 g carbohydrates, 15 g fat, 4 g saturated fat, 864 mg sodium, 5 g fiber

Perfect for a low-carb diet, eggplant takes the place of toast in these delicious breakfast stacks.

Dilly Egg and Salmon Wrap

1 whole wheat flour tortilla
  (8" diameter)

3 tablespoons salmon
  cream cheese spread

1 hard-cooked egg, sliced

¼ teaspoon dried dill

  Ground black pepper
  (optional)

3 leaves baby spinach

PLACE the tortilla on a paper towel or a piece of waxed paper. Spread with the cream cheese. Top with the egg and dill. Season to taste with pepper, if desired. Top with the spinach. Roll into a cylinder.

Total time: 5 minutes ✱ Makes 1 serving

Per serving: 303 calories, 13 g protein, 23 g carbohydrates, 19 g fat, 11 g saturated fat, 566 mg sodium, 3 g fiber

NUTRITION NEWS TO USE

It's never too early to prevent dementia—and one of the best ways to do so is to eat more fish, according to a study of 14,960 people ages 65 and older in seven countries. Results show that those who consume fish of any variety at least a few days a week are 19 percent less likely to have dementia than those who eat none at all.

Garden Breakfast Wrap

4 spinach-flavored flour tortillas (12" diameter)

4 eggs, beaten

4 egg whites, beaten

½ cup (2 ounces) crumbled reduced-fat lemon, garlic, and herb feta cheese or ¼ cup (1 ounce) grated Parmesan cheese

2 teaspoons trans-free margarine or spread

4 cups (4 ounces) baby arugula or baby spinach

Hot-pepper sauce (optional)

PREHEAT a grill pan over medium-high heat. Lightly toast 1 tortilla in the pan for about 30 seconds, turning once. Set aside on a plate and cover with a slightly damp paper towel. Repeat with the remaining tortillas. Whisk together the eggs, egg whites, and cheese in a medium bowl.

MELT the margarine or spread in a large nonstick skillet over medium heat. Pour in the egg mixture. Cook, stirring, for 2 minutes. Add the arugula or spinach. Continue cooking, stirring, for about 1 minute, or until the eggs are set and the greens are wilted. Mound one-quarter of the mixture on the bottom half of 1 tortilla, flap up the 2 sides, and roll into a cylinder. Repeat with the remaining tortillas and filling. Halve the wraps diagonally and serve with hot-pepper sauce, if desired.

Total time: 10 minutes ✸ Makes 4 servings

Per 4 serving: 516 calories, 24 g protein, 67 g carbohydrates, 17 g fat, 5 g saturated fat, 900 mg sodium, 5 g fiber

If you can't find spinach tortillas, replace them with 100 percent whole wheat tortillas.

—Jade Mason, Lynn, Massachusetts

Good Morning Sunshine

1 tablespoon fresh lemon juice

1 teaspoon olive oil

Sea salt

Cracked black pepper

½ cup arugula

¼ cup shaved fennel

2 tablespoons finely diced red onion, optional

1 whole grain bagel, halved and toasted

2 ounces mascarpone cheese

2 slices cooked thick country bacon

4 ounces smoked salmon (lox)

WHISK together the lemon juice, oil, salt, and pepper in a medium bowl. Add the arugula, fennel, and onion (if using). Toss to coat well.

PLACE each bagel half on a plate. Top each with half of the cheese, bacon, salmon, and arugula mixture.

Total time: 10 minutes ✳ Makes 2 servings

Per serving: 381 calories, 27 g protein, 20 g carbohydrates, 23 g fat, 9 saturated fat, 397 mg sodium, 3 g fiber

This recipe was inspired by my love of all things breakfast and brunch! I incorporated heart-healthy olive oil, lemon juice, and the omega-3-rich smoked salmon to create this mouthwatering, satisfying creation!

—Jade

Breakfast Bean Burritos

4 whole wheat tortillas (8" diameter)

2 teaspoons olive oil

1 small onion, chopped

1 large garlic clove, minced

1 can (16 ounces) reduced-sodium black beans

1 teaspoon chili powder

2 tablespoons finely chopped fresh cilantro

½ cup salsa

¼ cup fat-free or low-fat plain yogurt

¼ cup fat-free or low-fat sour cream

6 tablespoons shredded reduced-fat Monterey Jack or Cheddar cheese

PREHEAT the oven to 350°F. Coat a small baking dish with cooking spray. Wrap all 4 tortillas in 1 piece of foil. Bake for 10 minutes to heat through.

MEANWHILE, heat the oil in a medium nonstick skillet over medium heat. Cook the onion and garlic for 3 minutes. Stir in the beans (with liquid) and chili powder. Simmer, stirring occasionally, for 10 minutes. Stir in the cilantro.

COMBINE the salsa, yogurt, and sour cream in a small saucepan. Stir over very low heat just until warm (do not boil). To assemble the burritos, divide the bean mixture evenly among the tortillas. Sprinkle each with the cheese and roll to enclose the filling. Place the burritos seam side down in the baking dish. Top with the salsa mixture. Bake for 10 minutes, or until heated through.

Total time: 45 minutes ✱ Makes 4 servings

Per serving: 255 calories, 15 g protein, 44 g carbohydrates, 8 g fat, 3 g saturated fat, 809 mg sodium, 8 g fiber

Here, beans provide protein to start your day off right.

Swiss and Turkey Bacon Strata

2 eggs

2 egg whites

1¾ cups low-fat milk

1 tablespoon Dijon mustard

¼ teaspoon ground black pepper

1 small red onion, chopped

½ green bell pepper, chopped

½ red bell pepper, chopped

2 slices extra-lean turkey bacon, chopped (cut into ¼" pieces)

4 slices (1 ounce each) multigrain bread, cut into ½" cubes

⅓ cup shredded reduced-fat Swiss cheese

PREHEAT the oven to 375°F. Coat an 11" × 7" baking dish or four 2-cup casserole dishes with cooking spray and set on a baking sheet. Whisk together the eggs, egg whites, milk, mustard, and black pepper in a medium bowl. Set aside.

HEAT a nonstick skillet coated with cooking spray over medium heat. Cook the onion and bell peppers, stirring occasionally, for 8 minutes, or until the vegetables are almost tender. Stir in the bacon and cook for 2 minutes. Remove from the heat and stir in the bread cubes.

SPOON the vegetable mixture into the baking dish or casserole cups, dividing evenly. Sprinkle the cheese over the vegetables. Pour the eggs over the cheese. Let stand for at least 20 minutes, or cover and refrigerate for up to 12 hours.

BAKE for 35 minutes, or until a knife inserted in the center comes out clean. Let stand for 10 minutes.

Total time: 1 hour 10 minutes ✳ Makes 4 servings

Per serving: 227 calories, 18 g protein, 27 g carbohydrates, 6 g fat, 3 g saturated fat, 524 mg sodium, 4 g fiber

This delicious dish will keep you immune to the midmorning munchies.

Monterey Strata

8 ounces broccoli florets, chopped

2 eggs

2 egg whites

2 cups fat-free milk

2 teaspoons salt-free seasoning blend

¼ teaspoon salt

4 slices (5 ounces) 7-grain sourdough whole wheat bread, cut into ½" cubes

¼ cup minced scallions or onion

½ cup (2 ounces) shredded Swiss or Gruyère cheese

PREHEAT the oven to 325°F. Coat an 11" × 7" baking dish with cooking spray. Fill a skillet with ½" water. Cover and bring to a boil. Add the broccoli. Cover and cook for 1 to 2 minutes, or until crisp-tender. Drain.

COMBINE the eggs and egg whites in the baking dish. Beat with a fork until smooth. Stir in the milk, seasoning blend, and salt until blended. Add the bread, scallions or onion, and broccoli. Press with the back of a fork to submerge. Let stand for 5 minutes, or until the bread is soaked. Sprinkle with the cheese. Bake for about 45 minutes, or until puffed and golden.

Total time: 1 hour ✳ Makes 6 servings

Per serving: 168 calories, 12 g protein, 18 g carbohydrates, 5 g fat, 2 g saturated fat, 306 mg sodium, 3 g fiber

You can put this strata together and chill it overnight. Just pop it into the oven before serving. Any type of 100 percent whole grain bread can replace the 7-grain sourdough whole wheat bread.

Fiber Fun

- 1 cup low-fat raspberry, blueberry, or strawberry yogurt
- 1 cup fresh raspberries, blueberries, or diced strawberries
- ⅔ cup high-fiber cereal, such as All-Bran or Kashi GoLean

SPOON ¼ cup of the yogurt into each of 2 parfait or tall glass dishes. Top each with ½ cup of the berries and 2½ tablespoons of the cereal. Spoon the remaining yogurt over the berries and sprinkle with the remaining cereal.

Total time: 5 minutes ✳ Makes 1 serving

Per serving: 196 calories, 6 g protein, 46 g carbohydrates, 3 g fat, 1 g saturated fat, 101 mg sodium, 10 g fiber

I love this recipe because it is easy to make, requires very little preparation time, and it's healthy yet satisfying and versatile. It can also be enjoyed for breakfast, lunch, or dessert.
—**Bertha**

METABOLISM BOOSTER!
WHOLE GRAIN BREAKFAST

Eat a morning meal of whole grains and fresh fruit to help burn 50 percent more fat during a workout than you would with a breakfast of refined carbs, say researchers from the University of Nottingham. When we consume refined carbs (like bagels), blood sugar spikes and muscles store more glycogen, which the body uses instead of fat for fuel. But eating foods that keep blood sugar in check (like whole grains) helps muscles store less glycogen so the body can stoke its engine with fat.

Berry Parfaits

2 cups blackberries, raspberries, blueberries, or strawberries

2 tablespoons honey

1 container (8 ounces) fat-free lemon yogurt

SET 4 berries aside for garnish. Place the remainder in a blender. Add the honey and blend until smooth. Evenly layer the berry mixture and yogurt in 4 parfait glasses. Garnish with the reserved berries.

Total time: 5 minutes ✱ Makes 4 servings

Per serving: 115 calories, 4 g protein, 26 g carbohydrates, 0 g fat, 0 g saturated fat, 40 mg sodium, 4 g fiber

For a change of pace, substitute lime or vanilla yogurt for the lemon.

Cherry Cream of Rye Cereal

1¼ cups apple cider

1¼ cups water

¼ teaspoon salt

1 cup cream of rye cereal

1¼ tablespoons cherry fruit spread

⅛ teaspoon ground nutmeg

⅛ teaspoon ground cardamom

1½ tablespoons chopped hazelnuts (optional)

COMBINE the cider, water, and salt in a saucepan and bring to a boil over medium heat. Stir in the cereal and reduce the heat to low. Cook uncovered, stirring occasionally, for 3 to 5 minutes, or until thick. Remove from the heat and stir in the fruit spread. Spoon into bowls and sprinkle with the nutmeg, cardamom, and hazelnuts (if using). Serve hot.

Total time: 10 minutes ✳ Makes 4 servings

Per serving: 197 calories, 6 g protein, 41 g carbohydrates, 3 g fat, 1 g saturated fat, 155 mg sodium, 6 g fiber

Look for cream of rye in a canister near the oatmeal section of your supermarket or in the natural food section.

Creamy Quinoa

2½ cups low-fat milk

⅛ teaspoon salt

1 cup quinoa, rinsed

¼ cup chopped dried figs or dates

2 tablespoons butter

⅛ teaspoon ground cardamom

8 drops liquid stevia

4 tablespoons chopped toasted walnuts

BRING the milk and salt to a boil in a medium saucepan. Stir in the quinoa and reduce the heat to low. Cover and cook for 15 minutes, or until all the liquid has evaporated and the grains are tender-crunchy.

STIR in the figs or dates, butter, cardamom, and stevia. Remove from the heat. Divide among 4 bowls. Sprinkle each bowl with 1 tablespoon of the walnuts.

Total time: 20 minutes ✳ Makes 4 servings

Per serving: 381 calories, 12 g protein, 45 g carbohydrates, 18 g fat, 7 g saturated fat, 184 mg sodium, 4 g fiber

Always rinse quinoa under cold running water until the water is clear, removing the bitter coating.

Oatmeal with Ricotta, Fruit, and Nuts

2 cups apple cider

2 cups water

2 cups old-fashioned rolled oats

⅛ teaspoon salt

½ teaspoon ground cinnamon

¼ cup ricotta cheese

1 large peach or plum, chopped

2 tablespoons sunflower seeds or toasted almonds, chopped

COMBINE the cider, water, oats, and salt in a medium saucepan. Bring to a boil over medium heat. Reduce the heat to low. Cook uncovered, stirring occasionally, for 4 minutes, or until thick and creamy.

SPOON into bowls and sprinkle with the cinnamon. Top with the ricotta, peach or plum, and seeds or nuts.

Total time: 10 minutes ✷ Makes 6 servings

Per serving: 187 calories, 7 g protein, 31 g carbohydrates, 4 g fat, 1 g saturated fat, 67 mg sodium, 3 g fiber

NUTRITION NEWS TO USE

A normal body mass index doesn't necessarily mean a slim chance of diabetes and heart disease. In a recent study published in the *Archives of Internal Medicine*, one-quarter of normal-weight adults had a trio of symptoms—high blood pressure, triglycerides, and blood glucose—that put them at risk of cardiovascular and metabolic disease. Talk with your doctor about preventing heart disease or diabetes, particularly if you have any of these risk factors: a family history of either disease; an apple-shaped body; or African American, Native American, or Hispanic ethnicity. She may recommend staying active, not smoking, and consuming more heart-healthy foods.

Crepes with Banana and Kiwifruit

Crepes

- **1 cup whole grain pastry flour**
- **¼ teaspoon salt**
- **1 egg**
- **1 cup unsweetened soy milk or whole milk**
- **3 tablespoons unsweetened soy milk or whole milk**
- **1½ teaspoons vanilla extract**
- **2 teaspoons butter**
- **2 tablespoons water**

Filling

- **½ cup plain yogurt**
- **1 banana, cut into 16 diagonal slices**
- **2 kiwifruit, peeled, halved lengthwise, and sliced**
- **2 teaspoons lime juice (optional)**
- **½ teaspoon ground cinnamon**

To make the crepes:

COMBINE the flour and salt in a large bowl. Whisk together the egg, milk, and vanilla extract in a small bowl. Stir into the flour mixture.

MELT ½ teaspoon of the butter in an 8" nonstick skillet over medium heat. Pour 3 tablespoons of batter into the skillet and tilt the skillet to coat the bottom in a thin layer (if the batter seems too thick, add 1 to 2 tablespoons water). Cook the first side for about 2 minutes, or until nicely browned. Turn the crepe using a spatula and cook for 1 to 2 minutes (the second side will look spotty). Slide the crepe onto a plate and cover with foil to keep warm. Continue making crepes, rebuttering the pan after every second crepe, until all the butter and batter are used.

To make the filling and assemble:

PLACE a crepe on a serving plate, attractive side down, and spread with 1 tablespoon of the yogurt. Arrange 2 banana slices and one-quarter of a kiwifruit in strips one-third of the way from 1 edge. Sprinkle with ¼ teaspoon of the lime juice (if using) and a pinch of the cinnamon, and roll up. Repeat to fill 3 more crepes.

Total time: 55 minutes ✳ Makes 4 servings

Per serving: 236 calories, 9 g protein, 36 g carbohydrates, 7 g fat, 3 g saturated fat, 227 mg sodium, 4 g fiber

To make the crepes ahead of time, cook the crepes, stack, cover with foil, and chill or freeze. Thaw if frozen, then reheat the foil-wrapped stack on a baking sheet at 350°F for 5 minutes, or until the crepes are warm and pliable.

Whole Grain Pancakes with Berry Cream Syrup

Syrup

- ¼ cup red or black raspberry fruit spread
- 2 tablespoons heavy cream
- 4 teaspoons orange juice or apple cider

Pancakes

- ¾ cup whole grain pastry flour
- ¼ cup buckwheat flour
- 1½ teaspoons baking powder
- ½ teaspoon baking soda
- ⅛ teaspoon salt
- 1 cup buttermilk
- 1 large egg, at room temperature, separated
- 3 tablespoons melted butter
- 8 drops liquid stevia

To make the syrup:

HEAT the fruit spread, cream, and juice or cider in a small saucepan over medium-low heat until warm. Set aside.

To make the pancakes:

PREHEAT the oven to 200°F.

WHISK together the pastry flour, buckwheat flour, baking powder, baking soda, and salt in a large bowl. Stir together the buttermilk, egg yolk, butter, and stevia in a glass measure. Stir into the flour mixture until well combined.

BEAT the egg white in a bowl with an electric mixer on high speed until stiff peaks form. Fold into the batter. (The batter will be light but not fluid.)

HEAT a large skillet or griddle coated with cooking spray over medium-high heat. For each pancake, spread ¼ cup of the batter onto the skillet. Cook for 3 minutes, or until bubbles form around the edges. Flip and cook for 2 to 3 minutes, or until lightly browned. Place on a large plate and keep warm in the oven while preparing the remaining pancakes. Serve with the syrup.

Total time: 30 minutes ✳ Makes 4 servings

Per serving: 276 calories, 7 g protein, 33 g carbohydrates, 14 g fat, 8 g saturated fat, 560 mg sodium, 3 g fiber

To prepare an elegant blueberry variation on this dish, fold ⅓ cup blueberries into the finished batter and prepare as directed. Serve with low-calorie syrup, fresh berries, and a dollop of whipped cream.

Granola Pancakes with Fruit Sauce

Sauce

- 1 cup fresh berries (whole or sliced)
- 1 tablespoon maple syrup
- ½ teaspoon freshly squeezed lemon juice

Pancakes

- ¾ cup all-purpose flour
- 1 teaspoon baking soda
- 2 teaspoons sugar (optional)
- 1 cup low-fat buttermilk
- 1 egg, at room temperature
- 3 tablespoons melted butter
- ½ cup low-fat granola

To prepare the sauce:

COMBINE the berries, maple syrup, and lemon juice in a small saucepan. Cook over medium heat for 4 minutes, or just until the berries are soft and release their juices. Keep warm.

To prepare the pancakes:

WHISK together the flour, baking soda, and sugar (if using) in a medium bowl. Whisk together the buttermilk, egg, and butter in a small bowl. Add to the flour mixture and stir until just blended.

HEAT a large skillet or griddle coated with cooking spray over medium-high heat. For each pancake, spread 2 tablespoons of the batter onto the skillet. Sprinkle with 1 tablespoon of the granola. Cook for 3 minutes, or until the edges begin to look dry. Flip and cook for 2 to 3 minutes, or until bubbles form around the edges. Place on a large plate and keep warm in the oven while preparing the remaining pancakes. Serve with the sauce.

Total time: 25 minutes ✱ Makes 4 servings

Per serving: 290 calories, 8 g protein, 41 g carbohydrates, 11 g fat, 6 g saturated fat, 491 mg sodium, 2 g fiber

Granola adds a pleasant crunch and added fiber to these fruit-laced pancakes.

Banana-Stuffed Cinnamon French Toast

Filling

- 1 ripe banana, thinly sliced
- 2 tablespoons low-fat cream cheese, at room temperature
- 1 tablespoon confectioners' sugar
- 1 teaspoon lemon zest
- 2 pinches of ground nutmeg

French Toast

- 8 thin slices whole wheat cinnamon-raisin bread
- 1 cup 1% milk
- 1 egg
- 1 egg white
- ¾ teaspoon vanilla extract
  Confectioners' sugar
- ¼ cup sugar-free pancake syrup

To make the filling:

MASH 2 rounded tablespoons of the banana slices in a small bowl with the back of a spoon. (You should have about 2 tablespoons mashed.) Stir in the cream cheese, sugar, lemon zest, and nutmeg until smooth.

To make the French toast:

PREHEAT the oven to 200°F.

DIVIDE the banana filling among 4 slices of the bread. Top with the remaining banana slices and bread slices to make 4 sandwiches.

WHISK together the milk, egg, egg white, and vanilla extract in a shallow dish or pie plate. Dip the sandwiches into the egg mixture, turning with a spatula to coat both sides.

MEANWHILE, heat a large nonstick skillet or griddle coated with cooking spray over medium-low heat. Add the sandwiches and cook for 4 to 5 minutes, turning once, or until golden brown.

DUST with the confectioners' sugar. Drizzle with the syrup and serve hot.

Total time: 25 minutes ✳ Makes 4 servings

Per serving: 270 calories, 12 g protein, 51 g carbohydrates, 4 g fat, 2 g saturated fat, 242 mg sodium, 5 g fiber

Bananas lend an incredibly creamy, satisfying texture to this French toast dish, and they also help keep each serving virtually fat-free.

Strawberry-Banana–Topped French Toast

1 egg

¼ cup fat-free milk

¼ teaspoon ground cinnamon

1 slice whole grain bread

1 teaspoon trans-free margarine or spread

¼ cup sliced strawberries

¼ cup sliced banana

WHISK together the egg, milk, and cinnamon in a shallow bowl. Dip both sides of the bread into the milk mixture.

MELT the margarine in a nonstick skillet over medium heat. Cook the bread for 4 minutes, turning once, or until golden and cooked through. Halve diagonally. Place 1 French toast half on a plate. Top with half of the strawberries and bananas. Cover with the other French toast half and the remaining strawberries and bananas.

Total time: 10 minutes ✳ Makes 1 serving

Per serving: 255 calories, 14 g protein, 30 g carbohydrates, 10 g fat, 3 g saturated fat, 268 mg sodium, 5 g fiber

This breakfast is so delicious that you'll think you're eating dessert!

—Barbara Hullihen, Chardon, Ohio

Buckwheat Waffles

- 1 ripe banana
- 2 egg whites
- 1 cup whole grain pancake and waffle mix
- 1 cup light buckwheat flour
- 1½ teaspoons ground cinnamon
- 2 cups raspberries, blueberries, or sliced strawberries
- ¾ cup maple syrup
- 6 tablespoons chopped pecans

MASH the banana in a large bowl with a fork until smooth. Stir in the egg whites and 1¼ cups water until well blended. Stir in the pancake and waffle mix, flour, and cinnamon until blended. Let stand for 10 minutes.

PREHEAT the oven to 200°F. Heat a nonstick waffle iron coated with cooking spray over medium-high heat. Prepare waffles using ½ cup batter according to manufacturer's directions.

PLACE the waffles on a large plate and keep warm in the oven while preparing the remaining waffles.

PLACE 1 waffle on each of 6 plates. Top each with ⅓ cup of the berries, 2 tablespoons of the syrup, and 1 tablespoon of the pecans.

Total time: 40 minutes ✳ Makes 6 servings

Per serving: 318 calories, 8 g protein, 63 g carbohydrates, 5 g fat, 0 g saturated fat, 197 mg sodium, 8 g fiber

Light buckwheat is lighter in color and texture than traditional buckwheat, producing a milder flavor. Traditional buckwheat will work just as well, if desired. —**Barbara**

QUICK TIP: THE JUICE THAT "OUT-C'S" OJ

An apple juice a day may keep the doctor away, according to Spanish researchers. When they used a new, more accurate technique to analyze the levels of vitamin C in 17 fruit juices and soft drinks, apple juice came out on top—beating orange juice by as much as 14 milligrams per ounce. Extra ascorbic acid may have been added to the apple juices during production to increase levels of vitamin C, say researchers. Look for 100 percent apple juice (with no additional sweeteners), and stick to 8 ounces.

Cocoa-Espresso Waffles

1½ cups whole grain pastry flour

½ cup unsweetened cocoa powder

½ cup packed brown sugar

2 teaspoons baking powder

2 teaspoons espresso powder

¼ teaspoon baking soda

1 cup 1% milk

3 tablespoons light olive oil

3 egg whites

⅛ tablespoon salt

2 tablespoons mini chocolate chips

Maple syrup

PREHEAT the oven to 200°F.

WHISK together the flour, cocoa powder, sugar, baking powder, espresso powder, and baking soda in a large bowl. Make a well in the center of the flour mixture and add the milk and oil. Whisk together until blended.

HEAT a nonstick waffle iron coated with cooking spray over medium-high heat.

MEANWHILE, beat the egg whites and salt with an electric mixer at high speed just until soft peaks form. Fold the whites into the chocolate batter in 3 additions, folding in the chocolate chips with the last addition of whites just until blended.

ADD enough batter to almost cover the waffle grids (¾ cup) and cook for 3 to 4 minutes.

PLACE the waffles on a large plate and keep warm in the oven while preparing the remaining waffles. Serve with the maple syrup.

Total time: 35 minutes ✳ Makes 5 servings

Per serving: 306 calories, 9 g protein, 50 g carbohydrates, 11 g fat, 2 g saturated fat, 346 mg sodium, 6 g fiber

These chocolaty treats pack a healthy wallop of fiber and monounsaturated fats. They'll keep you smiling for hours.

Healthy Pumpkin Muffins

1 cup 100% pure pumpkin puree

2 eggs

1 cup fat-free milk

½ cup brown sugar

¼ cup canola oil

1 cup old-fashioned oats

1 cup whole grain pastry flour

½ cup light spelt flour

2 tablespoons ground flaxseed

1 tablespoon baking powder

1 teaspoon baking soda

1 teaspoon ground cinnamon

½ teaspoon ground nutmeg

½ teaspoon ground ginger

¼ teaspoon ground cloves

1 package (6 ounces) dried fruit mix, chopped

½ cup bittersweet chocolate chips

½ cup chopped walnuts or almonds (optional)

PREHEAT the oven to 375°F. Line 16 muffin cups with paper liners or coat with cooking spray.

STIR together the pumpkin, eggs, milk, sugar, and oil in a medium bowl.

WHISK together the oats, pastry flour, spelt flour, flaxseed, baking powder, baking soda, cinnamon, nutmeg, ginger, and cloves in a large bowl. Stir in the pumpkin mixture just until blended. Stir in the fruit mix, chocolate chips, and nuts (if using).

PLACE ⅓ cup of the batter into the muffin cups. Bake for 25 to 30 minutes, or until a wooden pick inserted in the center comes out clean. Cool on a rack for 10 minutes. Remove from the pan and cool completely.

Total time: 1 hour ✳ Makes 16 muffins

Per muffin: 195 calories, 4 g protein, 32 g carbohydrates, 6 g fat, 1 g saturated fat, 187 mg sodium, 3 g fiber

I make these muffins every other week and individually freeze them for my husband and myself to take to work each day. We used to eat prepackaged granola bars, but since I started making these muffins, we can't imagine a day at work without them.
—Susan

—Jessica Gerschitz, Jericho, New York

Sweet Potato–Corn Muffins

1 cup yellow cornmeal

¼ cup old-fashioned oatmeal

¼ cup all-purpose flour

⅓ cup sugar

2 teaspoons baking powder

1 teaspoon salt

½ teaspoon cinnamon

½ teaspoon nutmeg

1 cup hot, cooked, mashed sweet potato (1 large)

3 tablespoons trans-free margarine

1¼ cups fat-free milk

⅓ cup unsweetened applesauce

1 egg, lightly beaten

PREHEAT the oven to 425°F. Line a 12-cup muffin pan with paper liners or coat with cooking spray.

WHISK together the cornmeal, oatmeal, flour, sugar, baking powder, salt, cinnamon, and nutmeg in a large bowl.

PLACE the potato in a medium bowl and stir in the margarine until it melts. Stir in the milk, applesauce, and egg. Gradually stir into the cornmeal mixture just until blended.

SPOON into the muffin pan and bake for 25 to 30 minutes, or until a wooden pick inserted in the center comes out clean. Cool on a rack for 10 minutes. Remove from the pan and cool completely.

Total time: 50 minutes ✳ Makes 12 muffins

Per muffin: 134 calories, 3 g protein, 24 g carbohydrates, 3 g fat, 1 g saturated fat, 308 mg sodium, 1 g fiber

Here's a wonderful recipe for a superhealthy, high-fiber, low-fat, and low-sugar muffin. I work long hours as a health care administrator and need to reach for good things to eat that stave off my hunger. Eating food that tastes good and is good for you helps keep life in the balance! —Jessica

—Carmen Gane, Nipawin, Saskatchewan

Moist Bran Muffins

- ½ cup pitted dates, chopped
- ½ cup raisins
- 1 cup boiling water
- 1¼ cups low-fat buttermilk
- ½ cup brown sugar
- ⅓ cup canola oil
- 2 eggs
- 2 teaspoons vanilla extract
- 1½ cups whole wheat flour
- 1 cup bran
- 2 teaspoons baking powder
- 1 teaspoon baking soda
- ½ teaspoon salt

PLACE the dates and raisins in a small bowl and cover with the boiling water. Preheat the oven to 400°F. Line a 12-cup muffin pan with paper liners or coat with cooking spray.

STIR together the buttermilk, sugar, oil, eggs, and vanilla extract in a medium bowl. Stir together the flour, bran, baking powder, baking soda, and salt in a large bowl. Drain the raisins and dates. Stir the buttermilk mixture, raisins, and dates into the flour mixture just until blended.

DIVIDE the batter between the muffin cups. Bake for 20 to 25 minutes, or until a wooden pick inserted in the center comes out clean. Cool on a rack for 10 minutes. Remove from the pan and cool completely.

Total time: 55 minutes ✳ Makes 12 muffins

Per muffin: 210 calories, 5 g protein, 34 g carbohydrates, 8 g fat, 1 g saturated fat, 148 mg sodium, 5 g fiber

Studded with dates and raisins, these muffins are a hearty way to start the day. Freeze a batch for a grab-and-go breakfast.

—Carmen

Peanut Butter and Banana Streusel Muffins

Streusel

- 3 tablespoons whole grain pastry flour
- 3 tablespoons packed brown sugar
- 1 tablespoon butter, melted
- 1 teaspoon honey

Muffins

- 2 cups whole grain pastry flour
- 2 teaspoons baking powder
- 1 teaspoon ground cinnamon
- ½ teaspoon salt
- ½ cup pureed ripe banana (about 1 medium banana)
- ½ cup unsweetened applesauce
- ⅓ cup peanut butter
- ½ cup packed brown sugar
- 1 egg
- ¾ cup low-fat milk
- 1 teaspoon vanilla extract

PREHEAT the oven to 400°F. Line 18 muffin cups with paper liners or coat with cooking spray.

To make the streusel:
STIR together the flour, sugar, butter, and honey in a small bowl with a spoon until the mixture forms wet crumbs. Set aside.

To make the muffins:
WHISK together the flour, baking powder, cinnamon, and salt in a medium bowl until combined. Whisk together the banana, applesauce, peanut butter, sugar, and egg in a large bowl until blended. Whisk the milk and vanilla extract into the banana mixture until combined. Stir in the flour mixture just until blended.

DIVIDE the batter between the muffin cups. Divide the streusel mixture on top of the muffins. Bake for 16 to 18 minutes, or until a wooden pick inserted in the center comes out clean. Cool on a rack for 10 minutes. Remove from the pan and serve warm.

Total time: 30 minutes ✳ Makes 18 servings

Per muffin: 125 calories, 4 g protein, 21 g carbohydrates, 4 g fat, 1 g saturated fat, 147 mg sodium, 2 g fiber

Peanut butter is a powerhouse of nutrition! It not only contains fiber and protein to help balance your blood sugar, it is also an excellent source of monounsaturated fats.

Streusel Muffins

Topping

- ¼ cup fat-free cottage cheese
- 6 tablespoons reduced-fat cream cheese
- ¼ cup confectioners' sugar
- ½ teaspoon vanilla extract

Muffins

- ½ cup dried cranberries, chopped
- ½ cup boiling water
- 1½ cups whole grain pastry flour
- 2 teaspoons baking powder
- 1 teaspoon ground cinnamon
- 1 teaspoon orange zest
- ¼ teaspoon nutmeg
- 1 cup 100% pure pumpkin puree
- ¼ cup trans-free margarine or spread, at room temperature
- 2 eggs
- 3 tablespoons packed brown sugar

Streusel

- ¼ cup finely chopped pecans
- 2 tablespoons packed brown sugar
- 1 tablespoon wheat germ
- 1 tablespoon oat bran
- 1 tablespoon trans-free margarine or spread, at room temperature

To make the topping:

COMBINE the cottage cheese, cream cheese, confectioners' sugar, and vanilla extract in a blender or food processor. Blend or process until smooth. Set aside.

To make the muffins:

PLACE the cranberries in a small bowl and cover with the boiling water. Preheat the oven to 400°F. Line a 12-cup muffin pan with paper liners or coat with cooking spray.

STIR together the flour, baking powder, cinnamon, orange zest, and nutmeg in a large bowl. Stir together the pumpkin, margarine, eggs, and brown sugar in a medium bowl. Stir into the flour mixture just until blended. Drain the cranberries and stir into the batter.

To make the streusel:

COMBINE the pecans, brown sugar, wheat germ, oat bran, and margarine in a small bowl. Blend with your fingers or a fork to form crumbs.

DIVIDE the batter between the muffin cups. Spoon 1 tablespoon of the cottage cheese mixture over each. Sprinkle with about 2 teaspoons of the streusel. Bake for 20 to 25 minutes, or until a wooden pick inserted in the center comes out clean. Cool on a rack for 10 minutes. Remove from the pan and cool completely.

Total time: 1 hour ✳ Makes 12 muffins

Per muffin: 197 calories, 4 g protein, 27 g carbohydrates, 8 g fat, 2 g saturated fat, 221 mg sodium, 3 g fiber

I am a barber. Having a nutritious snack around that is easy to eat keeps me on my feet with more energy. My grandchildren like them for a quick-out-the-door breakfast.

—Candice

Grandma's Multigrain Breakfast Bread

1½ cups whole grain pastry flour

½ cup oat flour

⅓ cup sugar

2 teaspoons baking powder

½ teaspoon baking soda

¾ cup chopped stone fruit, such as peach, apricots, or plums (about 2)

¼ cup chopped almonds

1 cup low-fat buttermilk

¼ cup canola oil

2 eggs

PREHEAT the oven to 375°F. Coat a 9" × 5" loaf pan with cooking spray.

WHISK together the pastry flour, oat flour, sugar, baking powder, and baking soda in a large bowl. Stir in the fruit and almonds. Add the buttermilk, oil, and eggs. Stir just until blended. Pour into the pan.

BAKE for 50 minutes, or until a wooden pick comes out clean. Cool on a rack for 10 minutes. Remove from the pan and cool completely.

Total time: 1 hour 30 minutes ✱ Makes 12 slices

Per serving: 168 calories, 4 g protein, 22 g carbohydrates, 7 g fat, 1 g saturated fat, 153 mg sodium, 2 g fiber

I switched to multigrain flours for health reasons and found this whole grain recipe that looked good. I added the fruit and nuts to make it tastier and healthier. It was a big success, so I continued to bake it. It is loved by the whole family, even the kids! —Marietta

> **QUICK TIP: DRINK UP**
> **278** Milligrams of heart-healthy flavonoids that can be found in a cup of green tea

—Marcia Leigh Dier, Estacada, Oregon

Glazed Pumpkin-Date Bread

1 cup unbleached flour

⅔ cup whole grain pastry flour

2 teaspoons cinnamon

1 teaspoon baking soda

½ teaspoon salt

¼ teaspoon ground cloves

1 cup 100% pure pumpkin puree

½ cup unsweetened applesauce

½ cup sugar

¼ cup canola oil

½ cup chopped walnuts

½ cup chopped dates

½ cup confectioners' sugar

1 tablespoon low-fat milk

1½ teaspoons trans-free margarine or spread, at room temperature

PREHEAT the oven to 350°F. Coat a 9" × 5" loaf pan with cooking spray.

WHISK together the unbleached flour, pastry flour, cinnamon, baking soda, salt, and cloves in a large bowl. Stir together the pumpkin, applesauce, sugar, and oil in a medium bowl. Stir into the flour mixture just until combined. Stir in the walnuts and dates. Pour into the pan.

BAKE for 1 hour, or until a wooden pick inserted in the center comes out clean. Cool on a rack for 10 minutes. Remove from the pan and cool completely.

MEANWHILE, stir together the sugar, milk, and margarine in a small bowl until smooth. Drizzle over the cooled bread.

Total time: 1 hour 30 minutes ✳ Makes 12 slices

Per serving: 223 calories, 3 g protein, 37 g carbohydrates, 9 g fat, 1 g saturated fat, 222 mg sodium, 3 g fiber

This recipe is one I prepare during the holidays and share with our family. Every year they look forward to "Grandma's" pumpkin bread. They eat it for breakfast and as a dessert at dinner. It's great for an afternoon snack.

—Marcia

Lemon Coffee Cake

2½ cups whole grain pastry flour

2½ teaspoons baking powder

½ teaspoon salt

⅔ cup honey

⅓ cup canola oil

1 cup liquid egg substitute

1 tablespoon lemon zest

1½ teaspoons lemon extract

1 cup fat-free lemon yogurt

1 cup coarsely chopped dried cherries or blueberries

PREHEAT the oven to 325°F. Coat a 10-cup Bundt pan with cooking spray.

WHISK together the flour, baking powder, and salt in a small bowl. Beat the honey and oil in a large bowl with an electric mixer on medium speed until creamy. Beat in the egg substitute, lemon zest, and lemon extract. On low speed, beat in one-third of the flour mixture and one-half of the yogurt. Repeat, beginning and ending with the flour. Beat for 2 minutes, or until smooth and thick. Fold in the cherries or blueberries. Pour into the pan.

BAKE for 30 to 35 minutes, or until a wooden pick inserted in the center comes out clean. Cool on a rack for 10 minutes. Remove from the pan and place on the rack to cool completely.

Total time: 50 minutes ✳ Makes 12 servings

Per serving: 254 calories, 6 g protein, 42 g carbohydrates, 7 g fat, 1 g saturated fat, 250 mg sodium, 5 g fiber

Look for lemon extract in the spice section of the supermarket. You may substitute 2 tablespoons lemon juice for the extract.

Cranberry Coffee Cake

Topping

- ¾ cup packed light brown sugar
- ½ cup whole grain pastry flour
- ¼ cup chopped toasted walnuts
- 2 teaspoons ground cinnamon
- 2 tablespoons butter, at room temperature

Coffee Cake

- 2 cups whole grain pastry flour
- 1 teaspoon baking powder
- 1 teaspoon baking soda
- ½ teaspoon salt
- ¼ cup canola oil
- 1 cup granulated sugar
- 1 large egg
- 1 large egg white
- 1 tablespoon orange zest
- 1 teaspoon vanilla extract
- 1 cup reduced-fat sour cream
- 2 cups cranberries, coarsely chopped

To make the topping:

COMBINE the brown sugar, flour, walnuts, cinnamon, and butter in a small bowl. Mix with your fingers to form crumbs. Set aside.

To make the coffee cake:

PREHEAT the oven to 350°F. Coat a 13" × 9" baking dish with cooking spray.

WHISK together the flour, baking powder, baking soda, and salt in a medium bowl.

BEAT the oil, sugar, egg, and egg white in a mixing bowl with an electric mixer on medium speed for 3 minutes, or until light in color. Beat in the orange zest and vanilla extract. Beat in one-third of the flour mixture and half of the sour cream on low speed. Repeat, beginning and ending with the flour. Beat for about 2 minutes, or until smooth and thick.

POUR into the baking dish. Scatter the cranberries on top. Sprinkle with the topping. Bake for 40 to 45 minutes, or until a wooden pick inserted in the center comes out clean. Cool on a rack for 30 minutes to serve warm. Or, cool completely before serving.

Total time: 50 minutes   ✳   Makes 12 servings

Per serving: 304 calories, 4 g protein, 48 g carbohydrates, 11 g fat, 3 g saturated fat, 281 mg sodium, 3 g fiber

Enjoy this cake in the summer by replacing the cranberries with fresh blueberries.

Ginger-Granola Breakfast Bars

1 egg

1¼ cups lukewarm water

1 box (14 ounces) gingerbread mix

3 cups reduced-fat granola cereal

PREHEAT the oven to 350°F. Coat a 12" × 8" baking pan with cooking spray.

WHISK together the egg and water in a large bowl. Stir in the gingerbread mix just until moistened. Stir in the granola. Pour into the pan.

BAKE for 25 minutes, or until the top springs back when pressed with a finger. Cool in the pan on a rack.

Total time: 30 minutes ✳ Makes 12 servings

Per serving: 231 calories, 4 g protein, 42 g carbohydrates, 14 g fat, 2 g saturated fat, 278 mg sodium, 2 g fiber

For instant breakfasts, store the cooled bars in an airtight container for up to 4 days.

Protein Latte

¼ cup almond, coconut, or rice milk

1 medium banana

2 tablespoons vanilla whey protein powder

2 teaspoons almond, cashew, or peanut butter

1 cup hot tea, such as white, green, or chai

LAYER the milk, banana, protein powder, and nut butter in a blender. Top with the tea and blend just until combined. Drink immediately.

Total time: 5 minutes ✳ Makes 1 serving

Per serving: 285 calories, 22 g protein, 33 g carbohydrates, 8 g fat, 1 g saturated fat, 131 mg sodium, 5 g fiber

This hot protein breakfast is the best metabolism booster I've found. It is quick and easily varied for different personal tastes. But don't skip the banana: Its potassium with the hot tea is the key for digestive energy.

—Candice

BE SWEET SAVVY FOR BETTER BP

People who consume more than 74 grams of added fructose a day (that's two to three sweetened soft drinks) are 87 percent more likely to have severely elevated blood pressure than those who get less, according to a recent study. Researchers believe excess fructose may reduce the production of nitric oxide, a gas that helps blood vessels relax and dilate. Our swaps target the worst offenders (drinks and baked goods) and offer substitutions sweetened with fruit, which has less fructose and more healthy nutrients.

Swap out soda

Swap in 12 ounces seltzer with frozen lemon slices

Swap out banana-nut muffin

Swap in 1 whole wheat English muffin with 2 tablespoons natural peanut butter and ½ banana, sliced

Swap out oatmeal-raisin cookie

Swap in ½ cup oatmeal with 1 tablespoon raisins and 1 teaspoon cinnamon

Green Tea, Blueberry, and Banana Smoothie

1 bag green tea

3 tablespoons boiling water

2 teaspoons honey

1½ cups frozen blueberries

½ medium banana

¾ cup calcium-fortified light vanilla soy milk

PLACE the tea bag in a glass measuring cup and cover with the boiling water. Brew for 3 minutes. Remove the tea bag. Stir the honey into the tea until it dissolves.

COMBINE the blueberries, banana, and soy milk in a blender. Add the tea and blend on the highest setting until smooth. (Some blenders may require additional water to process the mixture.)

Total time: 5 minutes ✻ Makes 2 servings

Per serving: 125 calories, 2 g protein, 29 g carbohydrates, 1 g fat, 0 g saturated fat, 32 mg sodium, 4 g fiber

Need to fix this smoothie and bring to the office? No problem. Just store for several hours in a Thermos, then shake vigorously before pouring. The smoothie will be tasty but thinner than when freshly made.

Peanut Butter Breakfast Shake

1 cup fat-free milk

1 ripe banana, sliced

2 tablespoons creamy peanut butter

COMBINE the milk, banana, and peanut butter in a blender. Blend until smooth.

Total time: 5 minutes ✳ Makes 1 serving

Per serving: 391 calories, 17 g protein, 46 g carbohydrates, 17 g fat, 2 g saturated fat, 249 mg sodium, 5 g fiber

This quick and easy shake is a delicious way to start the day.

NUTRITION NEWS TO USE

Your toast or cereal could be hiding excessive salt, an additive known to jack up blood pressure. Research says bread and cereal are among the top contributors of sodium to our diet. Getting more than 2,300 milligrams per day—a mere 1 teaspoon of table salt—increases your risk of hypertension. For a heart-healthy morning meal, Dave Grotto, RD, recommends choosing 100 percent whole grain bread and cereals that contain no more than 150 milligrams of sodium per serving.

[it worked for me]

72 lbs lost!

❋ TANZY KILCREASE

Having leaned on her loved ones, Tanzy Kilcrease got serious weight loss results—72 pounds, to be exact.

My Story

At the age of 30, I became the principal of an elementary school and went back to graduate school—all while raising my three children. I was too busy to cook, so we ate out for every meal. When I was stressed, I grabbed any sweet I could find. Soon the scale edged upward. I enrolled in diet and exercise programs, but nothing stuck. Instead of slimming down, I gained 70 pounds in 6½ years.

On January 1, 2007, my mother, aunt, and I were sitting around talking about how fat and tired we all were, and I couldn't stand it anymore. I said, "We can beat this. Let's start a group. We'll meet once a week, weigh in, and talk about what we've done to be healthy." We started convening every Sunday at my mother's house.

VITAL STATS

Pounds lost: 72

Age: 40

Height: 5'3"

Weight then: 214 pounds

Weight now: 142 pounds

It was like our own private Weight Watchers meeting. We'd each get on the scale, then discuss strategies to help us meet our goals: Write in a journal to track food intake, increase our fiber by adding beans to our salads, or snack on fruit instead of chocolate to satisfy a sweet tooth. It was such great motivation. We screamed and gave each other high fives when we met our exercise or weight-loss goals for the week.

I lost 40 pounds the first 6 months; by the time I returned to school in the fall, I'd shed 55 pounds—my students didn't even recognize me! I've maintained my weight for more than 2 years, and people stop me all the time to ask how I did it. My answer: I'm still doing it. Losing weight and staying healthy is a lifelong journey.

My Top Tips

* Rise and shine . . . I squeeze in a 3-mile walk before work. It's the only time of day when I don't have appointments or social obligations to distract me.

* Get tech savvy . . . Online calorie trackers let you look up foods and keep tabs on daily intake with minimal calculations on your part. For a similar tool, go to www.prevention.com/myhealthtracker.

* Find a friend . . . My neighbors are my walking buddies. I look forward to their company each morning, which means I'm more likely to stick with it.

* Make room for splurges . . . I was a sugar addict, so I chose to give up daily processed sugar like candy, cookies, soda, and baked goods. But I still eat dessert on birthdays and special occasions so I don't feel deprived.

* Clean out your closet . . . When I dropped a size, I donated everything in my closet that was too big. I didn't want any excuse to gain weight.

lunches

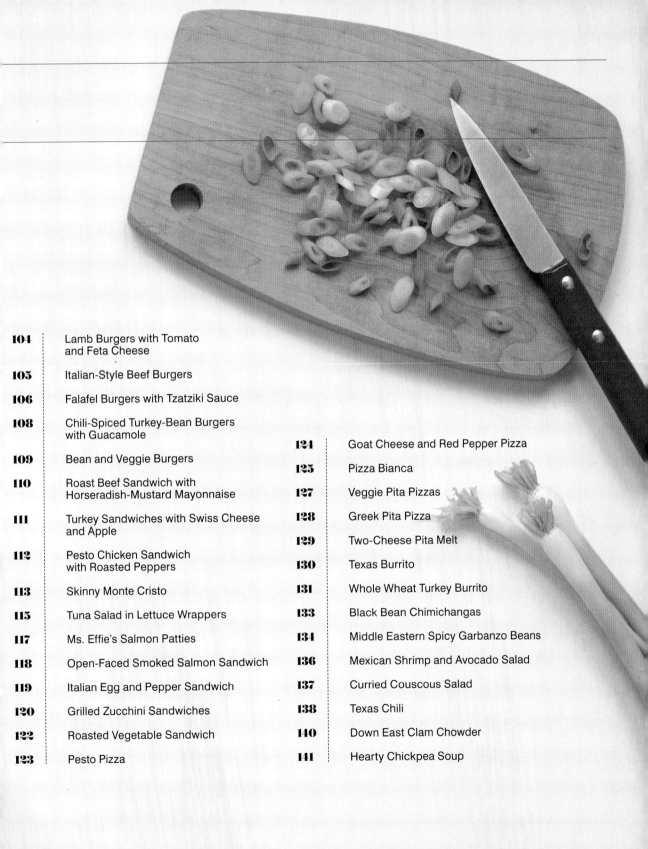

Lamb Burgers with Tomato and Feta Cheese

1¼ pounds ground lamb

2 garlic cloves, minced

1 tablespoon fresh chopped rosemary

½ teaspoon ground black pepper

¼ teaspoon salt

1 cup canned crushed tomatoes

Pinch of salt

⅓ cup crumbled feta cheese, at room temperature

COMBINE the lamb, garlic, rosemary, pepper, and salt in a large bowl. Shape into 4 burgers.

HEAT a large, heavy skillet over medium-high heat until drops of water skip over the surface. Cook the burgers for 6 minutes, turning once, or until browned. Pour off any fat, reduce the heat to low, and pour the tomatoes around the patties (the tomatoes will boil briefly).

COOK for 10 minutes, turning the burgers once, or until a thermometer inserted in the center registers 160°F. Place 1 burger on each of 4 plates. Season the tomatoes with the salt and spoon over the burgers. Sprinkle with the cheese.

Total time: 30 minutes ✽ Makes 4 servings

Per serving: 456 calories, 26 g protein, 6 g carbohydrates, 36 g fat, 16 g saturated fat, 488 mg sodium, 1 g fiber

Lamb is classic for these Greek-inspired burgers, but beef or turkey would also work nicely.

Italian-Style Beef Burgers

1½ pounds extra-lean
   ground beef

5 tablespoons grated
   Romano cheese

2 tablespoons pine nuts,
   toasted and finely chopped

1 teaspoon dried oregano

¾ teaspoon garlic powder

½ teaspoon salt

¼ teaspoon ground black
   pepper

PLACE the broiler rack 2" to 3" from the heat source and preheat the broiler.

COMBINE the beef, cheese, nuts, oregano, garlic powder, salt, and pepper in a large bowl. Shape into 4 burgers.

CAREFULLY place the burgers on a broiling pan and broil for 8 minutes, turning once, or until browned and a thermometer inserted in the center registers 160°F and the meat is no longer pink.

Total time: 15 minutes ✳ Makes 4 servings

Per serving: 260 calories, 26 g protein, 1 g carbohydrates, 13 g fat, 5 g saturated fat, 531 mg sodium, 0 g fiber

For burgers with the best texture, handle the ground meat as little as possible. You can grill or pan-fry the burgers instead of broiling them.

Falafel Burgers with Tzatziki Sauce

Tzatziki Sauce

- 1 container (8 ounces) reduced-fat sour cream
- 1 small cucumber, peeled, seeded, and finely chopped
- 2 tablespoons chopped fresh mint
- 2 tablespoons fresh lemon juice
- ¼ teaspoon salt

Falafel Burgers

- 1 pound extra-lean ground beef
- ½ cup dry falafel mix
- 1 teaspoon Greek seasoning or dried oregano
- ½ cup water
- 4 whole wheat pitas (6" diameter)
- 4 lettuce leaves
- 1 tomato, sliced
- ½ medium red onion, thinly sliced

To make the tzatziki sauce:

COMBINE the sour cream, cucumber, mint, lemon juice, and salt in a medium bowl. Cover and chill until ready to use.

To make the falafel burgers:

COMBINE the ground beef, falafel mix, seasoning or oregano, and water in a large bowl. Stir together until well blended. Shape into 4 patties.

HEAT a large skillet coated with cooking spray over medium-high heat. Cook the burgers for 10 minutes, turning once, or until a thermometer inserted in the center registers 160°F and the meat is no longer pink.

MEANWHILE, cut 1" off the top of each pita and open the pita. Divide the burgers, lettuce, tomato, and onion among the pitas. Drizzle the tzatziki sauce over each burger.

Total time: 35 minutes ✳ Makes 4 servings

Per serving: 421 calories, 36 g protein, 42 g carbohydrates, 16 g fat, 7 g saturated fat, 786 mg sodium, 11 g fiber

For a traditional treat, serve with an assortment of olives, peppers, and little pickles. To add kick to the burgers, top with a drop or two of hot chili sauce like the traditional harissa from the international section of your supermarket.

—Marla

Chili-Spiced Turkey-Bean Burgers with Guacamole

Guacamole

1 ripe avocado, halved, pitted, and peeled

2 tablespoons chopped sweet white onion

1 tablespoon salsa

1 tablespoon freshly squeezed lime juice

Pinch of salt

Burgers

⅔ cup canned black beans, rinsed and drained

1 pound lean ground turkey breast

1 large egg

2 teaspoons chili powder

½ teaspoon ground cumin

½ teaspoon salt

4 small whole grain hamburger buns, split

4 slices tomato

To make the guacamole:

MASH the avocado in a small bowl with a fork until fairly smooth. Mix in the onion, salsa, lime juice, and salt. Cover tightly and set aside.

To make the burgers:

PREHEAT the broiler. Coat the broiler pan rack with cooking spray.

MASH the beans in a medium bowl to a chunky texture. Stir in the turkey, egg, chili powder, cumin, and salt until well blended. Shape into 4 burgers.

BROIL the patties 4" to 6" from the heat for 12 minutes, turning once, or until a thermometer inserted in the center registers 165°F and the meat is no longer pink. Place on a plate.

PLACE the buns on the broiler pan and toast for 1 minute, or until lightly browned. Place toasted buns on each of 4 plates. On the bun bottom, place a tomato slice and a burger. Spoon ¼ of the guacamole over each and cover with the bun top.

Total time: 40 minutes ✽ Makes 4 servings

Per serving: 386 calories, 38 g protein, 37 g carbohydrates, 13 g fat, 2 g saturated fat, 831 mg sodium, 11 g fiber

These spirited burgers, loaded with spices and topped with a spoonful of guacamole, are love at first bite.

Bean and Veggie Burgers

Burgers

- ¼ cup bulgur
- 1 small onion, finely chopped
- ¾ cup shredded zucchini
- ½ cup shredded carrot
- ½ cup chopped red bell pepper
- 1 garlic clove, minced
- 2 cups chopped spinach
- 1½ teaspoons ground cumin
- ½ teaspoon salt
- 4 ounces firm tofu, drained and patted dry
- 1 can (15 ounces) chickpeas, rinsed and drained
- ¼ cup ground flaxseed
- 6 whole wheat buns, split
  Green leaf lettuce and sliced tomatoes

Sauce

- ⅓ cup low-fat plain yogurt
- 3 tablespoons chopped cilantro
- 1 scallion, finely chopped
- 1 jalapeño chile pepper, seeded and minced (wear plastic gloves when handling)
- ⅛ teaspoon salt

To make the burgers:

PREHEAT the oven to 400°F. Coat a baking sheet with cooking spray. Prepare the bulgur according to package directions and set aside.

HEAT a large nonstick skillet coated with cooking spray over medium heat. Cook the onion, zucchini, carrot, bell pepper, and garlic, stirring, for 8 minutes, or until the vegetables are crisp-tender.

INCREASE the heat to medium-high. Stir in the spinach, cumin, and salt. Cook for 2 minutes, or until the spinach wilts. Cool for 10 minutes.

CRUMBLE the tofu into a large bowl and add the chickpeas. Mash with a potato masher until smooth. Stir in the bulgur until well blended. Shape into 6 burgers. Place the flaxseed on a plate. Press the burgers into the flaxseed to coat. Place on the baking sheet and lightly coat with cooking spray. Bake for 25 minutes, turning once, or until browned.

To make the sauce:

STIR together the yogurt, cilantro, scallion, chile pepper, and salt in a small bowl. Serve each burger on a bun with lettuce, tomato, and the yogurt sauce.

Total time: 1 hour ✳ Makes 6 servings

Per serving: 296 calories, 13 g protein, 52 g carbohydrates, 5 g fat, 1 g saturated fat, 689 mg sodium, 11 g fiber

Topped with zippy yogurt sauce, these hearty burgers contain a boatload of flavorful vegetables, beans, and grains.

Roast Beef Sandwich
with Horseradish-Mustard Mayonnaise

3 tablespoons mayonnaise

2 teaspoons Dijon mustard

2 teaspoons prepared horseradish

8 slices light whole wheat bread

12 spinach or lettuce leaves

½ cucumber (3 ounces total), peeled and thinly sliced

12 slices (¾ pound) roast beef

½ teaspoon salt

¼ teaspoon ground black pepper

COMBINE the mayonnaise, mustard, and horseradish in a small bowl. Spread over the bread and cover 4 of the slices with the spinach or lettuce. Arrange the cucumber and roast beef over the spinach or lettuce. Season with the salt and pepper. Top with the remaining bread and cut in half.

Total time: 10 minutes ✽ Makes 4 servings

Per serving: 289 calories, 25 g protein, 28 g carbohydrates, 9 g fat, 2 g saturated fat, 907 mg sodium, 5 g fiber

You can change up this recipe by substituting chicken or turkey for the beef. You could also eliminate the bread. Instead, spread the meat with the mayonnaise, top with the cucumber, and wrap in the spinach or lettuce leaves.

┌─ **HEALTH HEARSAY**

Q: Does eating fat make you fat?

A: Not necessarily. There's nothing special about fat that packs on pounds. You gain weight when you eat more calories than you burn off, regardless of whether they're from fat, protein, or carbohydrates, says Diane McKay, PhD, an assistant professor at Tufts University. Getting enough fat in your diet—the Institute of Medicine recommends that it make up 20 to 35 percent of calories—is essential for good health, but the type of fat matters. Most should be mono- or polyunsaturated, which helps lower cholesterol, reduce inflammation, and decrease belly fat. Limit saturated fats and avoid trans fats. Both kinds can cause health problems. ─┘

Turkey Sandwiches
with Swiss Cheese and Apple

3 tablespoons macadamia or other nut butter

8 slices light whole wheat bread, lightly toasted

4 slices (4 ounces) Swiss cheese

8 slices (8 ounces) cooked turkey breast

¼ teaspoon salt

⅛ teaspoon ground black pepper (optional)

1 small apple, thinly sliced

½ bunch watercress sprigs

SPREAD the nut butter over the bread. Place the cheese on 4 slices of the bread, top with the turkey, and season with the salt and pepper (if using). Top with the apple, watercress, and the remaining bread. Cut in half.

Total time: 10 minutes ✳ Makes 4 servings

Per serving: 407 calories, 26 g protein, 33 g carbohydrates, 20 g fat, 7 g saturated fat, 898 mg sodium, 6 g fiber

This sandwich can be assembled ahead and refrigerated for up to 3 hours.

Pesto Chicken Sandwich
with Roasted Peppers

4 whole wheat tortillas
  (6" diameter)

¼ cup jarred pesto sauce

½ pound sliced cooked chicken
  breast, warmed

¼ teaspoon salt

¼ teaspoon ground black
  pepper

2 jarred roasted red bell
  peppers, drained and halved

4 thin slices mozzarella cheese

4 romaine leaves

PREHEAT the oven to 350°F. Arrange the tortillas on a baking sheet. Spread the pesto evenly over each. Arrange the chicken in a row down the center of each tortilla and sprinkle with the salt and black pepper. Top with the roasted bell peppers and cheese.

BAKE for 3 minutes, or just until the cheese melts. Top with a slice of the romaine, roll into a cylinder, and serve.

Total time: 10 minutes ✳ Makes 4 servings

Per serving: 353 calories, 31 g protein, 23 g carbohydrates, 17 g fat, 7 g saturated fat, 324 mg sodium, 3 g fiber

NUTRITION NEWS TO USE

Boosting your calcium intake may help curb your appetite and make slimming down easier, suggests research in the *British Journal of Nutrition*. When calcium-deficient women took a supplement, they lost four times more weight than those who didn't take the extra calcium. Researchers believe the brain compensates for a calcium shortage by initiating hunger to encourage eating foods rich in the mineral. Since most women fall short on calcium, aim to consume fat-free or low-fat yogurt and milk, beans, and dark leafy greens throughout the day, or talk with your doctor about supplements.

Skinny Monte Cristo

2 slices (¾ ounce) low-sodium deli ham

2 slices (¾ ounce) low-sodium deli turkey

2 slices Swiss cheese

4 slices 100 percent whole wheat thinly sliced bread, toasted

Ground black pepper

2 egg whites

2 pinches of ground nutmeg

¼ teaspoon confectioners' sugar

LAYER the ham, turkey, and cheese on 2 slices of toast. Season to taste with pepper. Top with the remaining toast.

HEAT a cast-iron skillet coated with cooking spray over medium heat for 2 minutes.

WHISK together the egg whites and nutmeg into a shallow bowl. Dip 1 side of a sandwich into the egg whites and let the excess drip off. Turn. Repeat with the other sandwich.

COOK for 6 minutes, turning once, or until the meat is warmed through, the cheese is melted, and the egg is cooked. Halve diagonally. Dust with the sugar and serve immediately.

Total time: 10 minutes ✽ Makes 2 servings

Per serving: 266 calories, 22 g protein, 24 g carbohydrates, 10 g fat, 5 g saturated fat, 564 mg sodium, 4 g fiber

This classic French sandwich consists of thin slices of cooked meat and cheese. It is dipped into egg and cooked until golden brown.

Tuna Salad in Lettuce Wrappers

- 2 cans (5 ounces each) solid white tuna packed in water, drained
- ¼ cup mayonnaise
- 1 teaspoon Dijon mustard
- 1 tablespoon lemon juice
- 2 tablespoons finely chopped red bell pepper or celery
- 2 teaspoons capers, drained
- 2 scallions, thinly sliced
- ¼ teaspoon salt
- ⅛ teaspoon ground black pepper
- 8 large lettuce leaves, such as Boston or leaf

FLAKE the tuna with a fork in a bowl. Stir in the mayonnaise, mustard, and lemon juice. Stir in the bell pepper or celery, capers, scallions, salt, and black pepper. Arrange the lettuce on a work surface with the rib end closest to you and the "cup" facing up. Spoon the tuna salad onto the leaf near the rib end and roll to enclose.

Total time: 25 minutes ✳ Makes 4 servings

Per serving: 178 calories, 21 g protein, 6 g carbohydrates, 8 g fat, 1 g saturated fat, 651 mg sodium, 1 g fiber

Try substituting canned or cooked salmon or boneless, skinless sardines for the tuna if you prefer. You can also add 3 or 4 thin slices of apple or a slice of Swiss or mozzarella cheese to the wrap for variety.

Ms. Effie's Salmon Patties

1 can (15 ounces) salmon, drained, skin removed

¾ cup oatmeal

⅓ cup low-fat milk

¼ cup Parmesan cheese

1 egg

1 tablespoon lemon juice

1 teaspoon salt-free seasoning
  Pinch of ground red pepper

6 cups salad greens

1 tomato, chopped

½ cup reduced-fat Caesar salad dressing

MASH the salmon with a fork in a medium bowl. Add the oatmeal, milk, cheese, egg, lemon juice, seasoning, and pepper. Stir to blend well. Let stand for 5 minutes. Shape into 4 patties.

HEAT a nonstick skillet coated with cooking spray over medium heat. Cook the patties for 6 minutes, turning once, or until browned and crisp.

DIVIDE the greens and tomato among 4 plates. Top each with 1 patty and drizzle with 2 tablespoons of the dressing.

Total time: 30 minutes　✳　Makes 4 servings

Per serving: 276 calories, 28 g protein, 20 g carbohydrates, 10 g fat, 3 g saturated fat, 780 mg sodium, 3 g fiber

I got the idea for these from a wonderful lady who ran an old-time luncheon diner in Clayton, Georgia. She made the best salmon patties and told me she used oatmeal instead of bread crumbs. **—Mary**

Open-Faced Smoked Salmon Sandwich

⅔ cup whipped cream cheese

2 teaspoons capers, drained

2½ tablespoons minced red onion

2 tablespoons chopped walnuts

8 slices rye crispbread

8 slices (½ pound) smoked salmon

¼ teaspoon ground black pepper

STIR together the cream cheese, capers, onion, and walnuts in a small bowl. Spread the mixture over the crispbread. Fold the salmon to fit on top of the cream cheese and sprinkle with the pepper.

Total time: 5 minutes ✱ Makes 4 servings

Per serving: 224 calories, 15 g protein, 19 g carbohydrates, 10 g fat, 4 g saturated fat, 614 mg sodium, 4 g fiber

Make the cream cheese mixture ahead and store it in a covered container in the refrigerator for up to 3 days. You can also store the assembled sandwiches in the refrigerator for up to 4 hours.

METABOLISM BOOSTER! VINEGAR

The primary substance that gives ordinary vinegar its sour taste and strong odor may fight fat, suggests new research presented at a recent meeting of the Japanese Society of Nutrition and Food Science. In a study of 175 overweight Japanese men and women, those who consumed a drink containing either 1 or 2 tablespoons of apple cider vinegar daily for 12 weeks had significantly lower body weight, body mass index, visceral fat, and waist circumference than the control group, which didn't consume any vinegar. Researchers credit vinegar's acetic acid, which may switch on genes that pump out proteins that break down fat.

Italian Egg and Pepper Sandwich

1 teaspoon olive oil
¼ cup sliced onion
¼ cup sliced green bell pepper
　Pinch of dried oregano
　Pinch of salt
1 egg
1 egg white
1 slice multigrain country bread, toasted

HEAT the oil in a nonstick skillet over medium heat. Add the onion, pepper, oregano, and salt. Cook, stirring occasionally, for 5 minutes, or until softened.

BEAT the egg and egg white in a small bowl with a fork. Add to the skillet. Cook for 3 minutes, or until set on the bottom. Flip the mixture. Fold if necessary to make the egg mixture the same size as the bread slice. Cook for about 2 minutes, or until cooked through. Set on the toast.

Total time: 15 minutes ✳ Makes 1 serving

Per serving: 223 calories, 14 g protein, 18 g carbohydrates, 11 g fat, 2 g saturated fat, 407 mg sodium, 5 g fiber

Even when the cupboard is almost bare, you can make this enjoyable sandwich.

Grilled Zucchini Sandwiches

1 lemon, juiced

3 tablespoons extra virgin olive oil

¼ teaspoon salt

¼ teaspoon pepper

4 medium zucchini, cut lengthwise into ¼" slices

1 large red onion, sliced

½ can great Northern beans, rinsed and drained

1 garlic clove, minced

1 teaspoon chopped fresh basil or ¼ teaspoon dried

Pinch of ground red pepper

1 tablespoon chopped walnuts

1 tablespoon crumbled goat cheese

4 sandwich rolls, split and toasted

PREHEAT a stove-top grill pan or skillet coated with cooking spray over medium heat. Combine the lemon juice, 2 tablespoons of the olive oil, ⅛ teaspoon of the salt, and ⅛ teaspoon of the pepper in a large bowl. Add the zucchini and onion to the bowl and toss to coat. Grill for 12 to 15 minutes, turning once.

MEANWHILE, place the beans, garlic, basil, red pepper, and the remaining 1 tablespoon olive oil, ⅛ teaspoon salt, and ⅛ teaspoon black pepper in a blender or food processor. Pulse until smooth. Fold in the walnuts and cheese.

DIVIDE the bean mixture onto each cut roll surface. Top with the grilled zucchini and onion.

Total time: 30 minutes ✳ Makes 4 servings

Per serving: 355 calories, 11 g protein, 46 g carbohydrates, 16 g fat, 3 g saturated fat, 618 mg sodium, 6 g fiber

I am always looking for and developing new recipes with lower fat and sugar that still are high in flavor. Just a little effort and thought can turn standard recipes into a dish that is lower in calories, while still being a flavorful, filling meal.

—Greg

Roasted Vegetable Sandwich

Tapenade

- 1 cup canned (in water) artichoke hearts, drained
- Juice of ½ lemon
- 1 tablespoon extra virgin olive oil
- 1 teaspoon minced garlic
- 1 teaspoon white wine vinegar
- ¼ teaspoon salt
- Ground black pepper

Sandwich

- 2 portobello mushroom caps
- 1 zucchini, sliced lengthwise and cut into 3" pieces
- 1 medium tomato, sliced
- 2 ounces fresh goat cheese
- 2 crusty multigrain rolls (4 ounces each), insides scooped out, or 2 slices whole grain bread

To make the tapenade:

COMBINE the artichokes, lemon juice, oil, garlic, vinegar, and salt in a food processor. Pulse, scraping down the sides of the bowl as needed, until the mixture is spreadable. Season to taste with pepper.

To make the sandwiches:

PREHEAT the oven to 400°F. Place the mushrooms and zucchini on a nonstick baking sheet. Roast for 10 minutes. Place the tomato slices on the same baking sheet and roast for 20 minutes, turning once, or until sizzling and any liquid is cooked away.

DIVIDE the mushrooms, zucchini, tomato, goat cheese, and tapenade among the rolls.

Total time: 40 minutes ✽ Makes 2 servings

Per serving: 232 calories, 12 g protein, 27 g carbohydrates, 11 g fat, 6 g saturated fat, 301 mg sodium, 9 g fiber

LABEL DECODER: "MADE WITH WHOLE GRAINS"

The USDA does not regulate this value-added claim, which often appears on processed foods such as crackers, cereals, and breads. Because labels usually don't indicate how many whole grains are included, this is a meaningless term. Instead, look for products that contain 100 percent whole grain, and read the ingredients list, which orders ingredients from most to least. Whole grain (wheat, oats) should be first, and enriched wheat flour—aka refined white flour—should not be included at all.

—Pamela James, Apple Valley, California

Pesto Pizza

- 1 container (6 ounces) fat-free Greek-style yogurt
- ¼ cup prepared pesto
- 1 whole wheat thin pizza crust (12" diameter)
- 1 large tomato, sliced
- 2 cups sliced vegetables, such as zucchini, bell pepper, and onion
- ¼ cup grated Parmesan cheese

PREHEAT the oven to 400°F.

STIR together the yogurt and pesto in a small bowl. Spread over the pizza crust. Arrange the tomato slices over the yogurt mixture. Top with the vegetables and sprinkle with the cheese.

BAKE for 15 minutes, or until heated through.

Total time: 25 minutes ✳ Makes 4 servings

Per serving: 325 calories, 17 g protein, 41 g carbohydrates, 13 g fat, 4 g saturated fat, 217 mg sodium, 8 g fiber

 I love this recipe because it is not only flavorful but healthy. I like pizza, but the tomato sauce doesn't agree with me, so I came up with another way to enjoy it. Delicious! —**Pamela**

Goat Cheese and Red Pepper Pizza

Dough

- ⅔ **cup warm water (105° to 115°F)**
- 1 **envelope (¼ ounce) active dry yeast (2¼ teaspoons)**
- 2 **cups whole wheat flour, preferably white whole wheat**
- ¼ **teaspoon salt**
- 2 **teaspoons extra virgin olive oil**

Pizza

- 5 **ounces low-fat soft goat cheese**
- 1 **garlic clove, minced**
- ½ **teaspoon chopped fresh oregano leaves or ¼ teaspoon dried**

  Ground black pepper
- 1 **cup (10 ounces) roasted red bell pepper strips**

  Slivered fresh basil leaves

To make the dough:

COAT a large bowl with cooking spray. Set aside.

COMBINE the water and yeast in a glass measuring cup and mix to dissolve. Combine 1¾ cups of the flour and the salt in a food processor. Pulse to mix. Add the oil to the yeast water. With the machine running, add the yeast mixture through the feed tube. Process for 1 to 2 minutes, or until the mixture forms a moist ball.

PLACE the dough on a work surface lightly floured with some of the remaining ¼ cup flour. With your hands, knead for about 1 minute, or until the dough is smooth. Use scant amounts of any remaining flour only to prevent surface sticking.

PLACE the dough in the prepared bowl. Coat lightly with cooking spray. Cover with plastic wrap. Set aside to rise for about 30 minutes, or until doubled in size.

To make the pizza:

COAT a 14" round pizza pan with cooking spray. Punch down the dough. Place on a lightly floured work surface. Let stand for 5 minutes. With floured hands or a rolling pin, pat or roll into a 14" circle. Place in the pan. Cover with plastic wrap and let stand for 15 minutes.

PREHEAT the oven to 375°F.

COMBINE the cheese, garlic, and oregano in a small bowl. Season with black pepper to taste. Dapple the crust with the crumbled cheese mixture. Scatter the bell pepper strips on top of the cheese. Bake for about 12 minutes, or until golden and bubbly. Remove the pizza from the oven and garnish with basil.

Total time: 1 hour 15 minutes ✱ Makes 4 servings

Per serving: 382 calories, 16 g protein, 54 g carbohydrates, 11 g fat, 6 g saturated fat, 279 mg sodium, 9 g fiber

A ready-made whole wheat crust may replace the from-scratch dough, but it will add considerably more sodium. Serve this pizza with a side spinach salad for extra fiber.

Pizza Bianca

Dough

- ²⁄₃ cup warm water (105° to 115°F)
- 1 envelope (¼ ounce) active dry yeast (2¼ teaspoons)
- 2 cups whole wheat flour, preferably white whole wheat
- ¼ teaspoon salt
- 2 teaspoons extra virgin olive oil

Pizza

- 1 tablespoon olive oil
- 1 onion, chopped
- 2 garlic cloves, minced
- ½ teaspoon dried oregano
- Pinch of salt
- ½ cup shredded Swiss or Gruyère cheese

To make the dough:

COAT a large bowl with cooking spray. Set aside.

COMBINE the water and yeast in a glass measuring cup and mix to dissolve. Combine 1¾ cups of the flour and the salt in a food processor. Pulse to mix. Add the oil to the yeast water. With the machine running, add the yeast mixture through the feed tube. Process for 1 to 2 minutes, or until the mixture forms a moist ball.

PLACE the dough on a work surface lightly floured with some of the remaining ¼ cup flour. With your hands, knead for about 1 minute, or until the dough is smooth. Use scant amounts of any remaining flour only to prevent surface sticking.

PLACE the dough in the prepared bowl. Coat lightly with cooking spray. Cover with plastic wrap. Set aside to rise for about 30 minutes, or until doubled in size.

To make the pizza:

COAT a 14" round pizza pan with cooking spray. Punch down the dough. Place on a lightly floured work surface. Let stand for 5 minutes. With floured hands or a rolling pin, pat or roll into a 14" circle. Place in the pan. Cover with plastic wrap and let stand for 15 minutes.

PREHEAT the oven to 375°F.

HEAT the oil in a large skillet over medium heat. Add the onion, garlic, oregano, and salt. Cook, stirring occasionally, for 5 minutes, or until golden. Spread the mixture evenly over the crust. Sprinkle with the cheese. Bake for 12 minutes, or until golden and bubbly. Cut into 8 slices.

Total time: 1 hour 15 minutes ✳ Makes 8 servings

Per serving: 184 calories, 6 g protein, 26 g carbohydrates, 6 g fat, 2 g saturated fat, 105 mg sodium, 5 g fiber

"White pizza" is a delightful alternative to the classic tomato-topped pie.

Veggie Pita Pizzas

2 whole wheat pitas
(8" diameter)

1 cup broccoli florets

1 scallion, sliced

½ cup sliced baby carrots

½ large green bell pepper,
chopped

½ cup spaghetti or pizza sauce

½ cup shredded part-skim
mozzarella cheese

PREHEAT the oven to 400°F. Place the pitas on a baking sheet. Bake for 5 minutes, or until lightly toasted.

HEAT a medium skillet coated with cooking spray over medium heat. Add the broccoli, scallion, carrots, and bell pepper. Cook, stirring often, for 5 minutes, or until the vegetables are crisp-tender.

SPREAD each pita with ¼ cup of the sauce. Divide the vegetable mixture between the pitas. Sprinkle half of the shredded cheese on each pita. Bake for 10 minutes, or until the cheese melts. Halve each pita.

Total time: 30 minutes ✱ Makes 4 servings

Per serving: 264 calories, 14 g protein, 38 g carbohydrates, 7 g fat, 2 g saturated fat, 734 mg sodium, 7 g fiber

As a nutrition consultant and an admitted pizza lover, I adapted this recipe for people who often crave gooey, cheesy, and often unhealthy food. It's so flavorful and filled with veggies and whole grains, so there's no guilt!
—**Linda**

To reel in weight gain, choose one of these combos:

1 Chunk light tuna + mixed greens + walnuts + balsamic vinaigrette

2 Salmon-avocado roll + edamame + miso soup + green tea

3 Shrimp + soba noodles + broccoli + light soy sauce

Why? Swedish researchers found that people who ate fish midday consumed 11 percent less at dinner—enough to lose 8 pounds in a year—compared with those who ate beef. Seafood's healthy fats may be the reason. "A meal high in omega-3 fatty acids can increase satiety for up to 2 hours," says Martha McKittrick, RD.

[**QUICK TIP: THREE HUNGER-BUSTING LUNCHES**]

Greek Pita Pizza

1 box (9 ounces) frozen artichoke hearts, thawed and chopped

1 medium zucchini, coarsely shredded

1 garlic clove, minced

¾ teaspoon dried oregano

6 pitted kalamata olives, chopped

4 whole wheat pitas (6½" diameter)

⅓ cup crumbled reduced-fat basil-tomato feta cheese

1 cup grape tomatoes, halved lengthwise

½ cup shredded reduced-fat mozzarella cheese

1 scallion, thinly sliced

PREHEAT the oven to 425°F. Pat the artichokes dry with paper towels.

HEAT a large nonstick skillet coated with cooking spray over medium-high heat. Cook the artichokes, zucchini, garlic, and oregano for 4 minutes, or until the zucchini is tender. Stir in the olives.

PLACE the pitas on a baking sheet and top with the zucchini mixture. Sprinkle with the feta cheese. Top with the tomatoes. Bake for 10 minutes, or until heated through. Sprinkle with the mozzarella and bake for 3 minutes, or until the cheese is melted. Sprinkle with the scallion.

Total time: 30 minutes ✱ Makes 4 servings

Per serving: 329 calories, 19 g protein, 46 g carbohydrates, 10 g fat, 3 g saturated fat, 805 mg sodium, 10 g fiber

There are many types of feta cheese sold in the supermarket, ranging from mild to very salty. Try salty Greek feta cheese for this recipe.

Two-Cheese Pita Melt

4 whole wheat pitas (4" diameter), split

4 teaspoons Dijon mustard

4 thin slices (3 ounces) mozzarella cheese

4 thin slices (3 ounces) Swiss cheese

1⅓ cups (4 ounces) sliced red or green cabbage

½ teaspoon dried oregano

½ teaspoon garlic powder (optional)

¼ teaspoon salt

¼ teaspoon ground black pepper

PREHEAT the oven to 400°F. Spread the inside of the pitas with the mustard and arrange the mozzarella and Swiss inside.

STIR together the cabbage, oregano, garlic powder (if using), salt, and pepper in a medium bowl. Stuff into the pitas. Place on a baking sheet and bake for 12 minutes, or until the cheese melts and the edges of the pitas are crisp.

Total time: 20 minutes ✳ Makes 4 servings

Per serving: 300 calories, 18 g protein, 21 g carbohydrates, 16 g fat, 10 g saturated fat, 694 mg sodium, 3 g fiber

Make these pitas with your favorite flavors. Replace 1 of the cheeses with feta cheese or goat cheese and substitute cooked broccoli for the cabbage, if desired.

Texas Burrito

3 tablespoons vegetable oil

1½ pounds cubed beef stew meat

1 onion, chopped

2 garlic cloves, minced

1½ small jalapeño chile peppers, seeded and finely chopped (wear plastic gloves when handling)

1¼ cups beef broth or hot water

1 tablespoon chili powder

1 tablespoon tomato paste

2 teaspoons ground cumin

½ teaspoon salt

¼ teaspoon ground black pepper

8 whole wheat tortillas (6" diameter)

1 cup (4 ounces) shredded Monterey Jack cheese

4 large lettuce leaves, shredded (optional)

1 large ripe tomato, finely chopped

HEAT the oil in a large saucepan over medium-high heat. Working in batches, cook the beef, stirring, for 5 minutes, or until browned. Remove to a plate.

REDUCE the heat to medium. Return the beef to the pan and stir in the onion, garlic, and chile peppers. Cook, stirring occasionally, for 5 minutes, or until the vegetables start to soften. Stir in the broth or water, chili powder, tomato paste, cumin, salt, and black pepper. Reduce the heat to low. Cover and cook for 1 hour, stirring occasionally. Remove the lid and cook for 30 minutes, or until the beef is tender.

MEANWHILE, preheat the oven to 375°F and wrap the tortillas in foil. Bake for 5 minutes, or until steaming and pliable. To assemble each burrito, place the tortillas on a work surface and divide the cheese down the center of each tortilla. Top with the beef mixture, lettuce (if using), and tomato. Fold 2 opposite sides over the filling, then fold 1 of the remaining sides over to enclose.

Total time: 1 hour 45 minutes ✽ Makes 8 servings

Per serving: 405 calories, 23 g protein, 24 g carbohydrates, 27 g fat, 10 g saturated fat, 461 mg sodium, 3 g fiber

Make a double batch of the filling and refrigerate or freeze it. Store in a covered container in the refrigerator for up to 5 days or in the freezer for up to 2 months. To reheat, thaw in the refrigerator, then cook in a saucepan over low heat, stirring occasionally, until heated through, about 10 minutes.

Whole Wheat Turkey Burrito

8 whole wheat flour tortillas (8" diameter)

12 ounces ground turkey breast

1 small green bell pepper, chopped

4 scallions, chopped

1 carrot, shredded

¼ cup low-sodium salsa

1 teaspoon mild chili powder

2 cups seeded and chopped plum tomatoes

8 romaine leaves

¼ cup (1 ounce) shredded reduced-fat Cheddar cheese

¼ cup fat-free sour cream

PREHEAT the oven to 200°F. Wrap the tortillas in foil and heat for 10 minutes, or until warm.

HEAT a large nonstick skillet coated with cooking spray over medium-high heat. Cook the turkey, pepper, and scallions, stirring to break up the meat, for 8 minutes, or until the turkey is no longer pink. Drain any fat.

ADD the carrot, salsa, chili powder, and half of the tomatoes. Reduce the heat to medium-low. Cover and simmer for 10 minutes, stirring occasionally. Remove the lid and continue to cook until any liquid is evaporated.

TRIM the romaine leaves so they are about 6" long. Place a leaf onto the center of a warm tortilla. Press lightly to flatten the center. Divide the turkey mixture among the tortillas. Divide the cheese and some of the remaining tomatoes over the turkey mixture. Top each with a dollop of sour cream. Roll up the tortilla to cover the filling and then fold in the ends. Repeat with the remaining tortillas.

Total time: 35 minutes ✳ Makes 4 servings

Per serving: 298 calories, 31 g protein, 48 g carbohydrates, 4 g fat, 1 g saturated fat, 483 mg sodium, 6 g fiber

QUICK TIP: MAKE IT A HABIT TO CUT YOUR PORTION BY ONE-FIFTH AT EVERY MEAL

40% The number of folks who say they are trying to lose weight and are not making an effort to reduce the calories they consume

—Kimberly Hammond, Kingwood, Texas

Black Bean Chimichangas

- 3 cans (15 ounces each) no-salt-added black beans, rinsed and drained
- 3 cups cooked brown rice
- 1 cup corn kernels
- 6 scallions, chopped
- ⅓ cup + 2 tablespoons chopped fresh cilantro
- 8 large whole wheat tortillas (10" diameter)
- 2 tablespoons olive oil
- 1 cup prepared salsa
- 1 avocado, cut into thin strips

PREHEAT the oven to broil. Coat a baking sheet with cooking spray.

COMBINE the beans, rice, corn, scallions, and ⅓ cup of the cilantro in a medium bowl. Toss to mix well.

PLACE the tortillas on a work surface. Place 1 cup of the bean mixture down the center of a tortilla. Fold in the sides, then roll tortillas into tight cylinders. Place the chimichangas seam side down on the baking sheet. Brush the tortillas with the oil.

BROIL in the center of the oven for 3 to 5 minutes, or until crisp and lightly browned.

PLACE 1 chimichanga on each of 8 plates. Sprinkle with the remaining 2 tablespoons cilantro. Serve with the salsa and avocado.

Total time: 15 minutes ✽ Makes 8 servings

Per serving: 428 calories, 14 g protein, 69 g carbohydrates, 10 g fat, 1 g saturated fat, 574 mg sodium, 13 g fiber

133

Lunches

Typically deep-fat-fried, chimichangas are a delicious alternative to a burrito. Here they're lightly brushed with healthy olive oil and broiled. Now that's a smart alternative! —Kimberly

Middle Eastern Spicy Garbanzo Beans

1 can (15.5 ounces) unsalted garbanzo beans, rinsed and drained

2 tablespoons freshly squeezed lemon juice

3 tablespoons white wine vinegar

1 tablespoon ground cumin

¼ teaspoon salt

Ground black pepper

4–5 dashes hot-pepper sauce (optional)

2 carrots, shredded

1 English cucumber, chopped

HEAT the beans, lemon juice, vinegar, cumin, salt, pepper, and hot-pepper sauce (if using) in a small saucepan over medium heat, stirring, for 5 minutes, or until heated through.

DIVIDE into 2 bowls and top each serving with half of the carrots and cucumber.

Total time: 10 minutes ✳ Makes 2 servings

Per serving: 312 calories, 16 g protein, 56 g carbohydrates, 3 g fat, 0 g saturated fat, 400 mg sodium, 13 g fiber

This is a favorite light lunch or dinner with my family. It is from my daughter, who has lived in the Middle East for several years. It is packed with fiber and is very healthy all around. **—Anne**

QUICK TIP: EAT SMART FOR ALL-DAY ENERGY

To put pep in your step and stay mentally sharp, eat less fat. A British study found that rats fed a diet of 55 percent total fat experienced a 50 percent drop in exercise stamina and significant short-term memory loss in as few as 9 days, compared with rats fed a low-fat diet. A "high-fat hangover" reduces heart and muscle efficiency, say researchers. Eat for maximum energy: Keep total fat intake between 20 and 35 percent of your daily calories—about 35 to 62 grams of fat—with most coming from the monounsaturated fatty acids in fish, nuts, and seeds.

Mexican Shrimp and Avocado Salad

1 pound shrimp, peeled and deveined

½ teaspoon lime zest

3 tablespoons lime juice

1 teaspoon ground cumin

½ teaspoon salt

¼ teaspoon ground black pepper

Ground red pepper

1 pound red tomatoes, chopped

1 small sweet white onion, chopped

2 tablespoons chopped pimiento-stuffed green olives

2 tablespoons minced jalapeño chile pepper, with seeds (wear plastic gloves when handling)

2 tablespoons olive oil

¼ cup + 2 tablespoons chopped fresh cilantro

1 ripe avocado, halved, pitted, peeled, and cut into chunks

4 cups mixed greens

STIR together the shrimp, lime zest, 1 tablespoon of the lime juice, ½ teaspoon of the cumin, ¼ teaspoon of the salt, the black pepper, and red pepper to taste in a medium bowl. Cover and set aside.

TOSS together the tomatoes, onion, olives, chile pepper, oil, ¼ cup of the cilantro, and the remaining 2 tablespoons lime juice, ½ teaspoon cumin, and ¼ teaspoon salt in another medium bowl. Let stand for 10 to 15 minutes to blend the flavors. Gently stir in the avocado.

PLACE the greens in a large shallow bowl and mound the avocado mixture in the center.

HEAT a nonstick skillet coated with cooking spray over medium-high heat. Cook the shrimp, turning often, for 4 minutes, or until just opaque in the thickest part. Add the shrimp and any pan juices to the salad and sprinkle with the remaining 2 tablespoons cilantro. Serve immediately.

Total time: 40 minutes ✳ Makes 4 servings

Per serving: 310 calories, 26 g protein, 15 g carbohydrates, 18 g fat, 3 g saturated fat, 572 mg sodium, 7 g fiber

Shrimp are a great low-fat, high-protein delicacy with a touch of omega-3 fatty acids.

Curried Couscous Salad

1¼ cups reduced-sodium chicken or vegetable broth

1 small zucchini, chopped

2 teaspoons green curry paste

¼ teaspoon ground black pepper

1 cup whole wheat couscous

⅓ cup chopped dried apricots

3 tablespoons golden raisins

1 can (15 ounces) small pink beans, chili beans, or red kidney beans, rinsed and drained

1 large tomato, chopped

½ cup chopped fresh flat-leaf parsley

1 small red onion, chopped

¼ cup lime juice

2 tablespoons olive oil

3 tablespoons slivered almonds, toasted

COMBINE the broth, zucchini, curry paste, and pepper in a medium saucepan. Cover and bring to a boil over high heat. Stir in the couscous, apricots, and raisins. Remove from the heat and let stand, covered, for 10 minutes.

FLUFF the couscous with a fork. Place in a large bowl, cover with a sheet of waxed paper, and let stand for 20 minutes, or until cooled.

STIR in the beans, tomato, parsley, onion, lime juice, and oil and gently toss to coat well. Cover and let stand for 30 minutes, or chill until ready to serve. Sprinkle with the almonds just before serving.

Total time: 25 minutes ✳ Makes 8 servings

Per serving: 364 calories, 14 g protein, 59 g carbohydrates, 11 g fat, 1 g saturated fat, 571 mg sodium, 13 g fiber

Couscous, a tiny pearl-like grain, is a staple in North African countries. Just a ½-cup serving of whole wheat couscous provides over 7 grams of protein, which will help you feel less tempted to snack. Some experts believe that combining protein with complex carbohydrates (like those found in beans) reduces cravings for sweets.

Texas Chili

3 large bell peppers (such as red, yellow, and/or green), chopped

1 onion, chopped

2 cans (10 ounces each) diced tomatoes with green chiles, such as Ro-tel

2 garlic cloves, minced

1 can (15 ounces) 99% fat-free turkey chili with beans

1 can (15 ounces) 99% fat-free turkey chili with no beans

HEAT a large saucepan coated with cooking spray over medium-high heat. Cook the peppers and onion for 10 minutes, or until very tender. Add the tomatoes and garlic and cook for 3 minutes, stirring. Stir in the chili with beans and the chili with no beans.

BRING to a simmer and reduce the heat to low. Cover and simmer for at least 1 hour, or until the flavors blend.

Total time: 1 hour 15 minutes ✳ Makes 6 servings

Per serving: 157 calories; 14 g protein; 22 g carbohydrates; 2 g fat; 1 g saturated fat; 1,010 mg sodium; 5g fiber

This recipe was passed on by fellow campmates at the Kerrville Folk Festival, but I added my own "secret ingredient"—the canned chili. It makes the chili milder in spice but still hot enough for anyone. —**Mary Lois**

Down East Clam Chowder

1 strip bacon

2 teaspoons canola oil

2 ribs celery, chopped

1 onion, chopped

1 garlic clove, minced

½ teaspoon dried thyme

1½ cups cubed Yukon gold potatoes

1½ cups clam juice

1½ tablespoons all-purpose flour

1½ cups 2% milk

3 cans (6½ ounces each) minced clams, drained

¼ cup chopped parsley

COOK the bacon in the microwave, per package directions, until crisp. Crumble into small pieces and set aside.

HEAT the oil in a large saucepan over medium-low heat. Cook the celery and onion for 5 minutes. Add the garlic and thyme and cook, stirring occasionally, for 3 minutes, or until the onion is softened but not browned. Add the potatoes and clam juice. The liquid should just cover the potatoes. (Add ½ cup water if necessary.) Bring to a simmer and cook for 10 minutes, or until the potatoes are tender but not mushy.

WHISK together the flour and ¼ cup of the milk in a small bowl until smooth. Stir into the chowder along with the remaining 1¼ cups milk. Increase the heat to high and simmer, stirring constantly, for 3 minutes, or until the soup has slightly thickened. Remove from the heat and add the clams.

DIVIDE into 4 bowls and sprinkle each serving with the crumbled bacon and parsley.

Total time: 50 minutes ✳ Makes 4 servings

Per serving: 214 calories; 14 g protein; 23 g carbohydrates; 7 g fat; 2 g saturated fat; 1,017 mg sodium; 2 g fiber

A warming bowl of soup as an appetizer not only prolongs the pleasure of a relaxing mealtime but also may help you eat fewer calories for the remainder of the meal.

Hearty Chickpea Soup

2 tablespoons olive oil

1 rib celery, finely chopped

1 carrot, chopped

1 onion, chopped

2 teaspoons minced garlic

1 teaspoon ground cinnamon

¼ teaspoon ground turmeric

¼ teaspoon ground ginger or grated fresh ginger

Pinch of saffron (optional)

2 cups vegetable broth

1 can (15 ounces) chickpeas, rinsed and drained

1 can (14½ ounces) no-salt-added diced or stewed tomatoes

2 cups baby spinach leaves

Lemon wedges

HEAT the oil in a medium saucepan over medium heat. Cook the celery, carrot, onion, and garlic, stirring occasionally, for 3 minutes, or until starting to soften. Add the cinnamon, turmeric, ginger, and saffron (if using). Cook for 1 minute, or until the spices are fragrant. Add the broth, chickpeas, and tomatoes (with juice). Bring to a boil.

REDUCE the heat to simmer. Cook, partially covered, for 25 minutes, or until the vegetables are tender. Stir in the spinach and cook for 2 minutes, or until wilted. Garnish with the lemon wedges, if desired.

Total time: 35 minutes ✳ Makes 4 servings

Per serving: 217 calories, 7 g protein, 27 g carbohydrates, 9 g fat, 1 g saturated fat, 421 mg sodium, 7 g fiber

The spicy, pungent mix of cinnamon and ginger is a warming backdrop for this healthy, colorful soup.

SUPERFOOD SPOTLIGHT: LENTILS

One-quarter cup of these tiny legumes is crammed with 13 grams of protein, 11 grams of belly-filling fiber, and 5 milligrams of fatigue-fighting iron—all for only 161 calories! Harvard School of Public health researchers found that women who ate lentils at least twice a week were 24 percent less likely to develop breast cancer than women who ate them less than once a month. And because lentils keep blood sugar steady, they may even cut back on hunger, boosting weight loss, according to a review of six studies.

Buy: Brown or green varieties in bulk—a pound costs about $3.

Try: Adding to soups or salads or mixing with whole grains. Rinse thoroughly, add to boiling water for 2 to 3 minutes, and simmer for 15 to 30 minutes before using.

[it worked for me]

85 lbs lost!

✳ PRISCILLA BARTLETT

She began eating right and exercising for the sheer joy of it. Her health bonus: Priscilla Bartlett's now a size 6.

My Story

When I was growing up, the family dinner was meat and potatoes. Though I was never an athletic girl, I was active, and that, combined with my youthful metabolism, kept my weight in check at 120 pounds—until I grew up and got married. My husband, George, and I continued to eat heavy, high-fat dinners—including take-out fried chicken and pizza accompanied by lots of beer! After 15 years, George had put on 20 pounds, but I'd gained 85.

Worried about my health, George suggested going on a diet together. We decided to replace breakfast and lunch with high-protein shakes. Along with controlling calories, it gave me the structure I needed after years of mindlessly snacking all day on junk. To supplement the shakes, we ate veggie-packed snacks and a sensible dinner.

VITAL STATS

Pounds lost: 85

Age: 41

Height: 5'2"

Weight then: 209 pounds

Weight now: 124 pounds

Still, I knew dieting alone wasn't enough, so I started walking a mile every day. After 3 months, I was covering 3 to 4 miles at a time—and looking for a new challenge. Then one day my husband, who'd cycled since before we got married, surprised me with a new bike. We soon started riding 15 to 18 miles every weekend and eventually began doing charity rides. The most challenging one was 50 miles. The last 8 miles included lots of hills, which have never been my strong suit. But I found my comfort zone and made it to the finish line. When I started biking, I'd already lost 59 pounds. After we started cycling regularly, the last 26 pounds flew off! Along the way, I transitioned from meal-replacement shakes to healthy, balanced meals, which helped fuel my exercise.

Today I ride every weekend and two or three times a week. I'm so much happier: I've dropped from size XXL shirts to small/medium. More important, I have lots more energy. I'm no longer ashamed of the way I look, and my husband can't keep his hands off me! He's proud of me, and I'm proud of him for supporting me in such a loving way. I could not have done it without him.

My Top Tips

* Exercise for joy, not just weight loss . . . Cycling was an epiphany for me. It gets me outdoors, clears my head, and helps maintain my weight. To stay on track, I also get on the scale every morning.

* Be a sounding board . . . Co-workers often come to me with their frustrations about losing weight. I never judge anyone because I've been there; I want only the best for them. It also reminds me that, wow, I actually did this!

* Make room for foods you love . . . When I started dieting, I incorporated chocolate—my weakness— into my new plan.

* Have a backup routine . . . When the weather's bad, I hook up my bike to a stationary indoor bike trainer so I can still get my workout.

* Retrain your taste buds . . . It took a while, but now I look forward to healthy foods such as salad, steamed broccoli, and grilled fish or chicken.

snacks & little

bites

Caesar Salad Spears

2 garlic cloves, peeled

1 tablespoon water

1 tablespoon light mayonnaise

1 tablespoon reduced-fat sour cream

1 tablespoon lemon juice

1 cup chopped cooked chicken breast

1 small rib celery, chopped

3 tablespoons grated Parmesan cheese

8 outer romaine leaves

¼ cup Caesar-flavored croutons

PLACE the garlic in a small custard cup and add the water. Microwave on high power for 1 minute, or until the garlic softens. Flatten the garlic by crushing it with the side of a knife and finely chop.

STIR together the garlic, mayonnaise, sour cream, and lemon juice in a medium bowl. Stir in the chicken, celery, and 2 tablespoons of the cheese until well blended.

ARRANGE the romaine on a serving plate. Spoon 2 tablespoons of the chicken mixture down the center of each leaf. Cut the croutons, if necessary, into approximately ½" pieces. Sprinkle the croutons over the chicken and top with the remaining 1 tablespoon cheese. Serve immediately or cover and chill for up to 3 hours.

Total time: 20 minutes ✳ Makes 8 servings

Per serving: 65 calories, 7 g protein, 4 g carbohydrates, 2 g fat, 1 g saturated fat, 96 mg sodium, 0 g fiber

Here's a great alternative to the traditional sandwich—crisp romaine wrapped around a delicious high-protein mix of chicken and cheese.

Fresh Spring Rolls

Dipping Sauce

- 2 tablespoons lime juice
- 2 tablespoons Asian fish sauce
- 1 tablespoon white wine or rice wine vinegar
- 2 tablespoons sugar
- 1 small garlic clove, finely chopped
- 2 teaspoons ketchup
- ¼ teaspoon ground red pepper

Spring Rolls

- 2 small carrots, shredded
- 2 scallions, finely chopped
- 24 deveined medium shrimp, cooked and peeled
- 24 fresh mint leaves
- 1 cup thinly sliced English cucumber, cut into half-rounds
- 8 fresh cilantro sprigs, thick stems removed
- 1 cup watercress, thick stems removed
- 3 tablespoons dry-roasted peanuts, coarsely chopped
- 8 round rice paper wrappers (8" diameter)

To make the dipping sauce:

STIR together the lime juice, fish sauce, wine or vinegar, sugar, garlic, ketchup, and pepper in a small bowl. Let stand for at least 20 minutes to allow the flavors to blend.

To make the spring rolls:

TOSS together the carrots, scallions, and 1 tablespoon of the prepared dipping sauce in another small bowl.

ARRANGE the shrimp, mint leaves, carrot mixture, cucumber, cilantro, watercress, and peanuts in piles in front of you on a board. Fill a large pie plate with very warm tap water. Set a clean kitchen towel nearby. Add one rice paper wrapper at a time to the water and soak for 30 to 45 seconds, or until it begins to soften. Repeat with the remaining wrappers.

PLACE in a stack on the towel and let stand for 2 minutes, or until soft and pliable. Layer the ingredients in a 4" line in the center of the rice paper, starting 3" up from the edge closest to you: 3 shrimp, 3 mint leaves, 1 rounded tablespoon carrot mixture, 1 rounded tablespoon cucumber, 1 sprig cilantro, 2 tablespoons watercress, and 1 teaspoon peanuts. Fold in the sides and roll up, envelope style. Set seam side down on a plate. Repeat with the remaining ingredients. Cover and refrigerate for up to 6 hours.

HALVE each roll on the diagonal and serve with the dipping sauce.

Total time: 40 minutes * Makes 8 servings

Per serving: 163 calories, 9 g protein, 27 g carbohydrates, 3 g fat, 0 g saturated fat, 596 mg sodium, 2 g fiber

pring rolls are traditionally served on the first day of the Chinese New Year and are smaller and more delicate than egg rolls. These are loaded with a medley of colorful ingredients.

Chicken "Not" Wings

8 boneless, skinless chicken thighs, trimmed

½ cup Buffalo wing sauce, such as Frank's RedHot

4 ribs celery, cut into thin 3" strips

¼ cup fat-free blue cheese dressing

PREHEAT the oven to 375°F.

CUT the thighs into wing-size strips, about 4 to 5 "wings" per thigh.

HEAT a large ovenproof skillet coated with cooking spray over high heat. Cook the thighs, stirring often, for 5 minutes, or until browned. Add the sauce, tossing to coat well.

PLACE the skillet in the oven and bake for 20 minutes, or until browned. Serve with the celery and dressing.

Total time: 35 minutes ✳ Makes 4 servings

Per serving: 270 calories; 40 g protein; 6 g carbohydrates; 8 g fat; 2 g saturated fat; 1,047 mg sodium; 2 g fiber

I love chicken wings—but I cannot have them due to the fat. I kind of played with this recipe to get the taste I love.

—Gordon

QUICK TIP: DRINK TO YOUR HEART'S CONTENT

People at high risk of heart disease who drink a mixture of no-sugar-added cocoa powder and fat-free milk twice a day have lower levels of inflammation—of which high levels are an indicator of atherosclerosis—compared with those who drink only milk, according to a Spanish study. Researchers believe the high concentration of polyphenols in the cocoa powder works as a natural anti-inflammatory. Drink chocolate milk or eat polyphenol-rich foods, such as dark chocolate, grapes, and berries, daily.

Ham and Grissini Roll-Ups

2 slices (2 ounces) deli-baked ham

4 teaspoons reduced-fat Boursin cheese

2 teaspoons chopped fresh parsley

6 grissini or Italian breadsticks, halved with a serrated knife

1½ tablespoons reduced-fat sour cream

1 tablespoon grainy deli-style mustard

ARRANGE the ham slices on a cutting board. Trim to square off the ham slices, if needed, to 6" × 4½" rectangles. Spread each piece with 2 teaspoons of the cheese. Sprinkle each piece with 1 teaspoon of the parsley. Cut the ham lengthwise into six ¾"-wide strips, using a pizza wheel or a sharp knife.

ROLL each strip of ham diagonally around a grissini half, pressing the cheese side to the grissini to adhere. Stir together the sour cream and mustard until smooth and serve as a dip for the grissini.

Total time: 15 minutes ✳ Makes 4 servings

Per serving: 110 calories, 6 g protein, 8 g carbohydrates, 5 g fat, 2 g saturated fat, 503 mg sodium, 1 g fiber

This robust snack is a deli delight! Enjoy a delicious roll-up of ham and cheese dipped in a zesty mustard dressing.

HEALTH HEARSAY

Q: "I keep getting e-mails about açai pills for weight loss. Is there anything to this?"

A: No. There's no proof that supplements made with açai help with weight loss or have any other miracle benefits, says Lona Sandon, RD. The berry is very high in antioxidants (similar to those in blueberries and red grapes) and contains some heart-healthy fats, but more research is needed before it can claim to fight cancer, lower cholesterol, or do anything else. Bottom line: "Açai is a healthful fruit you can add to your diet for variety," Sandon says. If you want to try it, buy fruit juice or pulp for smoothies, not capsules.

Mini Pita Pizzas with Caramelized Shallots

6 sun-dried tomato halves

1½ tablespoons pine nuts

1½ teaspoons olive oil

4 large shallots (6 ounces), peeled and thinly sliced crosswise

½ teaspoon sugar

1 teaspoon white wine vinegar

¼ cup herbed goat cheese

12 mini whole wheat pitas (2" diameter)

PREHEAT the oven to 350°F. Place the tomatoes in a small bowl. Add boiling water to cover and let stand for 15 minutes, or until softened. Drain well and finely chop.

MEANWHILE, cook the pine nuts in a small nonstick skillet over medium heat, stirring often, for 3 minutes, or until lightly toasted. Place on a plate and let cool.

HEAT the oil in the same skillet over medium heat. Cook the shallots, stirring occasionally, for 5 minutes, or until the shallots are softened. Add the sugar and cook for 2 minutes, stirring frequently, or until the shallots are golden brown. Stir in the vinegar and chopped tomatoes and cook for 1 minute.

SPREAD 1 teaspoon of the cheese on each mini pita and arrange on a baking sheet. Spoon 1 rounded measuring teaspoon of the shallot mixture onto each pita and sprinkle the pine nuts on top. Bake for 6 minutes, or until heated through.

Total time: 40 minutes ✳ Makes 6 servings

Per serving: 134 calories, 5 g protein, 21 g carbohydrates, 4 g fat, 1 g saturated fat, 189 mg sodium, 3 g fiber

These pita pizzas feature a sprinkling of pine nuts, which are extracted from certain kinds of pinecones. While these light and flavorful nuts are high in fat, most of it is monounsaturated. And just 1 ounce packs an impressive 4 grams of fiber.

Mustard-Glazed Snack Mix

4 cups bite-size whole grain cereal squares

1 cup broken whole wheat pretzel sticks (approximately 1" lengths)

½ cup unsalted almonds or peanuts

3 tablespoons yellow mustard

3 tablespoons honey

2 tablespoons butter, cut into 4 pieces

1 tablespoon Worcestershire sauce

⅛ teaspoon ground red pepper

PREHEAT the oven to 325°F. Line a jelly-roll pan with foil and coat with cooking spray.

TOSS together the cereal, pretzels, and almonds or peanuts in a large bowl. Set aside.

PLACE the mustard, honey, butter, Worcestershire sauce, and pepper in a medium microwaveable bowl. Cover with waxed paper and microwave on high power for 45 to 60 seconds, or just until the butter is melted. Stir together until smooth. Drizzle the mustard mixture, about one-third at a time, over the cereal mixture, tossing until evenly coated.

SPREAD the coated cereal mixture in a single layer on the pan. Bake for 30 to 35 minutes, stirring halfway through, until lightly browned. Cool in the pan on a rack for 30 minutes, or until completely cooled. Store in an airtight container for up to 2 weeks.

Total time: 45 minutes ✳ Makes 12 servings

Per serving: 165 calories, 5 g protein, 26 g carbohydrates, 6 g fat, 2 g saturated fat, 141 mg sodium, 5 g fiber

An eclectic combination of wholesome munchables and flavorful spices makes this mix perfect for packed lunches, late-night snacks, or party dishes.

Roasted Red Pepper Hummus with Cilantro

2 red bell peppers

4 large garlic cloves, unpeeled

1 can (15.5 ounces) chickpeas, rinsed and drained

2 tablespoons tahini

2 tablespoons lemon juice

1 tablespoon mild hot-pepper sauce

¼ cup chopped fresh cilantro

Assorted vegetable sticks, for dipping

PREHEAT the broiler. Place the bell peppers on a foil-lined baking sheet. Wrap the garlic in foil and place on the sheet. Broil the peppers 6" from the heat source for 15 to 20 minutes, turning occasionally, or until charred on all sides. Broil the garlic for 15 minutes. Place the peppers in a sealed paper bag and let stand for 10 minutes.

WHEN cool enough to handle, peel the garlic and finely chop in a food processor. When the bell peppers are cool enough to handle, peel, core, and seed them. Add the bell peppers, chickpeas, tahini, lemon juice, and hot-pepper sauce to the processor and blend until smooth. Add the cilantro and process just until combined.

FOR best flavor, chill for at least 4 hours or up to 3 days. Serve with the vegetable sticks.

Total time: 35 minutes ✻ Makes 4 servings

Per serving: 154 calories, 7 g protein, 22 g carbohydrates, 5 g fat, 1 g saturated fat, 277 mg sodium, 6 g fiber

Chickpeas are the main attraction in this Middle Eastern spread. Just ½ cup of this tasty snack delivers 7 grams of fiber.

—Millie Gentry, Cleveland, Ohio

Guilt-Free Brownies

1 can (15.5 ounces) black beans, rinsed and drained

½ cup unsweetened cocoa powder

½ cup 100% pumpkin puree

½ cup honey

¼ cup ground flaxseed

4 eggs

1½ teaspoons ground cinnamon

1 teaspoon vanilla extract

1 cup chopped walnuts

1 cup 60% cocoa bittersweet chocolate chips

PREHEAT the oven to 350°F. Coat an 8" × 8" baking pan with cooking spray.

COMBINE the beans, cocoa powder, pumpkin, honey, flaxseed, eggs, cinnamon, and vanilla extract in a blender or food processor. Blend or process until smooth. Pour into the pan and sprinkle with the walnuts and chocolate chips. Bake for 30 minutes, or until the top springs back when touched lightly in the center with a finger.

Total time: 1 hour ✳ Makes 16 brownies

Per serving: 202 calories, 6 g protein, 22 g carbohydrates, 13 g fat, 4 g saturated fat, 86 mg sodium, 4 g fiber

These brownies are high in protein, fiber, and flavor. They're a great way to beat a chocolate craving (and to sneak in some nutrition)!

—Millie

Chocolate-Almond Fudge Brownies

¾ cup fat-free plain yogurt

1 cup whole grain pastry flour

⅔ cup unsweetened cocoa powder

½ teaspoon salt

2 large egg whites

1 large egg

2 cups sugar

½ teaspoon almond extract

¼ cup miniature semisweet chocolate chips

LINE a sieve with a coffee filter or white paper towel and place over a deep bowl. Place the yogurt in the sieve and set aside to drain for 30 minutes (you should have about ½ cup drained yogurt). Discard the liquid in the bowl.

PREHEAT the oven to 350°F. Coat an 11" × 7" baking dish with cooking spray.

WHISK together the flour, cocoa powder, and salt in a medium bowl. Place the egg whites and egg in a large bowl. Beat with an electric mixer on medium speed until frothy. Add the sugar, almond extract, and reserved yogurt. Beat until the sugar dissolves. Add the flour mixture and beat on low speed just until combined. Stir in the chocolate chips. Pour into the baking dish. Bake for 30 minutes, or until a wooden pick inserted in the center comes out clean. Cool on a rack.

Total time: 50 minutes ✳ Makes 15 servings

Per serving: 161 calories, 3 g protein, 36 g carbohydrates, 2 g fat, 1 g saturated fat, 98 mg sodium, 2 g fiber

To make cutting sticky desserts easier, remove them from the pan and slice with unwaxed dental floss. Cut a piece of floss several inches longer than the dessert that you're cutting. Hold the floss taut over the dessert and lower your hands so the floss cuts through it. Let go of one end and pull the floss out through the other side.

Oatmeal-Date Bars

Filling

- 1 cup unsweetened applesauce
- 1 cup chopped dates
- ½ teaspoon ground cinnamon
- ½ teaspoon pumpkin pie spice
- 1 teaspoon vanilla extract

Crust

- 1 cup whole grain pastry flour
- 1 cup old-fashioned rolled oats
- ½ teaspoon baking powder
- ½ teaspoon baking soda
- ½ teaspoon salt
- ⅔ cup packed brown sugar
- 3 tablespoons butter, at room temperature
- 3 tablespoons reduced-fat sour cream

PREHEAT the oven to 375°F. Line an 11" × 7" baking dish with foil and coat with cooking spray.

To make the filling:
COMBINE the applesauce, dates, cinnamon, and pumpkin pie spice in a small saucepan. Bring to just a simmer and cook, stirring and mashing occasionally with a spatula, for 10 minutes, or until thickened. Stir in the vanilla extract. Set aside to cool.

To make the crust:
WHISK together the flour, oats, baking powder, baking soda, and salt in a medium bowl. Place the mixture on a sheet of waxed paper. Beat the sugar, butter, and sour cream in the same bowl, with an electric mixer on high speed, for 1 minute. Stir in the oat mixture with a wooden spoon until combined. Set a sheet of plastic wrap on a small baking sheet. Remove 1 cup of the dough and crumble it onto the plastic wrap. Cover loosely with the plastic and put in the freezer while assembling the bars. Drop the remaining dough by spoonfuls into the baking dish. Cover with a sheet of plastic wrap coated with cooking spray and press the dough into an even layer. Remove the wrap.

DROP the filling by spoonfuls over the dough and spread in an even layer. Crumble the chilled dough evenly over the filling. Bake for 25 minutes, or until golden brown. Cool completely in the pan on a rack. Remove from the pan and gently remove the foil. Cut into 18 pieces, cutting into thirds lengthwise and sixths crosswise. Store airtight for up to 1 week, or freeze for up to 2 months.

Total time: 1 hour 5 minutes ✳ Makes 18 servings

Per serving: 121 calories, 2 g protein, 24 g carbohydrates, 3 g fat, 1 g saturated fat, 118 mg sodium, 2 g fiber

Dates have a history that spans over 5,000 years. It's been said that the name comes from the Greek word for "finger," after the shape of this fruit. They have an intensely sweet flavor and are loaded with fiber, an ideal combination for fans of sugary snacks.

Oatmeal-Raisin Flax Cookies

1½ cups rolled oatmeal

1 cup whole grain pastry flour

2 tablespoons ground flaxseed

1 tablespoon ground cinnamon

1 teaspoon baking soda

6 tablespoons trans-free margarine

½ cup Splenda

½ cup unsweetened apple sauce

¼ cup egg substitute

1 teaspoon vanilla extract

¼ cup raisins

PREHEAT the oven to 375°F. Coat 2 cookie sheets with nonstick cooking spray.

WHISK together the oatmeal, flour, flaxseed, cinnamon, and baking soda in a medium bowl.

BEAT the margarine in a large bowl with an electric mixer on medium speed for 2 minutes, or until creamy. Beat in the Splenda, applesauce, egg substitute, and vanilla extract just until combined. Beat in the flour mixture for 3 minutes, or until well blended. Stir in the raisins.

DROP by teaspoons onto baking sheets. Bake for 15 to 17 minutes, or until lightly browned.

Total time: 30 minutes   ✳   Makes 24 servings

Per serving: 70 calories, 2 g protein, 9 g carbohydrates, 3 g fat, 1 g saturated fat, 81 mg sodium, 1 g fiber

I was diagnosed with diabetes 3½ years ago. I weighed 270 pounds. I felt terrible! I went to diabetes school and learned about my disease and a whole new lifestyle. I lost 107 pounds and control my blood sugar with diet and exercise.

—Alfred

Chocolate Chip Cookies

¾ cup Splenda–brown sugar blend

¾ cup sugar-free pancake syrup

2 tablespoons canola oil

2 containers (5 ounces each) pureed prunes (baby food)

4 eggs

1 teaspoon vanilla extract

3 cups old-fashioned oats

2 cups wheat bran

1⅔ cups all-purpose flour

⅓ cup unsweetened cocoa powder

1½ teaspoons baking soda

½ teaspoon baking powder

½ teaspoon salt

1 cup mini chocolate chips

PREHEAT the oven to 350°F. Coat a baking sheet with cooking spray.

COMBINE the sugar blend, syrup, oil, prunes, eggs, and vanilla extract in a large bowl. Add the oats, bran, flour, cocoa powder, baking soda, baking powder, and salt, stirring until well blended. Stir in the chocolate chips.

DROP the batter by tablespoons onto the cookie sheet. Bake for 10 to 12 minutes, or until the top of a cookie springs back when gently touched with a finger.

Total time: 45 minutes ❋ Makes 48 cookies

Per cookie: 103 calories, 3 g protein, 19 g carbohydrates, 3 g fat, 1 g saturated fat, 81 mg sodium, 2 g fiber

Sweets are my downfall. I can eat these cookies and be satisfied without craving the whole batch.

—Kathy

Triple Chocolate Drops

1¾ cups whole grain pastry flour

½ cup unsweetened cocoa powder

1 teaspoon baking powder

½ teaspoon baking soda

¼ teaspoon salt

1 ounce unsweetened chocolate

3 tablespoons canola oil

4 large egg whites

1 large egg

¾ cup granulated sugar

½ cup packed light brown sugar

¼ cup prune puree

1 teaspoon vanilla extract

¼ cup mini semisweet chocolate chips

Confectioners' sugar (optional)

WHISK together the flour, cocoa powder, baking powder, baking soda, and salt in a medium bowl. Place the chocolate and oil in a small microwaveable bowl. Microwave on high power for 1 minute. Stir until the chocolate is melted and smooth.

COMBINE the egg whites, egg, granulated sugar, and brown sugar in a large bowl. Beat with an electric mixer on high speed for 4 minutes, or until smooth and pale. Reduce the speed to low and add the melted chocolate, prune puree, and vanilla extract. Beat for 1 minute. Gradually beat in the flour mixture. Fold in the chocolate chips. Cover and refrigerate for 1 hour or up to 24 hours.

PREHEAT the oven to 350°F. Coat 2 large baking sheets with cooking spray.

LET the dough soften at room temperature for about 5 minutes. Drop by rounded teaspoons about 1½" apart onto the baking sheets. Bake one sheet at a time for 12 minutes, or until the centers just begin to set. Cool in the sheet on a rack for 2 minutes. Remove from the sheet and place on the rack to cool completely. Lightly dust with the confectioners' sugar (if using).

Total time: 30 minutes ✳ Makes 36 cookies

Per serving: 72 calories, 2 g protein, 13 g carbohydrates, 2 g fat, 1 g saturated fat, 60 mg sodium, 1 g fiber

Prune puree is a great fat replacer in chocolate baked goods as long as you don't use too much. Substitute the puree for up to two-thirds of the fat. To make your own, combine 12 ounces pitted prunes and 3 tablespoons honey in a food processor. Process for 10 seconds. Add ½ cup water and process until smooth. Refrigerate in an airtight container for up to 2 months. Or purchase pureed prune baby food.

Chocolate-Almond Meringue Cookies

½ cup blanched almonds

5 tablespoons sugar

3 large egg whites, at room temperature

¼ teaspoon cream of tartar

2 tablespoons unsweetened cocoa powder

¼ cup raspberry or strawberry all-fruit preserves

PREHEAT the oven to 250°F. Line a baking sheet with parchment paper or foil.

PLACE the almonds and 2 tablespoons of the sugar in a food processor. Process until finely ground. Beat the egg whites and cream of tartar in a large bowl with an electric mixer on high speed until frothy. Gradually beat in the remaining 3 tablespoons sugar until stiff, glossy peaks form. Gently fold in the cocoa powder and ground almonds.

SPOON the meringue into 1½" mounds on the baking sheet. Using the back of a spoon, depress the centers and build up the sides of each meringue to form a shallow cup. Bake for 1 hour. Turn off the oven and allow the meringues to stand with the oven door closed for 1 hour. Remove from the sheet and place onto a rack to cool completely. Store in an airtight container for up to 1 week.

FILL each meringue with ¼ teaspoon of the preserves.

Total time: 2 hours 15 minutes ✳ Makes 16 servings

Per serving: 53 calories, 2 g protein, 7 g carbohydrates, 2 g fat, 0 g saturated fat, 13 mg sodium, 1 g fiber

Light as a cloud, these crunchy, nutty treats are guaranteed to please a crowd. Why wait for a special occasion? Whip up a batch tonight!

—Angie Schneider, Louisville, Kentucky

Choco-Peanut Clusters

⅓ cup **60% bittersweet chocolate chips**

2 tablespoons **natural/organic peanut butter**

1½ cups **high-fiber cereal, such as All-Bran or Kashi GoLean**

LINE a baking sheet with waxed or parchment paper.

PLACE the chocolate chips in a medium microwaveable bowl. Microwave on high, stirring once, for 30 seconds to 1 minute, or until melted. Stir in the peanut butter until melted. Gently fold in the cereal until combined, being careful not to crush the cereal.

DROP the mixture by teaspoonfuls onto baking sheet. Chill for at least 45 minutes.

Total time: 1 hour ✷ Makes 16 servings

Per serving: 45 calories, 1 g protein, 7 g carbohydrates, 3 g fat, 1 g saturated fat, 23 mg sodium, 3 g fiber

I am someone who enjoys exercising and being active and likes to eat tasty food. Especially when it is good for you like these delicious snack bites! —**Angie**

Chocolate–Peanut Butter Balls

25 chocolate wafer cookies, finely crushed

1 cup + 2 tablespoons confectioners' sugar

⅓ cup honey

¼ cup + 2 tablespoons smooth peanut butter

STIR together cookie crumbs and 1 cup of the confectioners' sugar in a large bowl. Whisk together the honey and peanut butter in a medium bowl until well blended.

ADD to the cookie crumb mixture and stir well (the mixture may be crumbly).

SHAPE into 1" balls with your hands (the mixture should hold together as you shape it). Place in a single layer in an airtight container. Store in an airtight container at room temperature for up to 3 days. Just before serving, roll the balls in the remaining 2 tablespoons confectioners' sugar.

Total time: 10 minutes ✳ Makes 36 servings

Per serving: 58 calories, 1 g protein, 10 g carbohydrates, 2 g fat, 0 g saturated fat, 37 mg sodium, 0 g fiber

Snacks & Little Bites

The perfect fix for a candy craving, this classic combination of chocolate and peanut butter is satisfying with every bite.

Crunchy Peanut Squares

1 tablespoon butter

⅓ cup honey

¼ cup packed brown sugar

⅓ cup natural peanut butter

1 teaspoon vanilla extract

3 cups plain air-popped popcorn

2 cups crisp rice cereal

2 cups oat circle cereal

⅓ cup unsalted peanuts, chopped

⅓ cup 60% cocoa bittersweet chocolate chips

LINE a 13" × 9" baking pan with foil, extending the foil at the ends. Coat the foil with cooking spray.

MELT the butter, honey, and brown sugar in a large nonstick saucepan over low heat, stirring frequently. Remove the saucepan from the heat. Add the peanut butter and vanilla extract. Return the saucepan to the heat and cook, stirring constantly, for 2 minutes, or until the mixture is melted and well blended. Remove the pan from the heat. Stir in the popcorn, rice cereal, oat cereal, and peanuts. Stir until evenly coated.

PLACE into the prepared pan. Spray hands with cooking spray and press the mixture firmly into the pan. Sprinkle with the chocolate chips. Cool completely on a rack. Remove from the pan using the foil. Cut into 24 pieces.

Total time: 10 minutes ✽ Makes 24 servings

Per serving: 83 calories, 2 g protein, 12 g carbohydrates, 3 g fat, 1 g saturated fat, 38 mg sodium, 1 g fiber

These delicious squares dress up a common healthy and satisfying treat. Air-popped popcorn is usually lower in fat and calories than the kinds that are cooked in oil. For the healthiest popcorn, use a hot-air popper and omit any butter and salt.

QUICK TIP: POWER UP YOUR PEANUTS

For a bigger antioxidant punch per crunch, roast peanuts. The heat releases twice as many disease-fighting compounds, such as coumaric acid, which may help combat cancer, say USDA researchers.

HERE'S HOW: Roast shelled peanuts at 350°F for 21 minutes. Add to salads or stir-fries (include antioxidant-rich seed coats, which may shed during cooking).

Sweet Popcorn Treat

6 cups plain hot-air popped popcorn

½ cup colored melting chocolate wafers

PLACE the popcorn in a large bowl.

PLACE the wafers in a small microwaveable bowl and microwave on high for 1 minute. Remove and stir until melted. Using a spoon, drizzle over the popcorn.

LET cool, then break apart and place 1 cup in each of 6 resealable plastic bags. Store for up to 7 days.

Total time: 20 minutes ✳ Makes 6 servings

Per serving: 98 calories, 2 g protein, 15 g carbohydrates, 5 g fat, 3 g saturated fat, 2 mg sodium, 2 g fiber

I make this treat for every holiday using different colors of candy for each holiday, such as red, pink, and white for Valentine's Day.

—Margaret

METABOLISM BOOSTER! WATERMELON

The amino acid arginine, abundant in watermelon, might promote weight loss, according to a new study in the *Journal of Nutrition*. Researchers supplemented the diets of obese mice with arginine over 3 months and found that doing so decreased body-fat gains by a whopping 64 percent. Adding this amino acid to the diet enhanced the oxidation of fat and glucose and increased lean muscle, which burns more calories than fat does. Snack on watermelon in the summer, and eat other arginine sources, such as seafood, nuts, and seeds, year-round.

Blueberry Treat

1 **light multigrain English muffin,
   halved and toasted**

½ **cup fresh or frozen and
   thawed wild blueberries**

2 **tablespoons thawed frozen
   whipped topping**

PLACE 1 half of the muffin on 2 plates. Top each with ¼ cup of the blueberries and 1 tablespoon of the whipped topping,

Total time: 5 minutes　✽　Makes 2 servings

Per serving: 107 calories, 4 g protein, 23 g carbohydrates, 2 g fat, 1 g saturated fat, 90 mg sodium, 6 g fiber

This low-cal dish is my husband's and my favorite snack. Sometimes I sprinkle ground flaxseed meal on the cream—it looks and tastes like graham cracker crumbs.　　**—Marie**

FOR STRONG JOINTS: SESAME SEEDS

Two tablespoons provide more than 80 percent of your daily intake of copper, an anti-inflammatory that may help ease arthritis pain.

GET YOUR FILL: Mix tahini (sesame seed paste) with olive oil and use it as a salad dressing.

FOR YOUTHFUL SKIN: SUNFLOWER SEEDS

Two tablespoons supply nearly 40 percent of the Recommended Dietary Allowance (RDA) of vitamin E, an antioxidant that helps prevent sun damage.

GET YOUR FILL: For a healthier crunch, sprinkle these onto your salad instead of croutons.

FOR A HEALTHY HEART: FLAXSEED

Two tablespoons of ground flaxseed, which is rich in heart-healthy alpha-linolenic acid, help lower cholesterol, triglycerides, and blood pressure.

GET YOUR FILL: Add ground flaxseed to your cereal, oatmeal, or smoothie.

**[QUICK TIP:
SEEDS OF HEALTH]**

"Baked" Stuffed Pears

2½ tablespoons dried cranberries

5 teaspoons orange juice

3 teaspoons honey

2 Anjou or Bosc pears, halved lengthwise and cored

2 tablespoons chopped walnuts

½ teaspoon vanilla extract

⅛ teaspoon ground cinnamon

Pinch of grated nutmeg

2 tablespoons reduced-fat sour cream

COMBINE the cranberries, 3 teaspoons of the orange juice, and 1½ teaspoons of the honey in a small microwaveable bowl. Cover loosely with plastic wrap and microwave on high power for 1 minute. Set aside.

ARRANGE the pears in a spoke fashion, cut side up, in a microwaveable round baking dish or pie plate. Drizzle with the remaining 2 teaspoons orange juice and cover loosely with plastic wrap. Microwave on high power for 5 minutes. (The pears should be almost fork-tender.)

STIR the walnuts, vanilla extract, cinnamon, and nutmeg into the cranberries. Uncover the pears and divide the cranberry mixture among the pears. Cover loosely with plastic wrap. Microwave on high power for 2 minutes, or until the pears are fork-tender. Stir together the sour cream and the remaining 1½ teaspoons honey. Drizzle over the pears.

Total time: 15 minutes ✳ Makes 4 servings

Per serving: 220 calories, 2 g protein, 42 g carbohydrates, 7 g fat, 2 g saturated fat, 8 mg sodium, 5 g fiber

Enjoy baked pears without ever turning on the oven! The smooth, rich texture of the sauce is loaded with flavor.

Pumpkin Pie in a Cup

2 cups fat-free milk

1 box (1 ounce) fat-free, sugar-free instant vanilla pudding

¾ cup 100% pure pumpkin puree

1 teaspoon pumpkin pie spice

4 tablespoons thawed low-fat frozen whipped topping

WHISK together the milk and pudding mix in a medium bowl for 2 minutes, or until thickened. Whisk in the pumpkin and ½ teaspoon of the pumpkin pie spice until blended. Pour into 4 pudding cups or glasses.

CHILL until ready to serve. Top each with 1 tablespoon of whipped topping over the pudding and sprinkle with the remaining ½ teaspoon pumpkin pie spice.

Total time: 5 minutes ✳ Makes 4 servings

Per serving: 94 calories, 5 g protein, 18 g carbohydrates, 1 g fat, 1 g saturated fat, 378 mg sodium, 1 g fiber

66

99

I was feeling sorry for myself around the holidays, so I came up with this great dessert that I now offer right alongside my regular ones. Since it's delicious and looks so pretty, no one knows that it is a 'low-fat, sugar-free' dessert.

—**Margaret**

Dark Chocolate Mousse

1 package (12.3 ounces) light silken tofu

⅔ cup 60% cocoa bittersweet chocolate chips

¼ cup unsweetened cocoa powder

¼ cup water

¼ teaspoon almond extract

2 tablespoons Splenda

4 tablespoons low-fat whipped topping

4 tablespoons Spanish peanuts, chopped

PLACE the tofu in the blender or food processor and pulse until very smooth.

COOK the chocolate chips, cocoa powder, and water in a saucepan over low heat, stirring, until melted and well blended. Remove from the heat and stir in the almond extract. Stir in the Splenda, a little at a time, until smooth. Add the chocolate mixture to the tofu and puree until smooth and well blended.

SPOON the mousse into 4 serving dishes and chill for at least 1 hour. Serve each topped with 1 tablespoon whipped topping and 1 tablespoon peanuts.

Total time: 1 hour 10 minutes ✳ Makes 4 servings

Per serving: 245 calories, 11 g protein, 26 g carbohydrates, 14 g fat, 6 g saturated fat, 87 mg sodium, 3 g fiber

I am the wife of a diabetic who LOVES to eat and am constantly trying to find ways to make recipes that are 'diabetic friendly.' Here is a sweet treat I actually got from a Weight Watchers meeting and then modified it to be diabetic friendly.
—Linda

QUICK TIP: DIG INTO DARK CHOCOLATE TO BEAT BRAIN FOG

Cocoa flavonols—phytonutrients abundant in dark chocolate—may keep the brain alert by increasing bloodflow, found research presented at the British Psychological Society's annual conference. When adults consumed a drink containing cocoa flavonols, they reported less mental fatigue. For a brain boost, sip a cup of dark chocolate hot cocoa—we like Green and Black's Organic Hot Chocolate Drink—or nibble on a few small squares of dark chocolate containing at least 70 percent cocoa.

58 The percentage of women who crave chocolate when they "need a pick-me-up"

Strawberry-Pineapple Delight (photo on page 173)

1 package (0.44 ounce) sugar-free strawberry gelatin

1 can (8 ounces) pineapple chunks in juice, drained

1 package (16 ounces) fat-free frozen whipped topping

½ cup chopped walnuts (optional)

PLACE the gelatin in a large bowl. Stir in 1 cup boiling water and continue stirring for 2 minutes, or until completely dissolved.

STIR in the pineapple, whipped topping, and nuts (if using) until well blended. Chill for 3 to 24 hours, or until set.

Total time: 3 hours 10 minutes ✳ Makes 12 servings

Per serving: 74 calories, 0 g protein, 15 g carbohydrates, 0 g fat, 0 g saturated fat, 27 mg sodium, 0 g fiber

174

Snacks & Little Bites

My life is hectic and hurried most of the time. I like this recipe because it is simple and yet tastes almost sinful. My grandchildren love it as much as I do, and they don't even know it's healthy! —Sammie

Cranberry-Ginger Spiced Cider

¾ cup fresh or frozen cranberries

4 slices fresh ginger, cut into matchsticks (2 tablespoons)

6 whole cloves

11 cinnamon sticks, about 3" each

8 cups apple cider

⅓ cup honey

Brandy or applejack (optional)

CUT a 7" square from a double layer of cheesecloth. Place the cranberries, ginger, cloves, and 3 of the cinnamon sticks in the center of the cheesecloth. Gather up the edges of the cheesecloth and tie with kitchen twine.

PLACE the cider, honey, and spice bag in a large saucepan. Bring just to a simmer, cover, and cook for 30 minutes, or until the flavors meld. Place the spice bag in a strainer set over the pan and press with the back of a spoon to extract the liquids. Discard the bag.

LADLE the cider into mugs and serve with a cinnamon stick and a jigger of brandy or applejack, if desired.

Total time: 45 minutes ✳ Makes 8 servings

Per serving: 173 calories, 0 g protein, 44 g carbohydrates, 0 g fat, 0 g saturated fat, 27 mg sodium, 1 g fiber

You'll warm to this soothing cider. Accented with a festive mix of cranberries and ginger, it's the perfect drink for lounging by the fire or making a celebratory toast.

QUICK TIP: AVOID CHEMICALS IN YOUR CANS

Canned food alert: *Consumer Reports* found bisphenol A (BPA)—a chemical linked to reproductive problems, diabetes, and heart disease—in all 19 brand-name canned foods it tested, including those labeled "BPA-free." Because levels vary so widely, even among cans of the same product, there's no way to predict how much you're getting. To reduce your risk, opt for frozen fruits and vegetables and for beans and tuna sealed in plastic containers, bags, or pouches, or use fresh ingredients whenever possible to make homemade soups, stews, and sauces.

Alcohol-Free Sangria

- 3 cups Concord grape juice
- 2 cups orange juice
- ¼ cup lemon juice
- 2 tablespoons lime juice
- 1 orange, ends trimmed, sliced into half rounds
- 1 apple, cored and cut into thin wedges

STIR together the grape, orange, lemon, and lime juices in a 2-quart pitcher. Stir in the orange and apple wedges and refrigerate, covered, for 4 to 48 hours. Serve the sangria in tall glasses and spoon in some of the fruit.

Total time: 20 minutes * Makes 8 servings

Per serving: 92 calories, 1 g protein, 23 g carbohydrates, 0 g fat, 0 g saturated fat, 1 mg sodium, 1 g fiber

Chase away the heat with this refreshing cooler. Zesty orange slices and apple wedges float invitingly in this beautiful drink. For a reduced-alcohol version, combine this sangria with an equal amount of dry red wine.

[it worked for me]

136 lbs lost!

✳ SARAH MONTAGUE

Going from emotional eater to three-time triathlete, Sarah Montague lost 136 pounds along the way.

My Story

When I was a young girl in England, my parents went through a difficult divorce. I learned early on to medicate my feelings with food. I found comfort in feeling full and gorged myself on potato chips, chocolate, and cheese. So it's no surprise that when the pressure from my first job kicked in, I headed for the cupboard. Within 3 years, I gained 100 pounds, developed obesity-related asthma, and dislocated both knees. During that same time, I met my future husband. As we planned our wedding, it never occurred to me to try to lose the weight—instead, I had my wedding dress custom made. When I was 30, my husband and I moved across the Atlantic to Chicago. Within 6 months, I gained another 20 pounds. At a routine medical checkup, my doctor suggested I try Weight Watchers. I was shocked. Nobody had ever confronted me about my size, but it was the wake-up call I needed.

I started attending weekly Weight Watchers meetings and chose 136 pounds as my goal weight. I worried

VITAL STATS

Pounds lost: 136

Age: 40

Height: 5'3"

Weight then: 272 pounds

Weight now: 136 pounds

that it would be too difficult to drop a lifetime of bad habits, but I counted my points carefully and paid close attention to why I was eating: emotions or hunger. I began working out, and the more weight I lost, the easier—and more fun—it became. It took me 6 years to reach 136 pounds. Even then, I didn't consider myself athletic. So when friends approached me to train with them for a triathlon, I was hesitant. But I realized that losing so much weight was a huge accomplishment, and I needed a new challenge. I signed up for the race and finished in the middle of the pack but beaming with pride. For the first time, I was a player in the game—not a sideline spectator.

I've competed in three triathlons so far—and when I see the athletes at these events, it still amazes me that I'm one of them. I recently turned 40, and to mark the milestone, I participated in the Chicago Triathlon, my hardest race to date. I aimed to finish in 4 hours, but I did it in 3 hours 22 minutes. Training can be grueling, but I love working hard—I'll never numb my feelings with food again.

My Top Tips

✳ Think before you bite . . . Before I take seconds or have dessert, I remind myself that I won't regret what I don't eat.

✳ Plan, plan, plan . . . On busy days, I always pack a lunch—otherwise it's too likely that I'll rely on junk from the vending machines. I also stash stocked gym bags in my car and under my desk so I'm always ready to work out.

✳ Celebrate small victories . . . Competing has boosted my self-esteem, but smaller tests—like passing on the bread basket—are just as empowering.

✳ Stick to a routine . . . I buy similar groceries weekly— that way, I get in and out with no temptation from the snack aisle.

✳ Think big picture . . . I used to fill up without thinking about the consequences. Now I approach the week as a whole and make adjustments as needed. If I'm planning on a big dinner, I'm perfectly happy eating a light lunch.

dinners

Herbed Butterflied Leg of Lamb

¼ cup dry red wine

1 tablespoon extra virgin olive oil

2 tablespoons coarsely chopped fresh rosemary

2 bay leaves

¾ teaspoon dried oregano, crumbled

¾ teaspoon dried mint, crumbled

½ teaspoon coarse-ground black pepper

1 butterflied leg of lamb (2 pounds), well trimmed

¾ teaspoon salt

STIR together the wine, oil, rosemary, bay leaves, oregano, mint, and pepper in a shallow glass dish. Add the lamb and turn to coat. Cover and marinate in the refrigerator for 2 to 3 hours or overnight, turning once or twice.

PREHEAT the grill. Remove the lamb from the dish, reserving the marinade, and sprinkle both sides with the salt. Place the lamb on the grill rack and spoon some of the reserved marinade over. Discard the remaining marinade and bay leaves. Cover the lamb and grill for 25 minutes, turning 2 or 3 times and moving it away from any hot spots, or until a thermometer inserted in the center registers 145°F for medium-rare/160°F for medium/165°F for well-done. Let stand for 10 minutes before slicing.

Total time: 40 minutes   ✽   Makes 8 servings

Per serving: 169 calories, 23 g protein, 1 g carbohydrates, 7 g fat, 2 g saturated fat, 289 mg sodium, 0 g fiber

Begin this dish the night before you plan to serve it and you'll have the most amazing flavors come together on your grill.

HEALTH HEARSAY

Q: "Are baby carrots preserved with bleach?"

A: Not exactly . . . and there's no reason to stop eating them, says Randy Worobo, PhD, an associate professor of food microbiology at Cornell University. Carrots are rinsed (not preserved) in a chlorine wash recommended by the FDA to kill bacteria like salmonella and E. coli, which cause foodborne illness. Most precut produce, including frozen veggies and fruit salad, is washed with this or a similar sanitizer. Other e-mail rumors posit that baby carrots are made from large rotted ones, but that's not true, either. They are whittled down from misshapen carrot roots, which aren't rotted or deformed. These mini carrots have the same nutrients as the picture-perfect, long and straight ones.

All-American Pot Roast

4 tablespoons unbleached or all-purpose flour

¾ teaspoon dried oregano

½ teaspoon dried thyme

½ teaspoon salt

¼ teaspoon ground black pepper

1½ pounds boneless eye of round roast, trimmed of all visible fat

1 can (15½ ounces) reduced-sodium, fat-free beef broth

½ cup red wine or nonalcoholic wine or water

1 teaspoon Worcestershire sauce

2 teaspoons olive oil

1 bay leaf

¾ pound red new potatoes, washed and cut into eighths

¾ pound white turnips, peeled and cut into eighths

1 cup frozen small white onions, thawed

1 cup baby carrots

PREHEAT the oven to 400°F.

STIR together the flour, oregano, thyme, salt, and pepper in a large bowl. Dredge the beef to coat, shaking off the excess, and place on a plate. Whisk the broth, wine or water, and Worcestershire sauce into the remaining flour mixture until smooth.

HEAT the oil in an ovenproof pot or Dutch oven over medium-high heat. Working in batches, cook the beef for 8 minutes, turning, or until browned. Stir in all the beef, the broth mixture, and bay leaf. Cover and bake for 1½ hours. Add the potatoes, turnips, onions, and carrots. Cover and bake for 45 minutes, or until the meat and vegetables are tender. Remove the bay leaf and serve.

Total time: 2 hours   ✳   Makes 6 servings

Per serving: 248 calories, 29 g protein, 19 g carbohydrates, 5 g fat, 1 g saturated fat, 460 mg sodium, 3 g fiber

Researchers in France found that people feel happier after eating a meal with protein, and this savory dish delivers plenty. Now that is something to smile about!

London Broil Marinated in Soy Sauce and Mustard

1 tablespoon dry mustard

4 teaspoons soy sauce

2 teaspoons red wine vinegar

1 teaspoon onion powder

¼ teaspoon garlic powder

1 tablespoon olive oil

1 top round or sirloin London broil (1½ pounds), 1" thick

¼ teaspoon salt

¼ teaspoon ground black pepper

WHISK together the mustard, soy sauce, vinegar, onion powder, and garlic powder in a large glass baking dish. Whisk in the oil. Add the meat, turning to coat. Cover and chill for 2 to 24 hours.

REMOVE from the refrigerator 15 minutes before cooking. Place the broiler rack 2" to 3" from the heat source and preheat the broiler. Coat a broiling pan with cooking spray.

PLACE the beef on the pan and sprinkle with the salt and pepper. Broil for 10 minutes, turning once, or until a thermometer inserted in the center registers 145°F for medium-rare/160°F for medium/165°F for well-done. Let stand for 10 minutes before slicing.

Total time: 30 minutes ✱ Makes 4 servings

Per serving: 331 calories, 39 g protein, 2 g carbohydrates, 18 g fat, 6 g saturated fat, 583 mg sodium, 39 g fiber

Chill any leftovers in a covered container for up to 3 days. Use them for superfast suppers and lunches. To reheat, slice the beef and dip into simmering beef broth for a minute, or until heated through.

Filet Mignon with Tomatoes and Rosemary

2 teaspoons soy sauce

1½ teaspoons Dijon mustard

1½ teaspoons minced fresh rosemary

⅛ teaspoon garlic powder

2 tomatoes (8 ounces), finely chopped

2 teaspoons olive oil

4 filet mignons (6 ounces each), each 1½" thick

¼ teaspoon salt

½ teaspoon ground black pepper

PREHEAT the oven to 400°F.

COMBINE the soy sauce, mustard, rosemary, and garlic powder in a bowl. Fold in the tomatoes. Heat the oil in a large, oven-safe skillet over high heat. Sprinkle the beef with the salt and pepper. Cook for 4 minutes, or until browned, turning once.

PLACE the skillet in the oven for 10 minutes, or until a thermometer inserted in the center of the steaks registers 145°F for medium-rare/160°F for medium/165°F for well-done. Serve topped with the tomatoes.

Total time: 35 minutes ✽ Makes 4 servings

Per serving: 304 calories, 39 g protein, 5 g carbohydrates, 14 g fat, 5 g saturated fat, 461 mg sodium, 2 g fiber

Broil or grill the beef instead of pan-searing it if desired. Simply rub the meat with 1 to 2 teaspoons olive oil before cooking. Replace the beef with buffalo or ostrich fillets for a change of pace. Check with your local butcher or supermarket for these meats.

┌ **QUICK TIP: BEEF UP**
YOUR HEALTHY FAT INTAKE

Americans are eating too few heart-healthy omega-3 fatty acids and too many inflammation-promoting omega-6s. And now data from a massive Chinese study finds that women who eat the most omega-6s and the fewest omega-3s have nearly double the risk of colorectal cancer, compared with those who consume the opposite. For the healthiest ratio, eat fewer processed foods, in which omega-6s are abundant, and more natural sources of omega-3s, such as leafy greens, grass-fed beef, and fatty fish. ┘

Taste of Summer
Steak and Spinach Salad

¼ cup olive oil

¼ cup balsamic vinegar

1 tablespoon fresh lime juice

1 shallot, minced

¼ teaspoon salt

Cracked black pepper

1 pound flat iron (top blade) or top round steak

1 bag (9 to 10 ounces) baby spinach

1 cup cherry or grape tomatoes, halved

1 cup sprouts

1 avocado, peeled and sliced

4 ounces goat cheese, crumbled

½ cup dried cranberries

1 lime, sliced (optional)

WHISK together the oil, vinegar, lime juice, shallot, salt, and pepper in a sealable jar. Shake well.

PLACE the meat in a large resealable plastic bag and cover with about ½ of the oil mixture. Seal and shake to coat. Chill for 1 to 24 hours. Cover and chill the remaining dressing.

PREHEAT the grill or broiler. Remove the steak from the bag, discarding the marinade. Grill or broil for 7 minutes, turning once, or until a thermometer inserted in the center registers 145°F for medium-rare/160°F for medium/165°F for well-done. Let stand for 10 minutes before slicing.

DIVIDE the spinach, tomatoes, sprouts, and avocado onto 4 plates. Place one-quarter of the beef on top of each salad. Drizzle one-quarter of the remaining dressing over each salad. Divide the goat cheese and cranberries among the salads. Garnish with the lime slices.

Total time: 1 hour ✱ Makes 4 servings

Per serving: 506 calories, 32 g protein, 27 g carbohydrates, 31 g fat, 10 g saturated fat, 467 mg sodium, 7 g fiber

Flat iron steak is a flavorful, tender, and inexpensive cut of meat. Ask your butcher for it if you don't see it in the meat case.

—**Marla**

Chino-Latino Beef Kebabs

3 tablespoons reduced-sodium soy sauce

1 teaspoon Worcestershire sauce

1 teaspoon dried oregano

½ teaspoon ground cumin

½ teaspoon sesame oil

2 garlic cloves, minced

1 tablespoon grated fresh ginger

1 pound boneless sirloin London broil or top round steak, trimmed of all visible fat

1 sweet onion, such as Vidalia, cut into 16 pieces

1 medium green bell pepper, seeded and cut into 16 pieces

12 cherry tomatoes

¼ teaspoon salt

WHISK together the soy sauce, Worcestershire sauce, oregano, cumin, oil, garlic, and ginger in a large bowl.

CUT the sirloin with a sharp knife into twenty 1" cubes and add to the bowl, tossing to coat well.

COVER and chill for 2 to 24 hours.

PREHEAT the broiler and coat a broiler-pan rack with cooking spray. Alternately thread 5 beef cubes, 4 onion pieces, 4 bell pepper pieces, and 3 cherry tomatoes onto each of four 18" wooden or metal skewers. Place the skewers onto the broiler pan and sprinkle with the salt.

BROIL 4" from the heat source for 8 to 10 minutes, turning every 2 minutes, or until the vegetables are tender and the beef is cooked through.

Total time: 30 minutes ✲ Makes 4 servings

Per serving: 213 calories, 27 g protein, 12 g carbohydrates, 6 g fat, 2 g saturated fat, 635 mg sodium, 2 g fiber

Each kebab is studded with foods that help balance your blood sugar with a one-two punch. Lean beef provides protein to stop you from overeating, and the onions, green peppers, and tomatoes deliver fiber to block the digestion of excess calories.

QUICK TIP: SIMPLE HEART SAVER

99,000 The number of heart attacks that could be prevented each year if Americans consumed ½ teaspoon less salt daily (1,163 milligrams sodium), according to a report in the *New England Journal of Medicine*

Beef Fajitas

4 garlic cloves, minced

2 tablespoons lime juice

1 tablespoon olive oil

1 teaspoon grated lime zest

1 teaspoon ground cumin

1 pound top round steak, trimmed of all visible fat

¼ teaspoon salt

2 bell peppers, green and/or red, seeded and cut into ¼" strips

1 onion, cut into ¼" slices

4 whole wheat tortillas (8" diameter), warmed

½ cup medium-hot salsa

¼ cup fat-free sour cream

COMBINE the garlic, lime juice, oil, lime zest, and cumin in a resealable plastic bag. Add the steak and toss well to coat. Chill for 4 to 24 hours.

PREHEAT the grill or broiler. Remove the steak from the marinade, reserving any leftover marinade, and sprinkle with the salt. Grill or broil 4" from the heat for 10 minutes, turning once, or until a thermometer inserted in the center registers 145°F for medium-rare/160°F for medium/165°F for well-done. Let stand for 10 minutes before slicing.

HEAT a nonstick skillet coated with cooking spray over medium-high heat. Cook the peppers, onion, and reserved marinade, stirring often, for 8 minutes, or until the vegetables are softened.

SLICE the steak thinly across the grain on a slight angle. Place 1 tortilla on a plate and top with one-quarter of the sirloin, one-quarter of the vegetable mixture, 2 tablespoons salsa, and 1 tablespoon sour cream. Repeat with the remaining ingredients.

Total time: 35 minutes ✳ Makes 4 servings

Per serving: 322 calories, 29 g protein, 32 g carbohydrates, 11 g fat, 3 g saturated fat, 634 mg sodium, 4 g fiber

For many people, spicy foods are a great way to chase away those salty cravings. This Mexican favorite is guaranteed to heat things up around the dinner table.

Bison and Broccoli on Vegetable Pancake

8 ounces bison or beef sirloin steak, thinly sliced

3 garlic cloves, chopped

1½ teaspoons reduced-sodium soy sauce

1 teaspoon dry sherry

2 eggs

2 cups (6 ounces) broccoli slaw

4 scallions, chopped

3 teaspoons olive oil

2½ cups (6 ounces) broccoli florets

4 shiitake mushrooms, sliced

1 jalapeño chile pepper, sliced (wear plastic gloves when handling)

½ poblano chile pepper, julienned (wear plastic gloves when handling)

½ cup low-sodium beef broth

8 cherry tomatoes, halved

1 tablespoon oyster sauce

1 tablespoon fermented or salted black beans (optional)

SLICE the steak thinly against the grain using a sharp knife. Place the steak, garlic, 1 teaspoon of the soy sauce, and sherry in a large bowl. Toss to coat well. Set aside.

WHISK together the eggs with the remaining ½ teaspoon of soy sauce in a large bowl. Stir in the broccoli slaw and scallions until well blended.

HEAT 1 teaspoon of the oil in a wok or skillet coated with cooking spray over medium heat. Spoon ½ cup of the egg mixture into the wok or skillet and flatten slightly. Cook for 4 minutes, turning once, or until the eggs are completely set. Slide the pancake onto a dinner plate or roll it like a jelly roll before sliding onto the plate. Keep warm. Repeat with the remaining egg mixture.

HEAT the remaining 2 teaspoons oil in the same wok or skillet over medium heat. Add the steak and cook, stirring constantly, for 1 minute. Add the broccoli, mushrooms, chile peppers, and broth. Cook, stirring, for 4 minutes, or until the broccoli is crisp-tender. Stir in the tomatoes, oyster sauce, and beans (if using). Cook, stirring, for 2 minutes.

PLACE 1 pancake on each of 4 plates. Divide the steak mixture among the pancakes.

Total time: 50 minutes　✳　Makes 4 servings

Per serving: 185 calories, 20 g protein, 11 g carbohydrates, 7 g fat, 2 g saturated fat, 318 mg sodium, 4 g fiber

I love this recipe because it is fast, easy, healthy, and very delicious! I love bison and have been using it in all my Asian recipes that call for beef.

—**Randy**

Meat Loaf with Walnuts

1 large egg

¼ cup tomato paste

2 tablespoons Worcestershire sauce

½ teaspoon dried thyme

½ teaspoon salt

½ teaspoon ground black pepper

½ onion, minced

1 large garlic clove, minced

⅔ cup ground walnuts

1½ pounds extra-lean ground beef

½ cup tomato sauce

PREHEAT the oven to 375°F.

COMBINE the egg, tomato paste, Worcestershire sauce, thyme, salt, and pepper in a large bowl. Gently stir in the onion, garlic, walnuts, and beef.

FORM into a loaf and place in a 9" × 5" × 3" loaf pan. Spread the tomato sauce evenly over the top. Bake for 50 minutes, or until a thermometer inserted in the center registers 160°F and the meat is no longer pink. Pour off the fat in the pan and slice the loaf.

Total time: 1 hour 10 minutes ✳ Makes 6 servings

Per serving: 210 calories, 25 g protein, 6 g carbohydrates, 11 g fat, 3 g saturated fat, 520 mg sodium, 2 g fiber

A rotary hand cheese grater is excellent for grinding nuts.

NUTRITION NEWS TO USE

USDA researchers have cracked the secret to a younger brain. Simply adding about seven to nine whole nuts to your daily diet may improve balance, coordination, and memory, finds new research in the *British Journal of Nutrition*. Scientists believe the polyphenols and other antioxidants in walnuts help strengthen neural connections and improve cognitive skills.

37 The percentage reduction in heart disease risk in people who consume nuts more than 4 times per week

Spicy Meatballs with Coconut Milk

1½ pounds extra-lean ground beef

3 scallions, finely chopped

1 large egg

5 tablespoons + ½ cup light coconut milk

2 tablespoons soy sauce

1½ teaspoons ground cumin

¾ teaspoon ground coriander seed

½ teaspoon crushed red-pepper flakes

PLACE the broiler rack 4" from the heat source and preheat the broiler. Coat a large broiling pan with cooking spray.

COMBINE the beef, scallions, egg, 5 tablespoons of the coconut milk, 1½ tablespoons of the soy sauce, the cumin, coriander, and red-pepper flakes in a large bowl. Gently form into 1½" meatballs and arrange on the pan, placing ½" apart.

BROIL for 10 minutes, or until browned and no longer pink.

REMOVE to a serving dish and discard the fat drippings in the pan. Pour the remaining ½ cup coconut milk into the pan and scrape up the browned bits, stirring until dissolved. Add the remaining ½ tablespoon soy sauce and pour over the meatballs.

Total time: 35 minutes ✽ Makes 6 servings

Per serving: 237 calories, 27 g protein, 2 g carbohydrates, 13 g fat, 9 g saturated fat, 428 mg sodium, 1 g fiber

Spoon over a bed of whole wheat couscous, brown rice, or buckwheat noodles (soba). Or tuck sliced meatballs into a sandwich. Sprinkle with 1 tablespoon chopped fresh cilantro just before serving.

Liver and Caramelized Onions with Mashed Potatoes

Mashed Potatoes

- **2 pounds russet potatoes, peeled and cut into 2" pieces**
- **Pinch of salt**
- **1 cup low-fat plain yogurt, at room temperature**
- **1 tablespoon butter, at room temperature**
- **4 scallions, minced**

Caramelized Onions

- **1 tablespoon olive oil**
- **1 large sweet yellow onion, sliced**
- **1 teaspoon packed light brown sugar**
- **Splash of dry white wine (optional)**
- **2 pinches of salt**
- **Pinch of ground black pepper**

Liver

- **1 cup egg substitute**
- **1 cup seasoned bread crumbs**
- **1¼ pounds baby calves' liver, cut into 2" × 1" strips**
- **2 tablespoons olive oil**
- **Butter-flavored cooking spray (optional)**

To make the mashed potatoes:

PLACE the potatoes and salt in a medium saucepan with enough cold water to cover. Bring to a boil. Reduce the heat to a simmer and cook for 20 minutes, or until tender. Drain the potatoes. Return to the pan. Add the yogurt and butter and mash with a potato masher until smooth. Stir in the scallions.

To make the caramelized onions:

HEAT the oil in a medium saucepan over medium-high heat. Cook the onion, stirring, for 5 minutes, or until browned. Sprinkle with the sugar and wine (if using). Cook until the onions are caramelized. Sprinkle with the salt and pepper. Remove the pan from the heat. Keep the pan on the stove top to keep warm until ready to serve.

To prepare the liver:

PLACE the egg substitute in a shallow bowl. Place the bread crumbs in another shallow bowl. Dip the liver strips into the egg substitute, then into the bread crumbs.

HEAT the oil in a large skillet over medium-high heat. Cook the liver, in batches if necessary, for 5 minutes, turning once, or until browned. Remove with a slotted spoon and place on paper towels.

TO SERVE, place a scoop of mashed potatoes on each dinner plate. Coat with the cooking spray, if desired. Add the liver and onions to each plate.

Total time: 1 hour　✱　Makes 6 servings

Per serving: 452 calories, 30 g protein, 51 g carbohydrates, 14 g fat, 4 g saturated fat, 662 sodium, 4 g fiber

I miss my grandmother's liver and onions, which she always served with a mountain of buttery mashed potatoes. I decided to re-create her famous meal using much healthier ingredients—ready in less than 1 hour.

—**Donna**

Roast Pork Tenderloin with Sherry, Cream, and Almonds

- 1 pork tenderloin (1½–1¾ pounds)
- ¾ teaspoon paprika
- ½ teaspoon ground black pepper
- ¼ teaspoon salt
- 1 tablespoon whole wheat flour
- 1 tablespoon olive oil
- 2 large shallots, sliced
- ⅓ cup dry sherry or chicken broth
- ⅓ cup + 2 tablespoons chicken broth
- ¼ cup half-and-half
- 2 tablespoons (1 ounce) sliced almonds

PREHEAT the oven to 350°F. Sprinkle the pork with the paprika, pepper, and salt. Coat with the flour.

HEAT the oil in a large roasting pan or a large, heavy, oven-safe skillet over medium heat. Add the pork and cook for 5 minutes, turning, or until lightly browned on all sides. Scatter the shallots in the pan and cook, stirring once or twice, for 1 minute. Pour the sherry or broth and ⅓ cup of the broth around the meat.

ROAST for 25 minutes, turning once or twice, or until a thermometer inserted in the center reaches 155°F and the juices run clear. Let stand for 10 minutes before slicing.

ADD broth to the pan if needed, to equal 3 tablespoons. Place over medium-low heat and stir in the half-and-half. Cook, stirring, for 2 minutes, or until slightly thickened. Slice the pork on a slight diagonal and place on a platter. Sprinkle with the almonds. Serve the cream sauce on the side.

Total time: 1 hour 5 minutes ✳ Makes 4 servings

Per serving: 347 calories, 44 g protein, 8 g carbohydrates, 14 g fat, 4 g saturated fat, 368 mg sodium, 1 g fiber

QUICK TIP: DON'T WORRY, EAT HAPPY

30% The drop in your risk of depression if you eat a Mediterranean diet rich in produce, whole grains, healthy oils, and nuts. Researchers say essential nutrients in these foods help brain cells bind to serotonin, a mood-boosting neurotransmitter.

Hoisin Pork Stir-Fry

- 2 tablespoons reduced-sodium soy sauce
- 1 tablespoon dry sherry
- 1 tablespoon cornstarch
- 1 pound pork tenderloin, trimmed and cut into 1½" × ¼" strips
- 1 tablespoon sesame oil
- 3 cups broccoli florets
- 1 carrot, sliced
- ¼ teaspoon crushed red-pepper flakes
- 1 tablespoon grated fresh ginger
- 2 garlic cloves, minced
- ½ cup orange juice
- 3 tablespoons hoisin sauce

WHISK together the soy sauce, sherry, and cornstarch in a large bowl. Add the pork, tossing to coat well.

HEAT the oil in a large nonstick skillet over medium-high heat. Cook the broccoli, carrot, red-pepper flakes, ginger, and garlic, stirring often, for 3 minutes. Remove to a plate.

STIR in the pork and cook for 4 minutes, or until the pork is no longer pink. Add the broccoli mixture and cook for 1 minute. Add the orange juice and hoisin sauce and bring to a boil. Cook, stirring, for 1 minute, or until slightly thickened.

Total time: 25 minutes ✳ Makes 4 servings

Per serving: 246 calories, 27 g protein, 16 g carbohydrates, 8 g fat, 2 g saturated fat, 543 mg sodium, 3 g fiber

This stir-fry boasts a medley of colorful, high-fiber vegetables and high-quality protein to delight your senses and keep your appetite controlled for hours.

Roast Chicken with Barley Stuffing

¾ cup pearl barley

1 large navel orange

2 tablespoons olive oil

1 medium onion, chopped

1 carrot, chopped

1 rib celery, chopped

4 slices whole wheat bread, toasted and cut into cubes (2½ cups)

¾ cup mixed chopped dried fruit

2 teaspoons dried thyme

1 teaspoon salt

½ teaspoon ground black pepper

1 cup chicken broth

3 garlic cloves, minced

1 whole frying chicken (4 pounds)

COOK the barley according to package directions. Drain and set aside. Grate the zest from the orange. Peel the orange and chop. Set aside.

PREHEAT the oven to 425°F. Coat a 2-quart baking dish with cooking spray.

HEAT 1 tablespoon of the oil in a large skillet over medium heat. Cook the onion, carrot, and celery, stirring occasionally, for 10 minutes, or until lightly browned. Remove the skillet from the heat. Add the bread, dried fruit, ¾ teaspoon of the thyme, ¾ teaspoon of the salt, ¼ teaspoon of the pepper, reserved barley, and reserved orange. Stir in the broth.

PLACE the stuffing in the dish and cover with foil.

COMBINE the garlic, reserved orange zest, and the remaining 1 tablespoon oil, 1¼ teaspoons thyme, ¼ teaspoon salt, and ¼ teaspoon pepper in a small bowl. Place the chicken on a rack set in a roasting pan. Rub the orange mixture under and over the skin and in the cavity. Tie the legs with kitchen string. Roast for 30 minutes.

PLACE the stuffing in the oven. Reduce the oven temperature to 350°F and cook the stuffing and chicken for 45 minutes, or until a thermometer inserted in a breast registers 180°F and the juices run clear. Let stand for 10 minutes before carving. Remove the foil from the stuffing after 25 minutes, or when hot.

Total time: 1 hour 50 minutes　✳　Makes 8 servings

Per serving: 475 calories, 54 g protein, 37 g carbohydrates, 11 g fat, 2 g saturated fat, 689 mg sodium, 6 g fiber

Fiber-rich barley is a great alternative to a traditional rice stuffing. Use any combination of your favorite dried fruits to create a signature dish.

Grilled Chicken with Zippy Bar-B-Q Sauce

1 small onion, minced

1 can (8 ounces) tomato sauce

¼ cup red wine vinegar

¼ cup Worcestershire sauce

2 teaspoons paprika

2 teaspoons chili powder

1 teaspoon white pepper

½ teaspoon cinnamon

⅛ teaspoon cloves

2 cups water

4 bone-in chicken breast halves, skinned

COMBINE the onion, tomato sauce, vinegar, Worcestershire sauce, paprika, chili powder, pepper, cinnamon, cloves, and water in a medium saucepan. Bring to a boil over high heat. Reduce the heat to low and simmer uncovered for 20 minutes, or until thickened. Remove from the heat and let cool for 30 minutes.

PLACE the chicken in a resealable plastic bag with ⅔ cup of the sauce. Seal and shake to coat. Refrigerate for 8 to 24 hours.

PREHEAT the grill. Remove the chicken from the marinade and place on the grill rack or broiler pan. Discard the marinade. Grill or broil for 20 minutes, or until a thermometer inserted in the thickest portion registers 170°F and the juices run clear, brushing with the remaining sauce during the last 15 minutes of cooking.

ALTERNATIVELY, to bake the chicken, bake in a 375°F preheated oven for 35 to 40 minutes, or until a thermometer inserted in the thickest portion registers 170°F and the juices run clear, brushing with the remaining sauce during the last 15 minutes of cooking.

Total time: 9 hours ✳ Makes 4 servings

Per serving: 169 calories, 28 g protein, 9 g carbohydrates, 2 g fat, 0 g saturated fat, 542 mg sodium, 2 g fiber

I'm just a guy who loves to eat. I am sure that is what got me in the shape I was at before I was diagnosed with diabetes . . . I am happy to say that I am still just a guy who likes to eat, but I do it a little healthier now!

—Jay

Grilled Citrus-Honey Chicken

1 teaspoon grated orange zest

½ cup fresh orange juice

3 tablespoons lemon juice

2 tablespoons honey

1 tablespoon olive oil

1 garlic clove, minced

½ teaspoon coarsely ground black pepper

¼ teaspoon salt

¼ teaspoon ground cinnamon

4 bone-in chicken breast halves, skinned and trimmed

COMBINE the orange zest, orange juice, lemon juice, honey, oil, garlic, pepper, salt, and cinnamon in a resealable plastic bag until well blended. Add the chicken breasts. Seal the bag and massage gently to coat the chicken with the marinade. Chill for 1 to 2 hours.

PREHEAT the grill to medium. Drain the chicken marinade into a small saucepan and bring to a boil over medium heat. Boil for 2 minutes, or until thickened to a glaze.

PLACE the chicken on the grill and brush with some marinade. Cover and grill for 20 minutes, basting 2 or 3 times more and turning once, or until golden and cooked through.

Total time: 25 minutes ✳ Makes 4 servings

Per serving: 232 calories, 32 g protein, 14 g carbohydrates, 5 g fat, 1 g saturated fat, 235 mg sodium, 0 g fiber

Balancing the bright flavors of oranges and honey with just the right hint of sweetness makes for a tasty glaze during grilling. It's excellent on grilled pork, too.

SUPERFOOD SPOTLIGHT: PARSNIP

Don't let its pale color fool you: A serving of this low-calorie veggie is packed with 7 grams of fiber (40 percent more than its brighter-colored cousin, the carrot), 30 micrograms of bone-building vitamin K, and 30 percent of the immune-boosting vitamin C you need daily.

Buy: Smooth, off-white, and firm varieties that are small to medium in size. Parsnip ripens after the first frost, so winter months are prime for buying. Store in the fridge.

Try: Peeled and diced, it's delicious in soups and stews or raw in salads. For a healthy side, boil and mash them as you would potatoes. Their sweet, mild flavor requires less butter.

Chicken Cutlets with Mozzarella, Peppers, and Olives

- 4 boneless, skinless chicken breast halves
- 1 tablespoon fresh basil or ½ teaspoon dried
- 4 slices smoked or regular mozzarella cheese, each ¼" thick
- ½ teaspoon salt
- ¼ teaspoon ground black pepper
- 2 tablespoons olive oil
- 1 large green and/or red bell pepper, cut into thin strips
- ⅓ cup dry white wine or chicken broth
- ⅓ cup (3 ounces) pitted ripe kalamata olives, quartered lengthwise

PREHEAT the oven to 350°F. Make a 3" horizontal pocket in each chicken breast. Sprinkle the basil over the cheese. Slip a cheese slice into each pocket, folding it as needed to fit. Close the edges and secure with wooden picks. Sprinkle with ¼ teaspoon of the salt and the pepper.

HEAT the oil in a large oven-safe skillet over medium heat. Cook the bell pepper and the remaining ¼ teaspoon salt, stirring occasionally, for 5 minutes, or until lightly browned and starting to wilt. Push the bell pepper to the edge of the skillet and add the chicken. Cook for 3 minutes, or until lightly browned. Turn and arrange the bell pepper around the chicken. Add the wine or broth and olives.

BAKE for 15 minutes, turning once, or until a thermometer inserted in the thickest portion registers 160°F and the juices run clear.

REMOVE the chicken with a slotted spoon to plates and top with the peppers and olives. There should be about 2 tablespoons of juices in the pan. If more, set the skillet over medium heat and cook for 3 minutes, or until the liquid is reduced. Spoon over the chicken.

Total time: 45 minutes ✱ Makes 4 servings

Per serving: 206 calories, 24 g protein, 2 g carbohydrates, 10 g fat, 4 g saturated fat, 384 mg sodium, 1 g fiber

Prepare extra portions of these stuffed breasts for a quick lunch or supper. Store in a covered container in the refrigerator for up to 2 days. To reheat, arrange the chicken in a baking dish, cover, and bake at 350°F for 10 to 15 minutes, or until heated through. Drizzle with a little olive oil to replace lost moisture.

Chicken Salad Casserole

- 1 tablespoon canola oil
- 1 onion, chopped
- 1 green bell pepper, chopped
- 1 red bell pepper, chopped
- 1 yellow bell pepper, chopped
- 1 can (10¾ ounces) reduced-fat cream of mushroom soup
- ½ cup light mayonnaise
- ½ cup fat-free sour cream
- 2 tablespoons lemon juice
- 2 cups cooked chopped chicken breast
- 2 cups cooked brown rice
- 2 hard-cooked eggs, chopped
- ¼ cup slivered almonds
- 1½ cups crushed baked potato chips

PREHEAT the oven to 350°F. Coat a 2½-quart baking dish with cooking spray.

HEAT the oil in a large skillet over medium-high heat. Cook the onion and bell peppers for 10 minutes, or until tender.

WHISK together the soup, mayonnaise, sour cream, and lemon juice in a large bowl. Stir in the onion-pepper mixture, chicken, rice, eggs, and almonds just until blended. Pour into the baking dish and sprinkle with the potato chips.

BAKE for 35 minutes, or until hot and bubbling. Let stand for 10 minutes before serving.

Total time: 1 hour 15 minutes ✳ Makes 6 servings

Per serving: 323 calories, 7 g protein, 36 g carbohydrates, 17 g fat, 3 g saturated fat, 654 mg sodium, 4 g fiber

This dish goes well with a side of steamed green beans and was adapted from a dish prepared by a friend.

—Jodi

Postmenopausal women who added ½ tablespoon of safflower oil to their daily diets lost up to 4 pounds of belly fat and gained about 1½ pounds of muscle in 4 months—without changing their diet or exercise habits, according to a study in the *American Journal of Clinical Nutrition*. The oil's linoleic acid may improve the way the body uses fuel. Try safflower oil in this tangy dressing from chef Jennifer Chandler, author of *Simply Salads*.

Citrus Dressing

- 3 tablespoons freshly squeezed lime juice
- 2 tablespoons freshly squeezed orange juice
- 3 tablespoons safflower oil

WHISK together the lime juice, orange juice, and oil in a small bowl until combined. Season with salt and pepper to taste. Makes about ⅓ cup.

[**METABOLISM BOOSTER: SAFFLOWER OIL**]

—Julie Nusbaum, Hamilton, Indiana

Chicken, Broccoli, and Rice Casserole

- 1 cup quick-cooking brown rice
- 2 teaspoons olive oil
- 1 small onion, chopped
- 1 rib celery, chopped
- 1 can (10¾ ounces) 98% fat-free cream of chicken soup
- 1 cup low-sodium chicken broth
- ½ teaspoon dried thyme
- 1 package (10 ounces) frozen broccoli, thawed
- 2 cups cooked chopped chicken breast
- ½ cup reduced-fat Cheddar cheese

PREHEAT the oven to 375°F. Coat a 2-quart baking dish with cooking spray. Prepare the rice according to package directions.

HEAT the oil in a large skillet over medium-high heat. Cook the onion and celery for 5 minutes, or until softened. Stir in the soup, broth, thyme, broccoli, and chicken. Pour into the prepared pan.

COVER and bake for 40 minutes. Uncover and sprinkle with the cheese. Bake for 10 minutes, or until the cheese melts.

Total time: 1 hour 10 minutes ✳ Makes 6 servings

Per serving: 240 calories, 21 g protein, 23 g carbohydrates, 7 g fat, 2 g saturated fat, 532 mg sodium, 3 g fiber

This dish goes well with a green salad topped with low-fat balsamic vinaigrette.

—**Julie**

QUICK TIP: TAKEOUT TRICKERY

Avoid this fast-food faux pas: In a recent experiment conducted by Duke University's Fuqua School of Business, simply seeing a salad listed on an otherwise less-than-healthy menu caused consumers to make a higher-calorie choice: french fries. Researchers say an effect called "vicarious goal fulfillment" leads people to feel good about the fact that they considered the greens—even if they opted for fries instead. Being aware of this effect can help you order more healthfully.

Chicken Tetrazzini

2 teaspoons + 1 tablespoon butter

1¼ cups (4½ ounces) whole wheat rotelle or other short pasta

2¼ cups chicken broth

¼ cup dry white wine or chicken broth

1 bay leaf

4 boneless, skinless chicken breast halves, cut crosswise into ¼" strips

8 large mushrooms (8 ounces), sliced

½ cup heavy cream

2 tablespoons cornstarch

¼ teaspoon ground black pepper

2 tablespoons water

⅔ cup grated Parmesan cheese

PREHEAT the oven to 425°F. Butter an 8" × 8" baking dish with 2 teaspoons of the butter. Prepare the pasta according to package directions. Drain well and remove to a warm, large bowl.

MEANWHILE, combine 1½ cups of the broth, the wine or broth, and bay leaf in a saucepan. Bring to a simmer over medium heat. Add the chicken and cook for 8 minutes, or just until cooked. Using a slotted spoon, remove the chicken to the pasta bowl. Add the mushrooms to the broth and cook for 4 minutes, or until tender. Remove the mushrooms to the pasta bowl. Discard the bay leaf.

MEASURE 1½ cups of the broth left in the pan. If it is more than 1½ cups, boil it until reduced. If it is less than 1½ cups, add more broth. Add the cream and simmer for 1 minute. Increase the heat to medium-high and bring to a boil.

COMBINE the cornstarch, pepper, and water in a cup. Whisk into the broth mixture and cook for 1 minute, whisking until thickened. Stir into the pasta bowl, tossing to mix. Pour into the baking dish. Sprinkle with the cheese and dot with the remaining 1 tablespoon butter, cut into small pieces. Bake on the top rack for 20 minutes, or until light brown and bubbling.

Total time: 1 hour　✳　Makes 6 servings

Per serving: 186 calories, 17 g protein, 11 g carbohydrates, 8 g fat, 4 g saturated fat, 196 mg sodium, 1 g fiber

Use turkey, fish, or seafood in place of the chicken. Add a fresh herb, such as chopped parsley or basil, or scallions to the pasta mixture.

Orange Chicken and Broccoli

1 large bunch broccoli (about 1½ pounds)

½ cup orange juice

2 tablespoons reduced-sodium soy sauce

2 tablespoons orange marmalade

2 teaspoons cornstarch

1 tablespoon canola oil

1 pound chicken tenders, trimmed and cut into 1" pieces

3 scallions, sliced

3 large garlic cloves, minced

1 tablespoon minced fresh ginger

Pinch of red-pepper flakes

⅓ cup reduced-sodium chicken broth

1 red bell pepper, thinly sliced

CUT the broccoli into small florets. Trim and discard about 2" of the tough broccoli stems. Thinly slice the remaining stems. Stir in the orange juice, soy sauce, orange marmalade, and cornstarch in a small bowl. Set aside.

HEAT the oil in a wok or large nonstick skillet over high heat. Cook the chicken, stirring, for 3 minutes, or until no longer pink and the juices run clear. Add the scallions, garlic, ginger, and red-pepper flakes and stir to combine.

REMOVE the chicken to a plate with a slotted spoon. Add the broth and broccoli to the wok and reduce the heat to medium. Cover and cook for 2 minutes. Increase the heat to high and add the bell pepper. Cook, stirring frequently, for 2 minutes, or until the broth evaporates and the vegetables are crisp-tender. Stir the reserved sauce and add to the wok along with the chicken. Cook, stirring constantly, for 1 to 2 minutes, or until the sauce thickens and the chicken is hot.

Total time: 30 minutes ✳ Makes 4 servings

Per serving: 261 calories, 33 g protein, 27 g carbohydrates, 5 g fat, 4 g saturated fat, 386 mg sodium, 6 g fiber

Broccoli is a star member of the cruciferous family. It has a respectable amount of fiber, along with myriad other nutrients that earn it top honors among food researchers.

Turkey Cutlets with Ham and Provolone

4 turkey cutlets (4 ounces each)

½ teaspoon salt

¼ teaspoon ground black pepper

¼ cup soy flour

1 tablespoon olive oil

4 thin slices (3 ounces) ham, halved

4 thin slices (4 ounces) provolone cheese, halved

4 lemon wedges

SPRINKLE the turkey with the salt and pepper. Coat in the flour and pat off the excess.

HEAT the oil in a large nonstick skillet over high heat. Cook for 3 minutes, or until browned on the first side.

TURN, reduce the heat to low, and layer the ham and cheese on top. Cover and cook for 3 minutes, or until the turkey is no longer pink, the juices run clear, and the cheese is melted. Serve immediately with the lemon wedges for squeezing.

Total time: 20 minutes ✻ Makes 4 servings

Per serving: 309 calories, 41 g protein, 3 g carbohydrates, 14 g fat, 6 g saturated fat, 911 mg sodium, 1 g fiber

Substitute Swiss or mozzarella cheese for the provolone and sprinkle the turkey with 1 tablespoon chopped fresh parsley or 1 teaspoon dried thyme. Serve with 2 tablespoons tomato sauce. If your skillet has an oven-safe handle, you can also broil the turkey after adding the ham and cheese.

QUICK TIP: THE RIGHT BREW FOR YOUR BONES

If you like to cool off with an ale, make it pale. According to a University of California, Davis analysis of 100 commercial brews, light-colored ales, such as India Pale Ale (IPA), contain the most silicon, a compound that increases bone mineral density in women with osteoporosis. Researchers believe it's due to the ale's high levels of silicon-rich hops and malted barley. Enjoy IPA in moderation and you could boost your bone mineral density by up to 16 percent. Cheers!

Savory Turkey Stroganoff

3 teaspoons olive oil

¾ pound turkey cutlets, cut into thin strips

2 large shallots, thinly sliced

1 package (10 ounces) cremini mushrooms, sliced

1 cup baby carrots, sliced

1 garlic clove, minced

1 teaspoon hot paprika

¼ teaspoon salt

1 cup chicken broth

2 teaspoons tomato paste

2 teaspoons Worcestershire sauce

2 teaspoons cornstarch

⅓ cup reduced-fat sour cream

HEAT 2 teaspoons of the oil in a large nonstick skillet over high heat. Add the turkey and cook, stirring, for 3 minutes, or until no longer pink and just cooked through. Remove to a plate.

REDUCE the heat to medium-high and add the remaining 1 teaspoon oil. Add the shallots to the skillet. Cook, stirring, for 1 minute, or until the shallots begin to soften. Add the mushrooms and carrots. Cook, stirring, for 4 minutes, or until the mushrooms soften. Stir in the garlic, paprika, and salt and cook for 1 minute. Remove the skillet from the heat.

COMBINE the broth, tomato paste, Worcestershire sauce, and cornstarch in a small bowl and stir until blended. Return the skillet to medium heat and stir in the broth mixture. Cook, stirring frequently, for 3 minutes, or until the sauce comes to a boil and thickens. Simmer for 2 minutes. Stir in the turkey and cook for 1 minute, or until hot. Remove the skillet from the heat and stir in the sour cream.

Total time: 30 minutes ✳ Makes 4 servings

Per serving: 213 calories, 27 g protein, 11 g carbohydrates, 7 g fat, 2 g saturated fat, 691 mg sodium, 1 g fiber

Turkey is a superb source of protein, so this meal has the staying power to keep you away from those late-night snacks. Serve over steamed brown rice, whole grain pasta, or whole wheat couscous.

—Andrea Peterson, Fairfax, Virginia

Stuffed Zucchini Boats

3 medium zucchini, halved lengthwise

1½ pounds 99% fat-free ground turkey

1 cup cooked brown rice

1 teaspoon allspice

1 teaspoon ground cinnamon

½ teaspoon salt

1 cup marinara sauce

½ cup reduced-fat feta cheese, crumbled

1 cup low-fat plain yogurt (optional)

PREHEAT the oven to 350°F. Coat a 13" × 9" baking pan with cooking spray.

SCOOP out the center of the zucchini to form "boats" and place in the pan. Chop the centers (you should have 3 cups of chopped zucchini).

HEAT the oil in a medium skillet over medium-high heat. Cook the chopped zucchini and turkey for 10 minutes, or until the zucchini is tender and the turkey is browned. Place in a large bowl. Add the rice, allspice, cinnamon, and salt in a large bowl. Toss to coat well.

DIVIDE the turkey mixture into the boats. Divide the marinara sauce over the zucchini. Sprinkle with the cheese. Cover and bake for 50 minutes. Uncover and bake for 10 minutes, or until the zucchini is tender. Serve with the yogurt, if desired.

Total time: 1 hour 20 minutes   ✳   Makes 6 servings

Per serving: 213 calories, 25 g protein, 15 g carbohydrates, 7 g fat, 2 g saturated fat, 559 mg sodium, 3 g fiber

The Middle Eastern spices (allspice and cinnamon) in this dish really enhance the flavor of the turkey meat, which can be very bland on its own. Because this is all in one dish, it reheats wonderfully and tastes even better the second time!

—Andrea

Baked Salmon with Oregano

2 teaspoons olive oil

4 skinless salmon fillets
(6 ounces each), each 1" thick

1 tablespoon + 1½ teaspoons
lemon juice

1 teaspoon dried oregano

½ teaspoon salt

¼ teaspoon ground black
pepper

1 tablespoon butter, cut into
small pieces

1 teaspoon chopped fresh
parsley (optional)

PREHEAT the oven to 375°F. Grease a shallow baking dish with the oil. Arrange the fish in the dish and turn to coat with the oil. Sprinkle with the lemon juice, oregano, salt, and pepper. Dot with the butter and cover with foil. Bake for 24 minutes, or until the fish is opaque. Serve topped with the pan juices and parsley (if using).

Total time: 25 minutes ✳ Makes 4 servings

Per serving: 359 calories, 34 g protein, 1 g carbohydrates, 24 g fat,
6 g saturated fat, 412 mg sodium, 0 g fiber

Make this dish ahead or make extras for fast meals. Store extra portions in a covered container in the refrigerator for up to 3 days. To reheat, arrange the fillets in a baking dish, cover, and bake at 350°F for 8 minutes, or until heated through. Or serve the fillets cold or at room temperature mixed with vinegar and oil for a fish salad.

GOTTA TRY IT! MILDER OMEGA OPTION

Sick of salmon? Grill some barramundi. it has a mild, sweet flavor and a hearty 500 milligrams of omega-3s per 3-ounce serving—about half as much as salmon but equivalent to what scientists recommend getting daily from fish to support brain health. Most of the barramundi available is farmed sustainably on a mainly vegetarian diet, which ensures low levels of potentially harmful contaminants such as mercury. Look for it in your grocer's freezer.

Breaded Baked Cod with Tartar Sauce

Tartar Sauce

- ½ cup reduced-fat mayonnaise
- 1½ tablespoons lemon juice
- 1 tablespoon finely chopped dill
- 2 teaspoons mustard
- 2 teaspoons capers, drained and chopped
- 2 teaspoons chopped parsley (optional)

Fish

- 2 slices whole wheat bread, torn
- 2 eggs
- 1 tablespoon water
- 1¼ pounds cod or scrod fillet, cut into 1"–1½" pieces
- ½ teaspoon salt
- ¼ teaspoon ground black pepper

To make the tartar sauce:

COMBINE the mayonnaise, lemon juice, dill, mustard, capers, and parsley (if using) in a small bowl. Cover and chill.

To make the fish:

PREHEAT the oven to 400°F. Coat a baking sheet with cooking spray.

PROCESS the bread in a food processor into fine crumbs. Place in a shallow bowl. Beat the eggs with the water in another bowl. Sprinkle the fish with the salt and pepper. Dip the fish into the eggs, then into the bread crumbs. Place on the baking sheet. Coat the breaded fish with cooking spray. Bake for 10 minutes, or until opaque inside. Serve with the tartar sauce.

Total time: 25 minutes ✳ Makes 4 servings

Per serving: 241 calories, 30 g protein, 11 g carbohydrates, 8 g fat, 2 g saturated fat, 819 mg sodium, 1 g fiber

The tartar sauce can be stored in a covered container in the refrigerator for up to a week.

Mandarin-Basil Shrimp Salad on Roasted Sweet Potatoes

- 1 orange
- 14 large shrimp (about 8 ounces), peeled and deveined
- 3½ tablespoons extra virgin olive oil
- 2 tablespoons chopped fresh basil
- 1 garlic clove, minced
- ¼ teaspoon salt
- ¼ teaspoon pepper
- 2 medium (about 12 ounces each) sweet potatoes, each cut lengthwise into 6 wedges each
- 3 tablespoons light mayonnaise
- 2 tablespoons reduced-fat sour cream
- 1 can (11 ounces) mandarin oranges in light syrup, drained, ¼ cup syrup reserved
- 4 cups mixed baby salad greens

PREHEAT the oven to 350°F. Coat a large baking sheet with nonstick cooking spray. From the orange, grate 1 teaspoon zest. Squeeze the juice to yield ¼ cup.

COMBINE the zest, 2 tablespoons of the orange juice, shrimp, 2 tablespoons of the oil, 1 tablespoon of the basil, the garlic, ⅛ teaspoon of the salt, and ⅛ teaspoon of the pepper in a resealable plastic bag. Seal and shake to coat. Chill for 1 hour.

PLACE the sweet potatoes on the baking sheet and drizzle with the remaining 1½ tablespoons oil, ⅛ teaspoon salt, and ⅛ teaspoon pepper. Toss to coat and place in a single layer. Bake for 50 minutes, turning once, or until tender and browned.

MEANWHILE, whisk together the mayonnaise, sour cream, the remaining 2 tablespoons orange juice, the reserved mandarin orange syrup, and the remaining 1 tablespoon basil. Chill until ready to serve.

REMOVE the shrimp from the marinade to a paper towel–lined plate to drain. Preheat a grill pan or skillet coated with cooking spray over medium-high heat. Cook the shrimp for 4 minutes, turning once, or until opaque.

ARRANGE the sweet potato wedges on 2 dinner plates to resemble petals on a flower. Top each "flower" with 2 cups of the greens, then the mandarin oranges. Divide the shrimp and place on the greens. Drizzle 1 tablespoon of the dressing on each salad. Serve the rest of the dressing in 2 small bowls as a dip for the sweet potato petals.

Total time: 1 hour 30 minutes ✳ Makes 2 servings

Per serving: 358 calories, 16 g protein, 51 g carbohydrates, 10 g fat, 2 g saturated fat, 652 mg sodium, 8 g fiber

This is a wonderful meal for a ladies' luncheon or dinner, or it could be served more 'manly' style with the potatoes on the side!

—**Laurie**

Herb and Mesclun Salad with Grilled Shrimp

- 4 tablespoons lime juice
- ½ teaspoon ground cumin
- ¼ teaspoon salt
- ¼ teaspoon red-pepper flakes
- 1 pound large shrimp, peeled and deveined
- 6 cups mesclun or other mixed baby greens
- 1 cup fresh mint leaves
- 1 cup cilantro leaves
- 1 cup flat-leaf parsley leaves
- 1 small red onion, thinly sliced
- 2 tablespoons olive oil

WHISK together 2 tablespoons of the lime juice, ¼ teaspoon of the cumin, ⅛ teaspoon of the salt, and a pinch of the red-pepper flakes in a medium bowl. Stir in the shrimp. Let stand to marinate at room temperature, stirring occasionally, for 20 minutes.

MEANWHILE, combine the greens, mint, cilantro, parsley, and onion in a large bowl. Chill until ready to serve.

WHISK together the oil and the remaining 2 tablespoons lime juice, ¼ teaspoon cumin, ⅛ teaspoon salt, and red-pepper flakes in a small bowl. Lightly oil a grill pan and preheat over medium heat. Grill the shrimp for 4 minutes, or until opaque. Toss the shrimp with the salad and dressing.

Total time: 55 minutes ✳ Makes 4 servings

Per serving: 219 calories, 26 g protein, 9 g carbohydrates, 10 g fat, 1 g saturated fat, 348 mg sodium, 3 g fiber

Plan ahead and save time preparing this main-dish salad. Cook the shrimp when you have the grill lit for another meal. Feel free to adapt by using salmon or chicken breast instead of the shrimp.

QUICK TIP: THE GOOD FATS

25 The percentage of your daily calories that should come from good-for-you fats, such as monounsaturated fatty acids. Some excellent sources are almonds, avocados, and olive oil.

Crab Casserole

- 2 tablespoons light olive oil
- 1 onion, finely chopped
- 1 green bell pepper, finely chopped
- 1 red bell pepper, finely chopped
- 1½ pounds lump crabmeat (thoroughly picked through)
- 1 cup evaporated milk
- 1 teaspoon prepared mustard
- 1 teaspoon Worcestershire sauce
- ½ teaspoon ground red pepper
- 8 whole wheat butter-flavored cracker crumbs, crushed
- 2 teaspoons trans-free margarine

PREHEAT the oven to 350°F. Coat a 2-quart baking dish with cooking spray.

HEAT the oil in a large skillet over medium-high heat. Cook the onion and bell peppers, stirring, for 10 minutes, or until softened.

REMOVE from the heat and stir in the crab, milk, mustard, Worcestershire sauce, ground red pepper, and salt. Gently stir until well blended.

POUR into the dish. Top with the cracker crumbs and dot with the margarine. Bake for 25 to 30 minutes, or until hot and bubbling. Let stand for 10 minutes before serving.

Total time: 50 minutes ✳ Makes 4 servings

Per serving: 414 calories, 45 g protein, 17 g carbohydrates, 16 g fat, 5 g saturated fat, 820 mg sodium, 2 g fiber

217

Dinners

This is a very filling and rich recipe. It is served well alone or with a tossed salad or even baked apple slices. It's a great way to hide crabmeat in this lovely casserole!
—Jodi

Tuna-Stuffed Peppers

1 cup quick-cooking barley

4 large red bell peppers, tops removed and seeded

1 tablespoon olive oil

2 cans (5 ounces each) solid white tuna, packed in water, drained

2 eggs, beaten

¼ cup grated Romano cheese

¼ cup finely chopped parsley

2 garlic cloves, minced

1 small onion, minced

½ teaspoon dried Italian seasoning

¼ teaspoon ground black pepper

PREPARE the barley according to package directions. Set aside.

PREHEAT the oven to 350°F. Coat a large baking pan with ½ table-spoon of the oil.

BRING 6 cups of water to a boil in a large saucepot. Add the bell peppers to the boiling water and reduce the heat to a simmer. Cook for 5 minutes. Remove the bell peppers to a colander in the sink and run under cold water to stop the cooking. Place the peppers in a baking pan and rub with the remaining ½ tablespoon oil.

STIR together the tuna, eggs, cheese, parsley, garlic, onion, Italian seasoning, black pepper, and reserved barley in a large bowl until well blended.

DIVIDE the tuna mixture among the bell peppers in the pan. Bake for 40 minutes.

Total time: 1 hour 10 minutes ✻ Makes 4 servings

Per serving: 300 calories, 28 g protein, 21 g carbohydrates, 11 g fat, 3 g saturated fat, 482 mg sodium, 4 g fiber

 Here's a recipe that goes over well with just about everyone. It's one I learned from my Italian mama many years ago. As far as I know, she invented the idea of stuffing the peppers with a canned tuna mixture instead of ground beef, and it's a delicious combination of flavors.

—Amy

—Lesley Pew, Lynn, Massachusetts

Crustless Caramelized Onion, Tomato, and Cheese Tart

1½ tablespoons olive oil

1 tablespoon butter

4 medium red onions, thinly sliced

⅛ teaspoon salt

1 teaspoon balsamic vinegar

1 cup reduced-fat Jarlsberg or Gruyère cheese, shredded

1 cup part-skim mozzarella cheese, shredded

3 eggs

4 egg whites

2 plum tomatoes or 1 beefsteak tomato, sliced

1 tablespoon grated Parmesan cheese

PREHEAT the oven to 425°F. Coat a 9" or 10" pie plate with cooking spray.

HEAT the oil and butter in a Dutch oven over medium heat. Cook the onions and salt, stirring occasionally, for 10 minutes, or until the onions are soft and translucent.

REDUCE the heat to medium-low and cook for 20 to 40 minutes, stirring occasionally, or until the onions are well browned. Add the vinegar and cook for 10 minutes, or until the onions are completely caramelized.

PLACE the onions on the bottom of the pan. Sprinkle with the Jarlsberg or Gruyère and mozzarella. Beat the eggs and egg whites in a small bowl. Pour over the cheese. Top with the tomato slices and Parmesan. Bake for 30 to 35 minutes, or until a knife inserted in the center comes out clean.

Total time: 1 hour 30 minutes ✳ Makes 6 servings

Per serving: 231 calories, 18 g protein, 8 g carbohydrates, 14 g fat, 5 g saturated fat, 318 mg sodium, 1 g fiber

I like this recipe because you can adapt it to low-fat by using low-fat cheese or low-carb by skipping the crust. My husband likes this recipe because it is less filling without a crust.

—Lesley

QUICK TIP: CARB COUNT

130 The minimum number of grams of carbohydrates your body needs per day

Tomato and Spinach Crustless Quiche

2 teaspoons olive oil

4 plum tomatoes, halved lengthwise

½ cup chopped red onion

1 garlic clove, minced

1 package (10 ounces) spinach, rinsed and drained, tough stems removed

¾ cup shredded reduced-fat Cheddar cheese

3 large eggs

1 cup 1% milk

2 tablespoons grated Parmesan cheese

1½ teaspoons Dijon mustard

⅛ teaspoon ground black pepper

PREHEAT the oven to 350°F. Coat a 9" pie plate with cooking spray.

HEAT the oil in a large nonstick skillet over medium-high heat. Cook the tomatoes cut side down for 5 minutes, or until browned. Turn the tomatoes over and add the onion and garlic. Cook, stirring occasionally, for 2 minutes, or until the onion softens. Arrange the tomatoes cut side up in the pie plate. Spoon the onion and garlic around the tomatoes. Add half of the spinach to the skillet and cook for 4 minutes, or until wilted, and drain in a colander. Repeat with the remaining spinach. When cool enough to handle, squeeze the spinach until dry. Coarsely chop. Sprinkle the spinach in between the tomatoes. Top with the Cheddar.

WHISK together the eggs, milk, Parmesan, mustard, and pepper in a medium bowl. Pour into the pie plate. Bake for 30 minutes, or until a knife inserted in the center comes out clean. Remove to a rack to cool for 10 minutes.

Total time: 1 hour 5 minutes ✳ Makes 6 servings

Per serving: 138 calories, 11 g protein, 7 g carbohydrates, 8 g fat, 3 g saturated fat, 250 mg sodium, 2 g fiber

Perfect for a weekend brunch or light supper, this tasty quiche is so satisfying that you won't miss the crust at all.

Macaroni and Cheese

8 ounces multigrain pasta

¼ cup unbleached flour

2½ cups 1% milk

1 garlic clove, halved

½ teaspoon mustard powder

¼ teaspoon salt

¼ teaspoon ground red pepper

1⅓ cups shredded low-fat extra-sharp Cheddar cheese

2 tablespoons dried bread crumbs

2 tablespoons grated Parmesan cheese

PREHEAT the oven to 350°F. Coat a medium baking dish with cooking spray. Prepare the pasta according to package directions.

MEANWHILE, place the flour in a medium saucepan. Gradually whisk in the milk, whisking constantly, until smooth. Add the garlic, mustard powder, salt, and pepper. Place over medium heat. Cook, whisking constantly, for 7 minutes, or until thickened. Remove from the heat. Remove the garlic and discard.

STIR the Cheddar into the milk mixture until smooth and melted. Stir in the pasta. Pour into the prepared baking dish. Combine the bread crumbs and Parmesan in a small bowl. Sprinkle over the casserole. Bake for 15 to 20 minutes, or until bubbling and lightly browned.

Total time: 50 minutes ✳ Makes 6 servings

Per serving: 306 calories, 19 g protein, 38 g carbohydrates, 9 g fat, 5 g saturated fat, 444 mg sodium, 3 g fiber

Usually America's favorite comfort food has ample supplies of fat, weighing in at 22 grams for a 1-cup serving. We've scaled back the fat considerably, increased the protein, and even added a touch of fiber without sacrificing the rich, creamy taste. Now you can really feel comforted!

Pasta-Ratatouille Casserole

8 ounces whole grain penne or rotini pasta

2 tablespoons extra virgin olive oil

1 large onion, chopped

3 garlic cloves, minced

4 cups unpeeled cubed eggplant

1 medium zucchini, chopped

1 medium yellow squash, chopped

1 small red bell pepper, sliced

1 small yellow bell pepper, sliced

1 small green bell pepper, sliced

1 cup thickly sliced mushrooms

2 cups marinara sauce

3 tablespoons minced fresh basil or 1 tablespoon dried

1 tablespoon minced fresh oregano or 1 teaspoon dried

2 tablespoons chopped fresh parsley

3 large fresh plum tomatoes, chopped

¼ teaspoon salt

¼ teaspoon ground black pepper

1½ cups reduced-fat mozzarella cheese

¼ cup (1 ounce) freshly grated Parmesan cheese

PREHEAT the oven to 375°F. Coat a 3-quart glass baking dish with cooking spray and set aside. Prepare the pasta according to package directions. Drain and set aside.

HEAT the oil in a Dutch oven over medium-high heat. Add the onion and garlic and cook for 3 minutes, or until the onion is translucent.

ADD the eggplant, zucchini, squash, bell peppers, mushrooms, and marinara sauce. Bring to a boil. Reduce the heat to low and simmer uncovered, stirring frequently, until the vegetables are crisp-tender, about 15 minutes. Add the basil, oregano, parsley, tomatoes, salt, and black pepper. Simmer uncovered, stirring, for 20 minutes, or until the vegetables are tender.

STIR in the reserved pasta. Pour into the prepared dish. Sprinkle evenly with the mozzarella and Parmesan. Bake for 20 minutes, or until heated through and the cheese melts.

Total time: 1 hour 30 minutes ✳ Makes 8 servings

Per serving: 286 calories, 14 g protein, 36 g carbohydrates, 11 g fat, 3 g saturated fat, 547 mg sodium, 5 g fiber

I have been making this recipe for years. Ratatouille is one of my son's favorite vegetable recipes. I decided to add the pasta to make it a complete entrée.   —Virginia

Pasta with Walnut-Basil Pesto

8 ounces multigrain angel hair pasta

1¼ cups packed fresh basil

¼ cup walnuts

1 garlic clove, peeled

1 tablespoon extra virgin olive oil

¼ teaspoon salt

⅛ teaspoon crushed red-pepper flakes

¼ cup chopped tomato (optional)

¼ cup freshly grated Parmesan cheese

PREPARE the pasta according to package directions. Drain, reserving ½ cup of the cooking water.

PLACE the basil, walnuts, garlic, oil, salt, and red-pepper flakes in a food processor. Process, stopping the machine once or twice to scrape down the sides, until finely pureed. Scrape into a serving bowl. Stir 2 or 3 tablespoons of the pasta water into the pesto to warm it and make it creamier. Add the pasta and toss, adding more pasta water if dry. Sprinkle with the tomato, if using, and cheese.

Total time: 20 minutes ✱ Makes 4 servings

Per serving: 308 calories, 14 g protein, 41 g carbohydrates, 11 g fat, 2 g saturated fat, 248 mg sodium, 5 g fiber

If you like, coarsely chop and toast 1 tablespoon of the walnuts. Sprinkle over the top for a little extra crunch.

—Cynthia Davis, Glendale, Arizona

Mushroom-Spinach Lasagna

½ package (8 ounces) no-boil lasagna noodles (6 noodles)

1 jar (24 ounces) mushroom spaghetti sauce

1 container (16 ounces) 1% cottage cheese

1 can (8 ounces) mushrooms, drained

2 garlic cloves, minced

2 packages (10 ounces each) frozen chopped spinach, thawed and squeezed dry

6 ounces part-skim mozzarella cheese, shredded

6 ounces reduced-fat Cheddar cheese, shredded

PREHEAT the oven to 375°F. Coat a 13" × 9" baking dish with cooking spray.

SPREAD ½ cup of the sauce over the bottom of the pan. Layer 3 noodles on the sauce. Spread with 1 cup of the cottage cheese and sprinkle with half of the mushrooms, garlic, and spinach. Top with half of the sauce. Sprinkle with ½ cup each of the mozzarella and Cheddar.

REPEAT the layering.

COVER with foil and bake for 1 hour. Uncover and bake for 15 minutes, or until the cheese melts.

Total time: 1 hour 30 minutes ✷ Makes 8 servings

Per serving: 319 calories, 25 g protein, 35 g carbohydrates, 9 g fat, 5 g saturated fat, 882 mg sodium, 4 g fiber

My family always enjoys this mouthwatering dinner.

—Cynthia

Roasted Vegetable Lasagna

3 medium zucchini, cut lengthwise into ¼" slices

2 large red bell peppers, cut into 1" strips

1 tablespoon olive oil

1 package (8 ounces) sliced mushrooms

4 carrots, coarsely shredded

1 package (10 ounces) frozen chopped spinach, thawed and squeezed dry

1 container (15 ounces) reduced-fat ricotta cheese

⅓ cup grated Parmesan cheese

1 large egg

1 jar (26 ounces) spaghetti sauce

9 no-boil lasagna noodles

1½ cups shredded reduced-fat mozzarella cheese

PREHEAT the oven to 450°F. Coat the bottoms and sides of 2 baking sheets with cooking spray. Arrange the zucchini and peppers on the baking sheets. Coat with cooking spray. Roast for 15 minutes, or until tender, moving the sheets to the opposite oven racks once. Remove the sheets and reduce the oven temperature to 350°F.

HEAT the oil in a large nonstick skillet over medium-high heat. Add the mushrooms and cook, stirring frequently, for 4 minutes, or until lightly browned. Stir in the carrots and cook for 1 minute. Stir in the spinach, ricotta, Parmesan, and egg until blended.

SPREAD ½ cup of the spaghetti sauce over the bottom of a 13" × 9" baking dish. Top with 3 of the noodles, overlapping if necessary. Spoon on half of the ricotta mixture, spreading to cover the noodles. Top with half of the roasted vegetables. Spoon ½ cup of the sauce over the vegetables and sprinkle with ½ cup of the mozzarella. Repeat the layering. Top with the remaining 3 noodles. Spread the remaining sauce over the noodles. Cover the dish with foil. Bake for 30 minutes. Uncover and sprinkle with the remaining ½ cup mozzarella. Bake for 20 to 25 minutes longer, or until hot and bubbling. Let stand for 15 minutes before serving.

Total time: 1 hour 45 minutes ✳ Makes 8 servings

Per serving: 315 calories, 20 g protein, 35 g carbohydrates, 12 g fat, 5 g saturated fat, 723 mg sodium, 6 g fiber

Ricotta cheese is an excellent source of protein. Combine it with a medley of fiber-rich vegetables and you have a perfect Italian meal!

—Jodi Striblin, Washington, North Carolina

Vegetable Casserole

- 7 tablespoons trans-free margarine
- ¾ cup seasoned bread crumbs
- 2 tablespoons all-purpose flour
- 1 cup fat-free milk
- 1 bag (6 ounces) spinach, chopped
- 3 medium red onions, cut into rings
- ½ pound mushrooms, sliced
- 2 small zucchini or yellow squash, thinly sliced
- 2 cups shredded reduced-fat mozzarella cheese
- 3 tomatoes, sliced

PREHEAT the oven to 375°F. Coat a 13" × 9" baking dish with cooking spray. Melt 1 tablespoon of the margarine in a small saucepan over medium heat. Cook the bread crumbs, stirring, for 3 minutes, or until browned. Set aside.

MELT 3 tablespoons of the margarine in a medium saucepan over low heat. Whisk in the flour and cook for 1 minute, whisking constantly. Slowly add the milk, whisking constantly until thickened. Stir in the spinach. Spread into the pan.

MELT the remaining 2 tablespoons margarine in a large skillet over medium-high heat. Cook the onions, mushrooms, and squash for 10 minutes, or until tender. Place over the spinach mixture and sprinkle with the cheese. Top with the tomato slices. Evenly sprinkle the crumbs over the tomatoes. Bake for 35 minutes, or until bubbling.

Total time: 1 hour 15 minutes ✳ Makes 8 servings

Per serving: 258 calories, 14 g protein, 23 g carbohydrates, 13 g fat, 5 g saturated fat, 534 mg sodium, 4 g fiber

Trying to get my young children to eat spinach, squash, or mushrooms used to be a major effort. The cheese makes for a gooey and yummy dish that's so delicious on a cold winter day!   —Jodi

Cauliflower Bake

1 large head cauliflower, cut into florets

1 medium onion, chopped

1 garlic clove, minced

½ cup shredded reduced-fat Cheddar or Parmesan cheese

¼ cup fat-free half-and-half

¼ cup trans-free margarine

Salt

Ground black pepper

BRING 4 cups of water to a boil in a large saucepan over high heat. Add the cauliflower, onion, and garlic. Reduce the heat to low, cover, and simmer for 25 minutes, or until very tender.

PREHEAT the broiler. Coat a 1½-quart baking dish or four 8-ounce ramekins with cooking spray.

DRAIN the cauliflower and return to the pot. Stir in ¼ cup of the cheese, the half-and-half, margarine, and salt and pepper to taste. Beat with an electric mixer until the consistency of mashed potatoes.

PLACE in the baking dish or divide among the ramekins. Sprinkle with the remaining ¼ cup cheese. Broil for 3 minutes, or until the cheese melts.

NOTE: For easy handling when broiling the ramekins, place on a baking sheet.

Total time: 40 minutes ✳ Makes 4 servings

Per serving: 198 calories, 8 g protein, 16 g carbohydrates, 13 g fat, 5 g saturated fat, 291 mg sodium, 6 g fiber

I came up with this recipe while attempting to replicate a similar dish from a restaurant. I wanted to replace potatoes or rice as a side dish and had seen this type of dish offered at a few restaurants under the low-carb menu. I think it makes a good replacement.

—Pam

Couscous with Almonds and Dried Cherries

- ¾ cup fat-free, reduced-sodium chicken or vegetable broth
- ¾ cup water
- 1 tablespoon olive oil
- ½ cup chopped red onion
- ¼ teaspoon ground cinnamon
- ¼ teaspoon salt
- ⅛ teaspoon ground black pepper
- ¾ cup whole wheat couscous
- ¼ cup dried unsweetened cherries
- 2 tablespoons slivered almonds, toasted
- 2 tablespoons unsalted pepitas (raw pumpkin seeds)

BRING the broth and water to a boil in a small saucepan.

MEANWHILE, heat the oil in a medium saucepan over medium heat. Cook the onion, stirring, for 5 minutes, or until tender. Stir in the cinnamon, salt, and pepper until blended. Stir in the couscous and cherries. Top with the broth mixture and return to a boil.

REMOVE the couscous from the heat, cover, and let stand for 10 minutes, or until tender and the water has been absorbed. Fluff the couscous with a fork. Sprinkle with the almonds and pepitas.

Total time: 20 minutes ✳ Makes 4 servings

Per serving: 188 calories, 5 g protein, 27 g carbohydrates, 8 g fat, 1 g saturated fat, 233 mg sodium, 6 g fiber

Perfect warm or at room temperature, alongside roast pork or as a filling for stuffed squash, this versatile side dish will have everyone asking for the recipe.

Quinoa and Vegetable Pilaf

1 tablespoon butter

1 small onion, finely chopped

1 small carrot, finely chopped

1 rib celery, finely chopped

½ cup quinoa, rinsed until the water runs clear and drained

¾ cup chicken or vegetable broth

⅛ teaspoon salt

⅛ teaspoon ground black pepper

2 teaspoons chopped parsley (optional)

MELT the butter in a saucepan over medium-low heat. Cook the onion, carrot, and celery, stirring occasionally, for 7 minutes, or until the vegetables are almost tender. Stir in the quinoa, increase the heat to medium-high, and cook, stirring, for 3 minutes, or until lightly toasted. Stir in the broth, salt, and pepper. Reduce the heat to low, cover, and cook for 15 minutes, or until the grains are tender-chewy and all the liquid is absorbed. Serve sprinkled with the parsley (if using).

Total time: 35 minutes ✽ Makes 4 servings

Per serving: 122 calories, 3 g protein, 18 g carbohydrates, 4 g fat, 2 g saturated fat, 289 mg sodium, 2 g fiber

Quinoa keeps well and cooks in 15 minutes. Make extras if you can and store in a covered container in the refrigerator for up to 4 days. To reheat, place in a baking dish, cover, and roast at 350°F until steaming, about 15 minutes.

NUTRITION NEWS TO USE

A diet rich in beans, whole grains, and soy products may help keep blood pressure in check. In a study of 4,680 adults, scientists found that a 5 percent higher intake of glutamic acid—the predominant amino acid in these nonanimal sources of protein—helped reduce blood pressure by up to 4.1 total points. To increase your glutamic acid intake, eat like a vegetarian once a week: Choose a black bean burger over beef, or stir-fry tofu instead of pork.

Glazed Turnips, Pearl Onions, and Carrots

4 turnips, peeled and cut into 8 wedges each

2 cups frozen small white onions, thawed

1 cup baby carrots

1¼ cups chicken broth

2 tablespoons balsamic vinegar

2 tablespoons packed brown sugar

4 teaspoons butter

½ teaspoon ground cumin

¼ teaspoon salt

⅛ teaspoon ground black pepper

2 tablespoons chopped fresh parsley

COMBINE the turnips, onions, carrots, broth, vinegar, sugar, butter, cumin, salt, and pepper in a large skillet over medium-high heat. Bring to a boil. Reduce the heat to medium and simmer, stirring occasionally, for 20 minutes, or until the liquid evaporates. Cook, stirring often, for 6 minutes, or until the vegetables are golden and shiny.

REMOVE from the heat and stir in the parsley.

Total time: 45 minutes   ✳   Makes 4 servings

Per serving: 143 calories, 2 g protein, 24 g carbohydrates, 4 g fat, 2 g saturated fat, 547 mg sodium, 4 g fiber

Flavorful enough for Thanksgiving dinner, easy enough for any night of the week, this attractive trio of vegetables also contains a powerful mix of complex carbohydrates and fiber.

Squash and Greens Gratin

1 tablespoon olive oil

3 leeks, white and pale green parts only, halved lengthwise, sliced, and rinsed

1 red bell pepper, thinly sliced

½ teaspoon salt

¼ teaspoon ground black pepper

3 large carrots, thinly sliced

1 large butternut squash (3 pounds), peeled, seeded, and cut lengthwise into ½"-thick slices

1 box (10 ounces) frozen chopped kale, thawed and squeezed dry

1 cup shredded Gruyère or Swiss cheese

½ cup grated Parmesan cheese

1 cup vegetable broth

PREHEAT the oven to 375°F. Coat a shallow 3-quart baking dish with cooking spray.

HEAT the oil in a large skillet over medium heat. Cook the leeks, bell pepper, ¼ teaspoon of the salt, and ⅛ teaspoon of the pepper, stirring frequently, for 5 minutes, or until softened. Stir in the carrots and cook for 5 minutes.

ARRANGE one-third of the squash in the prepared baking dish. Season with some of the remaining salt and pepper. Top with half of the kale, ½ cup of the Gruyère or Swiss, half of the carrot mixture, and 3 tablespoons of the Parmesan. Repeat the layering. Top with the remaining squash. Pour the vegetable broth over and sprinkle with the remaining salt and pepper. Cover the dish with foil and bake for 45 minutes.

REMOVE the foil and sprinkle with the remaining Parmesan. Bake for 15 minutes longer, or until the vegetables are tender. Let stand for 15 minutes before serving.

Total time: 1 hour 45 minutes ✳ Makes 8 servings

Per serving: 212 calories, 9 g protein, 31 g carbohydrates, 7 g fat, 4 g saturated fat, 675 mg sodium, 6 g fiber

Butternut squash deserves a spot on every plate! The sweet interior is high in fiber and deliciously sweet, which makes it perfect for any occasion.

Sweet Potato Casserole

4 **large sweet potatoes, baked, cooled, and peeled**

4 **large baking apples, unpeeled, cored, and cut into ¼" slices**

½ **cup walnuts**

⅓ **cup dried cranberries or raisins**

1 **teaspoon ground cinnamon, nutmeg, or allspice**

1 **tablespoon trans-free margarine**

Balsamic vinegar (optional)

PREHEAT the oven to 350°F. Coat a 13" × 9" baking dish with cooking spray.

CUT the sweet potatoes into ½" slices. Arrange the sweet potato and apple slices in a single layer in the dish, alternating and overlapping the slices. Sprinkle with the walnuts, cranberries, and cinnamon. Dot with the margarine. Cover with foil and bake for 30 minutes. Remove the foil and bake for 15 minutes more, or until the sweet potatoes are tender.

SERVE with a sprinkle of the vinegar, if desired.

Total time: 1 hour 20 minutes. ✳ Makes 6 servings

Per serving: 231 calories, 3 g protein, 41 g carbohydrates, 7 g fat, 1 g saturated fat, 55 mg sodium, 6 g fiber

Sweet potatoes are so healthy—this dish seems like dessert with no added sugar. Use red and/or green apples; they contrast nicely with the orange sweet potatoes. —Corri

Curried Sweet Potato Salad

2 **pounds sweet potatoes, peeled and cut into rough ¾" chunks**

3 **tablespoons pecans**

½ **cup fat-free plain yogurt**

2 **tablespoons light mayonnaise**

2 **tablespoons packed brown sugar**

½ **teaspoon curry powder**

⅛ **teaspoon salt**

1 **cup juice-packed canned pineapple tidbits, drained**

3 **scallions, sliced**

PLACE the sweet potatoes in a large saucepan and barely cover with cold water. Cover and bring to a boil over high heat. Reduce the heat to low and simmer, covered, for 10 to 12 minutes, or until tender. Drain and let cool.

MEANWHILE, cook the pecans in a small nonstick skillet over medium heat, stirring often, for 3 to 4 minutes, or until lightly toasted. Tip onto a plate and let cool. Chop coarsely.

WHISK the yogurt, mayonnaise, sugar, curry powder, and salt in a salad bowl until well blended. Add the pineapple, scallions, and sweet potatoes. Mix gently with a rubber spatula. Sprinkle with the toasted pecans and serve immediately, or cover and chill until ready to serve.

Total time: 35 minutes ✽ Makes 6 servings

Per serving: 226 calories, 4 g protein, 45 g carbohydrates, 5 g fat, 1 g saturated fat, 186 mg sodium, 6 g fiber

Put an end to those erratic blood sugar levels. Sweet potatoes are rich in complex carbohydrates and fiber, which will help your body maintain stable stores of energy.

Spinach Salad with Warm Bacon Vinaigrette

3 strips bacon

3 tablespoons walnut or olive oil

2 tablespoons red wine vinegar or other vinegar

1 teaspoon Dijon mustard (optional)

1 small garlic clove, minced

⅛ teaspoon salt

⅛ teaspoon ground black pepper

1 bunch (10 ounces) spinach, coarse stems trimmed (about 5 cups loosely packed)

1 McIntosh apple (4 ounces), peeled and cut into ½" pieces

8 shavings (¾ ounce) Romano cheese, each about 1" × 2"

COOK the bacon in a skillet over medium-low heat for 8 minutes, turning the slices occasionally or until crisp and browned. Drain on a paper towel–lined plate and keep warm.

MEASURE the fat in the pan (there should be 2 to 3 tablespoons). Add enough oil to equal 5 tablespoons of total fat in the pan. Whisk in the vinegar, mustard (if using), garlic, salt, and pepper. Keep warm.

COMBINE the spinach and apple in a large bowl. Spoon the warm bacon mixture over the spinach and apple. Toss to coat. Divide among 4 plates, crumble the bacon over the spinach, and top with the cheese.

Total time: 15 minutes ✳ Makes 4 servings

Per serving: 149 calories, 6 g protein, 8 g carbohydrates, 11 g fat, 2 g saturated fat, 368 mg sodium, 2 g fiber

The Romano cheese on this salad tastes best when cut into shavings (thin slices) rather than grated over top. To cut a shaving of Romano cheese, drag a vegetable peeler or cheese slicer along the broad side of the block of cheese to create thin slices about 1" wide and 2" long. To make a main-dish salad, garnish each serving with 2 or 3 wedges of tomato, a few slices of hard-cooked egg, and a slice of red onion. Or add cold, cooked chicken.

Crispy Celery and Pear Salad

4 ribs celery

2 tablespoons cider or pear vinegar

2 tablespoons honey

¼ teaspoon salt

2 red Anjou pears, cored and sliced

½ cup chopped walnuts, toasted

Ground black pepper

6 large leaves Butter or Bibb lettuce

1 ounce Parmesan cheese, cut into shards

HALVE the celery on the diagonal and immerse in a bowl of ice water for 15 minutes. Drain and pat dry. Cut diagonally into thin slices.

MEANWHILE, whisk together the vinegar, honey, and salt in a large bowl. Add the pears, walnuts, celery, and pepper. Toss to coat well.

DIVIDE the lettuce leaves among 4 plates. Top with one-quarter of the salad and the Parmesan.

Total time: 20 minutes ✳ Makes 4 servings

Per serving: 246 calories, 9 g protein, 26 g carbohydrates, 14 g fat, 3 g saturated fat, 420 mg sodium, 5 g fiber

If pears are out of season, substitute 1 can (15 ounces) pears in natural juices for the fresh pears.

—**Lillian**

Asian Slaw

- 2 tablespoons rice vinegar
- 1 tablespoon reduced-sodium soy sauce
- 2 teaspoons honey
- ¼ teaspoon sesame oil
- ½ small head Napa cabbage
- 1 cup snow peas, trimmed
- 1 carrot, peeled and grated
- 1 scallion, chopped

WHISK together the vinegar, soy sauce, honey, and oil in a large bowl until well blended.

THINLY shred the cabbage with a sharp knife and place in the bowl. Cut the snow peas into thin strips and add to the cabbage along with the carrot and scallion. Toss to coat well.

Total time: 15 minutes ✱ Makes 4 servings

Per serving: 40 calories, 2 g protein, 8 g carbohydrates, 0 g fat, 0 g saturated fat, 153 mg sodium, 2 g fiber

Perfect for a summer evening, the sweet and salty glaze that coats this dish is the perfect complement to the tangy bite of the crunchy Asian vegetables.

Cucumber and Radish Salad
with Sesame-Soy Dressing

3 tablespoons rice vinegar

2 tablespoons reduced-sodium soy sauce

1½ tablespoons orange juice

1 tablespoon toasted sesame oil

1 teaspoon peeled, grated fresh ginger

1 garlic clove, crushed

⅛ teaspoon hot-pepper sauce (optional)

4 small cucumbers (12 ounces), peeled and thinly sliced

8 radishes (about 1 cup), thinly sliced

½ small red onion, halved and thinly sliced

2 teaspoons toasted sesame seeds

WHISK together the vinegar, soy sauce, orange juice, oil, ginger, garlic, and hot-pepper sauce (if using) in a large bowl. Add the cucumbers, radishes, onion, and sesame seeds. Toss well and serve at room temperature or chilled.

Total time: 10 minutes ✽ Makes 4 servings

Per serving: 64 calories, 2 g protein, 6 g carbohydrates, 4 g fat, 1 g saturated fat, 284 mg sodium, 2 g fiber

Top with 1 tablespoon chopped fresh cilantro before serving.

QUICK TIP: FIBER UP

25 Amount of fiber (in grams) you should eat daily. Fiber-rich foods fill you up faster, so you eat less. Fiber also slows digestion, which stabilizes your energy levels.

Christmas Ribbon Salad

- 1 package (0.44 ounce) sugar-free instant lime gelatin
- ½ cup chopped celery
- 1 package (0.30 ounce) sugar-free instant lemon gelatin
- ¼ cup boiling water
- 1 package (8 ounces) reduced-fat cream cheese, at room temperature
- 1 cup fat-free half-and-half
- 1 can (20 ounces) crushed pineapple in its own juice, drained
- 1 package (0.44 ounce) sugar-free instant raspberry gelatin
- 1 cup chopped walnuts

PREPARE the lime gelatin according to package directions in a medium bowl. Stir in the celery. Pour into a 13" × 9" glass baking dish. Chill.

WHISK together the lemon gelatin and boiling water in a large bowl. Chill for 10 minutes, or until partially set. Beat with an electric mixer until frothy. Add the cream cheese and half-and-half and beat on low until smooth. Gently stir in the pineapple. Pour on top of the green layer. Chill for 1 hour, or until completely set.

PREPARE the raspberry gelatin according to package directions in a medium bowl. Chill for 1 hour, or until partially set. Stir in the nuts and spread over the lemon layer. Chill for 2 hours, or until completely set. Cut into 12 squares.

Total time: 4 hours 15 minutes   ✻   Makes 12 servings

Per serving: 143 calories, 5 g protein, 9 g carbohydrates, 9 g fat, 3 g saturated fat, 205 mg sodium, 1 g fiber

Change up the colors of this dish to match any holiday by using different flavors of gelatin. —**Hildegarde**

[it worked for me]

67 lbs lost!

✳ DEBRA LAMBERT

Giving birth to her daughter motivated Debra Lambert to take control of her health and start eating smart.

My Story

I was 43 years old and pregnant with my first child, but what should have been the happiest time of my life was one of the scariest. At the beginning of my pregnancy, I weighed more than 200 pounds and was quickly gaining. I developed gestational diabetes, and if I didn't get it under control, I could put my baby at risk of obesity and type 2 diabetes. I didn't want her to have to struggle with weight like I did. This was the wake-up call that I needed. I met with a dietitian and took control of my blood sugar. The gestational diabetes was gone as soon as I delivered my beautiful baby, but I was almost 280 pounds and at risk of type 2 diabetes. I knew I had to make a change if I wanted to see my daughter graduate from college.

VITAL STATS

Pounds lost: 67

Age: 46

Height: 5'4"

Weight then: 216 pounds

Weight now: 149 Pounds

By the time Madelyn was 2, I had shed the 60 pounds I gained during my pregnancy. But at 216 pounds, I was determined to slim down and get healthy once and for all. That's when I read about the Flat Belly Diet. Women lost weight adding dark chocolate and nuts to a well-balanced meal? Where do I sign up? I bought the book, and it didn't take me long to realize that fresh, healthy food was even tastier than the junk of my pre-pregnancy days. Eating four 400-calorie meals daily left me feeling satisfied. And when I needed motivation, I turned to Flatbellydiet.com; it connected me with people experiencing the same thing I was.

Almost daily, I was on the message boards, getting advice from other dieters. My first week I was com-pletely overwhelmed, but then someone on the boards said, "Take a deep breath. Just do what you can, and it will be good enough." That's exactly what I needed to hear. Week after week, the pounds kept dropping. But the best part is that I'm teaching my daughter about good nutrition. I'm still active on the site, but these days I'm the one encouraging others. The only thing better than losing the weight is knowing I'm helping others do the same.

My Top Tips

* Pick a realistic diet plan . . . I tried other diets where I ate less than 1,200 calories daily, but I couldn't keep up with them. This one was the perfect fit!

* Prepare to succeed . . . Every night I planned and assembled my meals for the following day. In the morning, I just had to grab them and go—no prep work to slow me down.

* Measure everything . . . When you're trying to lose weight, every calorie counts. Stick to correct portions or you could stall your weight loss.

* See beyond the scale . . . Relish small signs that the diet is working. Is it easier to cross your legs? Are your rings fitting better?

* Embrace mini challenges . . . I used to avoid working out, but on the diet I had much more energy. I started walking and realized exercising was easy. I just ran my first 5-K race!

247

Dinners

desserts

Orange and Poppy Seed Cake

Cake

- 2 cups whole grain pastry flour
- ½ cup poppy seeds
- ½ teaspoon baking powder
- ½ teaspoon salt
- 4 large egg whites, at room temperature
- 2 large eggs, at room temperature
- 1¼ cups sugar
- ¼ cup canola oil
- 2 tablespoons grated orange zest
- 1 teaspoon vanilla extract
- ¾ cup orange juice

Glaze

- ½ cup confectioners' sugar
- 2 tablespoons orange juice

To make the cake:

PREHEAT the oven to 350°F. Coat a 10" tube pan with a removable bottom with cooking spray. Dust with flour.

WHISK together the flour, poppy seeds, baking powder, and salt in a medium bowl. Beat the egg whites in a large bowl with an electric mixer on medium speed until soft peaks form. Beat the whole eggs and sugar in another large bowl with the same beaters on medium speed until pale yellow and fluffy. Beat in the oil, orange zest, and vanilla extract. On low speed, beat in one-third of the flour mixture and one-half of the orange juice. Repeat, beginning and ending with the flour.

STIR one-third of the egg whites gently into the batter. Fold in the remaining whites until no streaks of white remain.

POUR into the pan. Bake for 40 minutes, or until a wooden pick inserted in the center comes out clean. Run a knife around the rim of the cake to loosen it from the sides. Cool on a rack for 15 minutes. Remove from the pan and place on the rack to cool completely.

To make the glaze:

WHISK together the confectioners' sugar and orange juice until smooth in a small bowl. Drizzle over the cooled cake.

Total time: 1 hour 10 minutes ✳ Makes 12 servings

Per serving: 246 calories, 5 g protein, 41 g carbohydrates, 8 g fat, 1 g saturated fat, 146 mg sodium, 2 g fiber

Adding the glaze to this cake makes a lovely presentation, but it does add some extra sugar. Save this step for special occasions. Serve the cake unglazed for everyday events.

Apricot-Lemon Chiffon Cake

Cake

- 5 egg whites
- ½ teaspoon cream of tartar
- 1 package (18.25 ounces) white cake mix
- 3 egg yolks
- ¾ cup apricot nectar
- ½ cup canola oil
- 2 tablespoons lemon juice
- 1 teaspoon lemon zest

Glaze

- 2 cups confectioners' sugar, sifted
- 2 tablespoons lemon juice
- 1 tablespoon apricot nectar
- 1 teaspoon grated lemon zest

To make the cake:

PLACE a rack in the center of the oven. Preheat the oven to 325°F. Beat the egg whites and cream of tartar in a medium bowl with an electric mixer on high speed for 3 minutes, or until stiff peaks form. Set aside.

PLACE the cake mix, egg yolks, nectar, oil, lemon juice, and lemon zest in a large bowl. Beat with the same beaters on low speed for 1 minute. Stop and scrape down the side of the bowl with a rubber spatula. Increase the mixer speed to medium and beat for 2 minutes, or until well blended. Fold the whites into the batter until the mixture is light but well combined. Pour into an ungreased 10" tube pan, smoothing the top with the spatula.

BAKE for 45 minutes, or until the top is golden brown and springs back when lightly pressed with a fingertip. Remove the pan from the oven and immediately turn upside down over the neck of a glass bottle. Cool for 1 hour. Remove the pan from the bottle. Run a long, sharp knife around the edge of the cake and invert it onto a rack, then invert it again onto a serving platter so that it is right side up.

To make the glaze:

BEAT the sugar, lemon juice, nectar, and lemon zest in a medium bowl with an electric mixer on low speed for 1 minute. Spread the glaze on the top and sides of the cake with clean, smooth strokes. Let the glaze set for 20 minutes before serving.

Total time: 1 hour 25 minutes ✳ Makes 16 servings

Per serving: 284 calories, 3 g protein, 43 g carbohydrates, 11 g fat, 1 g saturated fat, 237 mg sodium, 0 g fiber

Look for apricot nectar in the juice section of your supermarket or the natural foods section. Often thicker than some juices, nectars should be shaken before being used.

—Cynthia J Saling, Louisville, Kentucky

Lemon-Lime Refrigerator Sheet Cake

1 (18.25 ounces) lemon cake mix

1 package (0.44 ounce) sugar-free lime gelatin

1 cup boiling water

½ cup cold water

1 package (1 ounce) fat-free, sugar-free instant lemon pudding

1¾ cup fat-free milk

1 container (8 ounces) fat-free frozen whipped topping, thawed

PREPARE the cake according to package directions for a 13" × 9" baking pan. Cool on a rack for 15 minutes. Pierce the cake with the back of a wooden spoon at 1" intervals.

STIR together the gelatin and boiling water in a small bowl for 2 minutes, or until completely dissolved. Stir in the cold water. Chill for 45 minutes, or until slightly set up. Pour over the cake. Chill for 3 hours.

WHISK together the milk and pudding mix in a large bowl for 2 minutes, or until thickened. Fold in the topping. Spread over the cake and chill for at least 2 hours.

Total time: 5 hours ✱ Makes 12 servings

Per serving: 241 calories, 4 g protein, 43 g carbohydrates, 5 g fat, 2 g saturated fat, 459 mg sodium, 0 g fiber

This colorful cake makes a wonderful summer desert! It's easy to prepare and simple to serve. —**Cynthia**

HEALTH HEARSAY

Q: "Is white flour bleached with dangerous chemicals?"

A: No. Some Web sites allege that flour is bleached with alloxan, a compound that caused diabetes in animal research, but experts tell us that's not true. Flour bleaches naturally on its own as yellow compounds called xantophylls react with oxygen in the air; this takes several weeks. To speed the whitening, processors bleach flour—turning it white from its natural straw color—with safe, FDA-regulated chemicals (some of the same ones used to sanitize veggies). Alloxan may form as a by-product, but the amount is minuscule (less than 0.03 milligrams per slice of bread) and harmless, says Julie Jones, PhD, professor emeritus of family, consumer, and nutritional sciences at St. Catherine University. Bottom line: White flour is not dangerous, but because processing strips away essential nutrients such as fiber, magnesium, and vitamin E, it is less nutritious.

Yummy Pineapple Cake

1 package (18 ounces) yellow cake mix

¾ cup liquid egg substitute or 3 large eggs

1 cup water

1 can (20 ounces) crushed pineapple in juice

1 package (8 ounces) fat-free cream cheese, at room temperature

2 cups fat-free milk

1 package (1 ounce) sugar-free instant vanilla pudding

⅛ teaspoon ground cinnamon

1 cup reduced-fat whipped topping

1 can (15½ ounces) mandarin oranges, drained (optional)

PREHEAT the oven to 325°F, or according to cake mix package directions. Coat a 13" × 9" baking dish with cooking spray.

PREPARE the cake mix according to package directions, using the egg substitute or eggs and water. Pour into the prepared baking dish. Bake according to package directions. Cool on a rack.

POKE holes all over the cake with a fork or the handle of a teaspoon. Pour the pineapple (with juice) over the cake.

BEAT the cream cheese in a large bowl with an electric mixer on medium speed until smooth. Add the milk, pudding mix, and cinnamon. Beat for 3 minutes. Pour over the pineapple. Top with the whipped topping. Decorate with the oranges (if using). Cover and chill for at least 4 hours.

Total time: 5 hours ✻ Makes 16 servings

Per serving: 248 calories, 6 g protein, 44 g carbohydrates, 6 g fat, 2 g saturated fat, 423 mg sodium, 2 g fiber

Perfect for a potluck, this cake will feed a crowd. Change it up with a variety of cake mixes, such as lemon, orange, or even coconut.

Peach Upside-Down Cake

⅔ cup sugar

2 tablespoons butter, at room temperature

2½ pounds large ripe peaches, peeled, halved, and pitted

1 cup whole grain pastry flour

1 teaspoon baking powder

½ teaspoon baking soda

½ teaspoon ground cinnamon

¼ teaspoon salt

1 tablespoon canola oil

1 large egg

1 teaspoon vanilla extract

1 teaspoon almond extract

½ cup low-fat buttermilk

PREHEAT the oven to 375°F.

COMBINE ⅓ cup of the sugar and 1 tablespoon of the butter in a 9" cast-iron skillet. Cook over medium heat for 3 to 5 minutes, or until the sugar begins to melt. Add the peaches, cut side up, in a single layer (the fruit should fit tightly). Remove from the heat.

WHISK together the flour, baking powder, baking soda, cinnamon, and salt in a medium bowl. Beat the oil and the remaining ⅓ cup sugar and 1 tablespoon butter in a large bowl with an electric mixer on medium speed until smooth. Add the egg, vanilla extract, and almond extract and beat until smooth. With the mixer on low speed, add the buttermilk and flour mixture, beating just until incorporated. Spoon evenly over the peaches in the skillet.

BAKE for 20 minutes, or until a wooden pick inserted in the center comes out clean. Cool on a rack for 5 minutes. Loosen the edges of the cake with a knife. Invert the cake onto a serving plate. If any of the peaches stick to the skillet, remove them with a knife and replace them on the cake.

Total time: 40 minutes ✳ Makes 8 servings

Per serving: 222 calories, 4 g protein, 40 g carbohydrates, 6 g fat, 2 g saturated fat, 258 mg sodium, 3 g fiber

For this delicious twist on the classic upside-down cake, apricots, plums, or nectarines work well in place of the peaches.

Orange–Olive Oil Cake with Fresh Berries

Cake

- ¾ cup whole grain pastry flour
- ¼ cup cornmeal
- 1 teaspoon baking powder
- ¼ teaspoon baking soda
- ¼ teaspoon salt
- ⅓ cup + 1 tablespoon sugar
- 3 tablespoons olive oil
- ½ cup fat-free plain yogurt
- 2 large eggs
- 2 tablespoons orange juice
- 1 tablespoon orange zest
- ¼ teaspoon ground cinnamon

Berries

- 1 cup fresh blackberries
- 1 tablespoon sugar
- 1 tablespoon orange juice
- 1 cup fresh blueberries
- 1 cup fresh raspberries

To make the cake:

PREHEAT the oven to 350°F. Coat a 9" springform pan with cooking spray.

WHISK together the flour, cornmeal, baking powder, baking soda, and salt in a small bowl. Beat ⅓ cup of the sugar and the oil in a large bowl with an electric mixer on high speed for 2 minutes. Add the yogurt, eggs, orange juice, and orange zest. Beat for 1 minute. Add the flour mixture and beat until blended. Pour the batter into the prepared pan.

STIR together the cinnamon and the remaining 1 tablespoon sugar in a small bowl. Sprinkle over the batter. Bake for 20 to 25 minutes, or until a wooden pick inserted in the center comes out clean. Cool completely in the pan on a rack.

To make the berries:

PUREE ¾ cup of the blackberries, the sugar, and the orange juice in a food processor or blender until smooth. Strain the puree through a sieve into a small bowl and discard the seeds. Cut the cake into wedges. Divide the sauce and the blueberries, raspberries, and the remaining blackberries among the slices.

Total time: 45 minutes ✳ Makes 8 servings

Per serving: 196 calories, 4 g protein, 31 g carbohydrates, 7 g fat, 1 g saturated fat, 203 mg sodium, 4 g fiber

Olive oil makes this dessert luxuriously rich and adds a healthy dash of monounsaturated fats. If fresh berries aren't available, substitute frozen.

Strawberry Shortcakes

- 2 cups whole grain pastry flour
- 4 tablespoons chilled butter, cut into small pieces
- 2 tablespoons packed light brown sugar
- 2 teaspoons baking powder
- ¼ teaspoon baking soda
- ⅔ cup + 1 tablespoon low-fat buttermilk
- 1 tablespoon + ⅓ cup granulated sugar
- 2 pints strawberries, sliced
- 3 tablespoons orange juice
- 1 cup low-fat Greek-style vanilla yogurt
- 1 teaspoon orange zest

PREHEAT the oven to 400°F. Coat a large baking sheet with cooking spray.

COMBINE the flour, butter, brown sugar, baking powder, and baking soda in a large bowl. Mix with your fingers to form crumbs. Add ⅔ cup of the buttermilk, stirring with a fork until the dough comes together. Turn the dough out onto a lightly floured surface. Gently pat or roll to ¾" thickness. Using a 3" round cutter or large glass, cut into 6 biscuits. (You may have to pat the dough scraps together to cut out all the biscuits.) Place on the prepared baking sheet. Brush with the remaining 1 tablespoon buttermilk. Sprinkle with 1 tablespoon of the granulated sugar.

BAKE for 12 minutes, or until golden. Cool on a rack for 10 minutes. Remove from the sheet and place on the rack to cool completely. Split in half crosswise.

STIR together the strawberries, orange juice, and the remaining ⅓ cup granulated sugar in a large bowl. Let stand for 10 minutes, stirring occasionally.

WHISK together the yogurt and orange zest in a medium bowl.

PLACE the bottoms of the biscuits on 6 plates. Divide the yogurt and strawberries among the biscuits. Top each with the biscuit tops.

Total time: 1 hour 30 minutes ✳ Makes 6 servings

Per serving: 367 calories, 10 g protein, 63 g carbohydrates, 10 g fat, 6 g saturated fat, 328 mg sodium, 5 g fiber

You never miss the calories and fat when low-fat vanilla yogurt replaces whipped cream in this classic summer dessert.

Heavenly Strawberry Cake

- 1 prepared angel food cake (10–14 ounces)
- 2 cups sliced strawberries
- 1 carton (8 ounces) frozen light whipped topping, thawed
- 1 can (1 pound) crushed pineapple, packed in its own juice, drained
- 3 large strawberries

SLICE the cake horizontally into 3 equal rings. Place the bottom layer on a serving plate. Spread with about one-third (about 1¼ cups) of the whipped topping. Top with half of the sliced strawberries and half of the pineapple. Repeat the layering. Top with the remaining cake ring and spread with the remaining topping. Garnish with the whole strawberries.

Total time: 15 minutes ✳ Makes 8 servings

Per serving: 203 calories, 3 g protein, 42 g carbohydrates, 4 g fat, 3 g saturated fat, 319 mg sodium, 2 g fiber

My dad used to love strawberry shortcake when my mom made it the old-fashioned way, with lots of butter, sugar, and whipping cream. I started making this healthier version, and he loves it—it's always the first dessert eaten at church socials.

—**Linda**

Pineapple-Carrot Cake

2¾ cups whole grain pastry flour

2 teaspoons baking powder

2 teaspoons baking soda

2 teaspoons ground cinnamon

1 teaspoon ground nutmeg

¼ teaspoon salt

2 large eggs

4 large egg whites

1 cup packed light brown sugar

1 cup fat-free plain or vanilla yogurt

¼ cup canola oil

2 cups grated carrots

1 cup drained canned crushed pineapple

⅔ cup currants

2 tablespoons confectioners' sugar

PREHEAT the oven to 325°F. Coat a 13" × 9" baking dish with cooking spray.

WHISK together the flour, baking powder, baking soda, cinnamon, nutmeg, and salt in a large bowl.

BEAT the eggs and egg whites in a large bowl with an electric mixer on medium speed until foamy. Add the brown sugar. Beat for 3 minutes. Add the yogurt and oil. Beat until creamy. Beat in the flour mixture on low speed. Stir in the carrots, pineapple, and currants.

POUR into the baking dish. Bake for 40 minutes, or until a wooden pick inserted in the center comes out clean. Cool completely on a rack. Sprinkle with the confectioners' sugar just before serving.

Total time: 1 hour   ✴   Makes 16 servings

Per serving: 195 calories, 5 g protein, 36 g carbohydrates, 4 g fat, 0 g saturated fat, 288 mg sodium, 3 g fiber

GOTTA TRY IT! THE PERFECT PLATE

What works better for weight loss than upping your exercise, consuming less fat, and increasing the amount of fruits and vegetables you eat? Plating proper portions, according to a study in *Obesity Research*. Slimware, a line of dishes with portion-control guidelines built discreetly into the design, can help eliminate the guesswork. Simply pile your veggies over the largest sunflower and place your meat on the smallest. The medium one is just right for pasta, corn, or other starches. ($36.50 for four; www.slimware.com)

Apple Delight

- 1 **package (18.25 ounces) yellow cake mix**
- ½ **cup trans-free margarine**
- 1 **teaspoon vanilla extract**
- 1 **can (21 ounces) apple pie filling**

STIR together the cake mix, margarine, and vanilla extract in a medium bowl until blended. Mixture will be crumbly. Place the pie filling in a 3- to 4-quart slow cooker. Top with the cake mixture.

COVER and cook on low for 3 hours, or until the top turns light golden. Cool slightly and scoop the warm cake onto a plate.

Total time: 3 hours 15 minutes ✳ Makes 12 servings

Per serving: 277 calories, 1 g protein, 48 g carbohydrates, 10 g fat, 3 g saturated fat, 374 mg sodium, 1 g fiber

Here's a great way to bake dessert while you're off taking care of other things. For variety, substitute blueberry or cherry pie filling.
—**Mary Ellen**

Rich Chocolate Layer Cake

Cake

- 1½ cups whole grain pastry flour
- ½ cup unsweetened cocoa powder
- 1 tablespoon instant espresso powder
- 1 teaspoon baking soda
- 8 tablespoons butter, softened
- 1 cup sugar
- 1 large egg
- 1 teaspoon vanilla extract
- ½ cup low-fat buttermilk
- ½ cup hot water

Frosting

- 1½ cups sugar
- ¼ cup water
- 3 large egg whites, at room temperature
- 1 teaspoon cream of tartar
- 1 teaspoon vanilla extract
- ¼ cup unsweetened cocoa powder

To make the cake:

PREHEAT the oven to 350°F. Coat two 8" round cake pans with cooking spray.

WHISK together the flour, cocoa powder, espresso powder, and baking soda in a medium bowl. Beat the butter and sugar in a large bowl with an electric mixer on medium speed for 3 minutes, or until creamy. Add the egg and vanilla extract. Beat on low speed until creamy. With the mixer on low speed, beat in one-third of the flour mixture and the buttermilk. Beat in half of the remaining flour mixture and the hot water. Beat in the remaining flour mixture. Pour into the prepared pans.

BAKE for 25 minutes, or until a wooden pick inserted in the center comes out clean. Cool on a rack for 10 minutes. Remove from the pans and place on a rack to cool completely.

To make the frosting:

COMBINE the sugar, water, egg whites, and cream of tartar in the top of a double boiler. Place over a saucepan of simmering water. Beat for 5 minutes with clean beaters and the mixer on high speed until soft peaks form. Add the vanilla extract and beat for 4 minutes, or until the mixture is thick and glossy and registers 160°F on an instant-read thermometer. Remove from the heat.

SIFT the cocoa powder over the frosting and gently fold in. Allow to cool completely, about 20 minutes. Place 1 cooled cake layer on a serving plate. Evenly spread the top with frosting. Top with the remaining cake layer and spread the top with frosting. Spread the remaining frosting over the sides.

Makes 16 servings

Per serving: 227 calories, 3 g protein, 41 g carbohydrates, 7 g fat, 4 g saturated fat, 144 mg sodium, 2 g fiber

A meringue frosting lightens up this decadent dessert. Enjoy with espresso or hot chai tea.

Peanut Butter Bundt Cake

Cake

- 1½ cups whole grain pastry flour
- 1 cup cake flour
- 2 teaspoons baking powder
- ½ teaspoon baking soda
- ½ teaspoon salt
- ½ cup reduced-fat peanut butter
- ½ cup butter, at room temperature
- 1 cup sugar
- 2 egg whites
- 1 tablespoon vanilla extract
- ⅓ cup mini chocolate chips
- 1½ cups low-fat buttermilk

Glaze

- 1 tablespoon unsweetened cocoa powder
- 2 tablespoons peanut butter
- 2 tablespoons water
- ½ teaspoon vanilla extract
- ½ cup confectioners' sugar
- Pinch of salt

To make the cake:

PREHEAT the oven to 350°F. Coat a 10" Bundt pan with cooking spray.

WHISK together the pastry flour, cake flour, baking powder, baking soda, and salt in a medium bowl. Beat together the peanut butter and butter in another medium bowl with an electric mixer at medium speed for 1 minute, or until creamy. Add the sugar, egg whites, and vanilla extract and beat for 2 minutes, or until light and fluffy. Beat in the chocolate chips on low speed, just until combined. With the mixer set on the lowest speed, alternately add the flour mixture and buttermilk in 3 additions. Spread into the pan.

BAKE for 55 minutes, or until a wooden pick inserted in the center comes out clean and the cake begins to pull away from the sides of the pan. Cool in the pan on a rack for 10 minutes. Loosen the sides with a spatula and invert onto a serving plate.

To make the glaze:

STIR together the cocoa powder, peanut butter, water, and vanilla extract in a small bowl until blended. Stir in the confectioners' sugar and salt until smooth. Slip strips of waxed paper under the edges of the cake. Drizzle the glaze over the cake using a spoon. Set aside until the glaze is firm. Remove the waxed paper strips.

Total time: 1 hour 20 minutes ✱ Makes 16 servings

Per serving: 267 calories, 6 g protein, 37 g carbohydrates, 11 g fat, 5 g saturated fat, 315 mg sodium, 2 g fiber

It's difficult to believe that peanut butter could be a diet food, but its creamy rich texture helps make this cake taste like a real indulgence—and it reduces the amount of butter typically called for in similar recipes.

Vanilla Cheesecake with Berry Sauce

3 large egg whites

1¼ cups vanilla wafer cookie crumbs

1 tablespoon butter, melted

3 tablespoons + 1¼ cups sugar

1½ pounds 1% cottage cheese

1 package (8 ounces) reduced-fat cream cheese, at room temperature

1 package (8 ounces) fat-free cream cheese, at room temperature

¼ cup whole grain pastry flour

1 large egg

1 tablespoon vanilla extract

1 pint mixed berries, such as blackberries, raspberries, and blueberries

¼ cup strawberry all-fruit syrup

PREHEAT the oven to 325°F. Coat a 9" springform pan with cooking spray.

PLACE 1 egg white in a medium bowl. Beat lightly with a fork. Add the cookie crumbs, butter, and 3 tablespoons of the sugar. Toss until the crumbs cling together. Press into the bottom and 2" up the sides of the prepared pan.

COMBINE the cottage cheese and cream cheese in a food processor. Process until smooth. Add the flour and the remaining 1¼ cups sugar. Process until the sugar is dissolved. Add the egg, vanilla extract, and the remaining 2 egg whites. Process just until blended. Pour over the prepared crust. Bake for 1 hour 15 minutes. Turn off the oven and leave the cheesecake in the oven for 30 minutes.

COOL on a rack. Cover and refrigerate for at least 6 hours.

COMBINE the berries and syrup in a medium bowl. Stir, crushing a few of the berries with the back of a wooden spoon. Let stand for 5 minutes, or until a light syrup forms. Serve over slices of the cheesecake.

Total time: 8 hours   ✳   Makes 12 servings

Per serving: 281 calories, 14 g protein, 41 g carbohydrates, 7 g fat, 4 g saturated fat, 443 mg sodium, 2 g fiber

QUICK TIP: A SERIOUSLY EASY WAY TO CUT CALORIES

119 The increase in daily calorie burn among adults who cut their TV viewing time in half—from 4½ hours a day—according to a recent *JAMA* study

Cherry Cheesecake

- 1 package (8 ounces) reduced-fat cream cheese, at room temperature
- 1 package (8 ounces) fat-free cream cheese, at room temperature
- 1 can (14 ounces) fat-free sweetened condensed milk
- 1 package (1.34 ounces) fat-free, sugar-free instant vanilla pudding
- 1 container (6 ounces) low-fat lemon yogurt
- 1 prepared reduced-fat graham cracker crust (9" diameter)
- 1 can (20 ounces) light cherry pie filling

BEAT the cream cheeses in a large bowl with an electric mixer on medium speed until smooth. Beat in the milk, pudding mix, and yogurt on low just until blended. Pour into the crust and chill for at least 1 hour. Top with the pie filling.

Total time: 2 hours ✳ Makes 10 servings

Per serving: 301 calories, 10 g protein, 49 g carbohydrates, 6 g fat, 3 g saturated fat, 571 mg sodium, 1 g fiber

This is my answer to cheesecake cravings without all the sugar and fat I shouldn't have. It's very easy to make and tastes rich and wonderful.
—**Marilyn**

—Victoria Ross, Ione, California

Lemon Cheesecake

- 7 graham cracker rectangles
- 2 tablespoons + 1¼ cups sugar
- 3 tablespoons trans-free margarine, melted
- 1 package (8 ounces) reduced-fat cream cheese, at room temperature
- 1 package (8 ounces) fat-free cream cheese, at room temperature
- 3 eggs, at room temperature
- 1 lemon, juiced
- 1 teaspoon vanilla extract

PREHEAT the oven to 350°F.

PLACE the graham crackers in a resealable plastic bag and crush with a rolling pin until finely crushed. Place in a 9" glass pie plate and stir in 2 tablespoons of the sugar and the margarine. Press onto the bottom and sides of the plate. Set aside.

BEAT the cream cheeses in a large bowl with an electric mixer on medium until smooth. Add the eggs, one at a time, mixing well after each addition. Stir in the remaining 1¼ cups sugar, the lemon juice, and vanilla extract. Pour into the shell. Bake for 20 minutes. Cover with foil and bake for 15 minutes.

REMOVE to a rack and let stand for 1 hour, or until cooled. Cover and chill for at least 8 hours.

Total time: 9 hours ✳ Makes 8 servings

Per serving: 230 calories, 6 g protein, 22 g carbohydrates, 11 g fat, 5 g saturated fat, 418 mg sodium, 0 g fiber

Prepare this cheesecake for holidays or potlucks topping with sliced berries for a nice presentation.

—Victoria

QUICK TIP: SORBET, HEALTH FRIEND OR FOE?

THE CLAIM

Fruity flavors and low fat content give the impression that sorbet is a health food.

THE TRUTH

The store-bought version is often loaded with sweeteners, including high fructose corn syrup. And many contain "natural flavor," chemically processed from fruits and meats, which many scientists argue has not been studied adequately for safety.

VERDICT

Make a homemade version in minutes that's full of fiber and antioxidants. Just grab a food processor and combine 1 pound of frozen blackberries, ½ cup of fat-free or low-fat plain yogurt, 2 tablespoons of sugar, and several tablespoons of water. Process until pureed. Enjoy or freeze for later. Makes 4 servings.

Creamy Chocolate Cheesecake

18 chocolate graham crackers, crushed

2 tablespoons butter, melted

3 packages (8 ounces each) reduced-fat cream cheese, at room temperature

1¼ cups sugar

2 large egg whites

1 large egg

¾ cup unsweetened cocoa powder

1 tablespoon vanilla extract

½ teaspoon almond extract

¼ teaspoon salt

PREHEAT the oven to 325°F. Coat a 9" springform pan with cooking spray.

STIR together the graham cracker crumbs and butter in a small bowl. Press onto the bottom and 2" up the sides of the pan. Bake for 10 minutes. Cool on a rack.

BEAT the cream cheese and sugar in a large bowl with an electric mixer on medium speed until smooth. Add the egg whites, egg, cocoa powder, vanilla extract, almond extract, and salt. Beat for 5 minutes, or until smooth. Pour into the crust. Bake for 1 hour 15 minutes.

TURN off the oven and leave the cheesecake in the oven for 1 hour. Cool on a rack. Cover and refrigerate for at least 2 hours.

Total time: 4 hours 30 minutes　✱　Makes 16 servings

Per serving: 257 calories, 7 g protein, 33 g carbohydrates, 11 g fat, 6 g saturated fat, 280 mg sodium, 2 g fiber

A simple way to crush graham crackers is to place them in a resealable plastic bag, seal the bag, and use a rolling pin to break them into coarse crumbs.

Key Lime Cheesecake Pie

1 package (0.44 ounce) fat-free, sugar-free lime gelatin

½ cup boiling water

2 limes

1 package (8 ounces) fat-free cream cheese, at room temperature

1 container (6 ounces) fat-free Key lime yogurt

1 container (8 ounces) fat-free frozen whipped topping, thawed

1 reduced-fat graham cracker crust (9" diameter)

WHISK together the gelatin and boiling water in a medium bowl for 2 minutes, or until dissolved. Place in the freezer for 15 minutes, or until almost set.

MEANWHILE, zest 1 lime and place the zest in a large bowl. Squeeze the juice of the lime and add to the bowl. Add the cream cheese and yogurt and beat with an electric mixer on medium speed until smooth. Whisk in the gelatin and ¾ of the whipped topping until blended.

POUR into the crust. Chill for at least 2 hours. Place 8 dollops of the remaining topping around the cake. Cut the remaining lime into 8 slices. Place the lime slices in the topping for garnish.

Total time: 2 hours 15 minutes ✳ Makes 8 servings

Per serving: 157 calories, 2 g protein, 26 g carbohydrates, 3 g fat, 0 g saturated fat, 157 mg sodium, 0 g fiber

This is one of our favorite quick desserts, and we like to substitute other flavors for lime—especially strawberry. Delish!

—Sue

METABOLISM BOOSTER: CITRUS

Researchers believe the flavonoid naringenin, abundant in citrus fruits such as oranges and grapefruit, might promote weight loss, according to a new animal study from the University of Western Ontario. Supplementing a high-fat diet with naringenin lowered elevated blood sugar and high cholesterol, thwarted the onset of insulin resistance, and prevented obesity. The researchers also found that adding large amounts of this flavonoid to the diet caused the liver to burn excess fat rather than store it.

Banana Pudding Pie

- **3** cups fat-free milk
- **2** packages (0.44 ounce each) sugar-free instant banana cream pudding
- **1** container (8 ounces) frozen whipped topping, thawed
- **1** prepared chocolate cookie or graham cracker crumb crust (9" diameter)

WHISK together the milk and pudding mix in a medium bowl for 2 minutes, or until thickened. Stir in the whipped topping. Spread into the crust. Chill for at least 4 hours before serving.

Total time: 4 hours 10 minutes ✳ Makes 8 servings

Per serving: 235 calories, 4 g protein, 31 g carbohydrates, 9 g fat, 6 g saturated fat, 469 mg sodium, 1 g fiber

Impress your family with this fantastic dessert that will have them thinking you've been in the kitchen for hours. Although the chill time is 4 hours, this classic pie comes together in just 10 minutes.

—**Sheri**

QUICK TIP: CHEW MORE, EAT LESS

New science proves an old wives' tale. People who chewed almonds 25 to 40 times absorbed more healthy unsaturated fat and felt more satisfied than when they finished in 10 chews, finds a study in the *American Journal of Clinical Nutrition*. Extra chewing breaks down fiber and sturdy cells, releasing nutrients that would otherwise pass through the digestive tract, explains researcher Richard Mattes, MPH, PhD, RD. Plus, steady chewers felt fuller, which may help promote weight loss.

Chocolate Cream Pie

- 2 cups low-fat milk
- 1 package (1.5 ounces) sugar-free chocolate pudding
- 1 package (8 ounces) reduced-fat cream cheese, at room temperature
- 1 container (8 ounces) sugar-free frozen whipped topping, thawed
- 1 prepared chocolate crumb pie crust (9" diameter)

WHISK together the milk and pudding mix for 2 minutes, or until thickened. Stir in the cream cheese until smooth. Fold in the whipped topping.

POUR into the crust. Chill for at least 4 hours before serving.

Total time: 4 hours 10 minutes ✳ Makes 8 servings

Per serving: 232 calories, 5 g protein, 9 g carbohydrates, 10 g fat, 4 g saturated fat, 295 mg sodium, 1 g fiber

Adding cream cheese to traditional chocolate cream pie cuts the sweetness while adding richness—delicious.

—**Ashley**

QUICK TIP: THE FRUIT SWAP FOR HEALTHY SMILES

Like raisins in your cereal? Add your own. In a recent University of Illinois at Chicago study, participants who ate bran cereal topped with fresh raisins developed significantly less dental plaque acidity, a risk factor for tooth decay, than those who ate store-bought raisin bran. When sugar is added to the in-cereal fruit, it may cause bacteria to stick to teeth. Add fresh raisins to breakfast grains to save your smile—and calories!

Strawberry Yogurt Pie

1 package (0.44 ounce) sugar-free instant strawberry gelatin

¼ cup boiling water

2 containers (6 ounces each) strawberry yogurt

1 container (8 ounces) fat-free frozen whipped topping, thawed

1 prepared reduced-fat graham cracker crust (9" diameter)

1 cup strawberries, sliced

WHISK together the gelatin and boiling water for 2 minutes, or until dissolved. Whisk in the yogurt until smooth. Whisk in the gelatin and topping until blended.

POUR into the crust. Chill for at least 2 hours. Top with the sliced strawberries.

Total time: 2 hours 15 minutes ✻ Makes 6 servings

Per serving: 256 calories, 5 g protein, 44 g carbohydrates, 5 g fat, 1 g saturated fat, 218 mg sodium, 1 g fiber

You can easily change up this recipe by substituting different flavored gelatin and yogurt. Go for peach, black cherry, or raspberry along with the same flavor yogurt or vanilla for a creamier flavor. **—Marlene**

Four-Berry Pie

2 cups whole grain pastry flour

½ teaspoon salt

4 tablespoons chilled butter, cut into small pieces

¼ cup canola oil

6 tablespoons fat-free sour cream

1½ tablespoons ice water

¼ teaspoon almond extract

2 cups halved strawberries

2 cups raspberries

1 cup blackberries

1 cup blueberries

3 tablespoons lemon juice

1 cup sugar (depending on sweetness of fruit, add from ¾ to 1 cup)

3 tablespoons cornstarch

3 tablespoons instant tapioca

PLACE the flour and salt in a food processor. Pulse until blended. Add the butter and oil. Pulse until the mixture resembles coarse crumbs. Add the sour cream, 1 tablespoon of the water, and almond extract. Pulse just until the dough forms large clumps. (If the dough seems too dry, add a few more drops of ice water.) Form into 2 equal balls and flatten each into a disk. Cover and refrigerate for at least 15 minutes and up to 1 day.

PREHEAT the oven to 400°F. Coat a 9" pie plate with cooking spray. Line a baking sheet with foil. On a well-floured surface, roll out each piece of dough into a 10" circle. Fit 1 circle into the pie plate, leaving the overhang. Slide the remaining circle onto a flat plate. Cover the dough and refrigerate until needed.

GENTLY toss together the strawberries, raspberries, blackberries, blueberries, and lemon juice in a large bowl. Stir together the sugar, cornstarch, and tapioca in a small bowl. Sprinkle over the fruit, tossing well. Let stand at room temperature for 15 minutes.

SPOON the berry mixture into the pie plate. Cut the remaining dough into ¾"-wide strips. Place half of the strips over the filling, spacing them evenly. Place the remaining strips at an opposing angle to the first strips to form a lattice pattern. Trim the ends of the lattice strips and the bottom crust to a ½" overhang. Fold the bottom crust over the lattice ends and flute. Place the pie on the prepared baking sheet and bake for 45 minutes, or until the crust is golden brown and the juices bubble. Cool on a rack.

Total time: 1 hour 30 minutes ✳ Makes 8 servings

Per serving: 353 calories, 5 g protein, 56 g carbohydrates, 14 g fat, 4 g saturated fat, 156 mg sodium, 7 g fiber

A lovely summer pie, this delicious dessert uses a total of 4 cups of berries. If you can't get all 4 types, substitute more of another berry to equal 4 cups.

Blueberry-Ginger Pie

1 cup gingersnap cookies (about 7 ounces)

1½ tablespoons packed brown sugar

2 tablespoons butter, melted

6 cups fresh or frozen and thawed blueberries

4 tablespoons cornstarch

¼ cup water

½ cup granulated sugar

PREHEAT the oven to 325°F. Place the gingersnaps in a food processor and process until the crumbs are fine. Add the brown sugar and butter and pulse until the mixture is just combined. Press into a 9" pie plate and bake for 8 to 10 minutes, or until lightly browned. Place on a rack to cool completely.

PLACE the blueberries, cornstarch, and water in a medium saucepan. Bring to a simmer over medium heat. Cook, stirring occasionally, for 5 minutes, or until slightly thickened. Add the granulated sugar and cook on low for 10 to 12 minutes, or until the sugar is dissolved. Remove from the heat and cool slightly. Pour the filling into the prepared crust. Cool for at least 1 hour before serving.

Total time: 1 hour 30 minutes ✳ Makes 8 servings

Per serving: 254 calories, 2 g protein, 51 g carbohydrates, 6 g fat, 2 g saturated fat, 185 mg sodium, 3 g fiber

One of the sweetest things about berries is that they have large amounts of fiber. When shopping for fresh blueberries, look for plump, firm berries with an indigo-blue color and a silvery frost. Rinse fresh berries just before you're ready to use them.

Sugar-Free Pumpkin Pie

- 1 package (0.25 ounce) unflavored gelatin
- 2 tablespoons cornstarch
- 1¼ teaspoons ground cinnamon
- ½ teaspoon ground nutmeg
- ½ teaspoon ground ginger
- ¼ teaspoon ground cloves
- ¼ teaspoon salt
- 1 can (15 ounces) 100% pure pumpkin puree
- 1 can (12 ounces) light evaporated milk
- 2 eggs, beaten
- ⅓ cup Splenda or granular sugar substitute
- 1 prepared pie crust (9" diameter), baked

COMBINE the gelatin, cornstarch, cinnamon, nutmeg, ginger, cloves, and salt in a large saucepan. Stir in the pumpkin and evaporated milk. Let stand for 5 minutes to soften the gelatin.

COOK over medium heat, stirring, for 4 minutes, or until the mixture bubbles. Continue cooking for 2 minutes, stirring constantly. Remove from the heat.

PLACE the eggs in a medium bowl and beat well. Gradually stir about 1 cup of the cooked mixture into the beaten eggs. Slowly stir back into the pumpkin mixture in a saucepan and cook over low heat for 2 minutes. Do not boil. Remove from the heat and stir in the Splenda.

POUR the mixture into the pie crust. Cover and chill for 6 hours or overnight.

Total time: 6 hours 20 minutes ✳ Makes 8 servings

Per serving: 167 calories, 6 g protein, 20 g carbohydrates, 7 g fat, 3 g saturated fat, 244 mg sodium, 2 g fiber

You don't have to wait for Thanksgiving to prepare this delicious pie—bursting with healthful antioxidants, it's a welcome addition to any meal.

—**Marshall**

QUICK TIP: 1-SECOND CONFIDENCE TRICK

For an instant mood lift, sit or stand up straighter. When Ohio State University researchers asked study participants to rate their skills related to job opportunities, they found that those who completed the task with proper posture were more secure in their abilities than those who were slumped over. "People feel confident when they're sitting upright, and they can attribute that confidence to their present thoughts," says study author and psychologist Richard E. Petty, PhD.

Crustless Pumpkin Pie

2 **eggs**

Pinch of salt

1 **can (15 ounces) 100% pure pumpkin puree**

1½ **cups low-fat vanilla almond milk**

¼ **cup sugar**

½ **teaspoon chopped fresh or crystallized ginger**

2 **teaspoons ground cinnamon**

1 **teaspoon pumpkin pie spice**

2 **teaspoons vanilla extract**

PREHEAT the oven to 350°F. Coat a 9" glass pie plate with cooking spray.

WHISK together the eggs and salt in a large bowl until fluffy. Add the pumpkin, milk, sugar, ginger, cinnamon, pumpkin pie spice, and vanilla extract. Whisk until well blended. Pour into the pie plate.

BAKE for 45 to 50 minutes, or until a knife inserted in the center comes out clean. Let cool for 1 hour.

Total time: 2 hours ❄ Makes 6 servings

Per serving: 111 calories, 3 g protein, 20 g carbohydrates, 3 g fat, 1 g saturated fat, 89 mg sodium, 3 g fiber

I look forward to a little me time every evening for about an hour—to relax, read, or watch TV and pamper myself a bit. This dessert is an indulgence I look forward to and can hardly wait to dig in.

—**Lynette**

Apple-Walnut Pie

- 1 package (1 pound) refrigerated pie crusts, softened as directed on package
- 8 medium apples, peeled and sliced
- ¼ cup Splenda or granular sugar substitute
- ½ cup walnuts or pecans, chopped
- 1 tablespoon all-purpose flour
- 1 teaspoon ground cinnamon
- ½ teaspoon ground nutmeg
  Pinch of salt
- 1 teaspoon melted butter

PREHEAT the oven to 450°F. Line a 9" pie plate with one of the crusts according to package directions.

GENTLY toss together the apples, Splenda or sugar substitute, nuts, flour, cinnamon, nutmeg, and salt in a large bowl.

POUR into the pie crust. Cover with the remaining crust and crimp to seal. Brush the top crust with the butter. Bake for 10 minutes. Reduce the temperature to 350°F and bake for 55 to 60 minutes, or until the crust is golden brown and the fruit is bubbling.

Total time: 1 hour 30 minutes ✳ Makes 10 servings

Per serving: 316 calories, 3 g protein, 43 g carbohydrates, 16 g fat, 5 g saturated fat, 179 mg sodium, 4 g fiber

281

Desserts

Once I get home from work, I don't have a lot of time to cook. My recipes have to be simple, healthy, and taste good. This can go in the oven before I make dinner and it's ready for dessert. —**Vicky**

NUTRITION NEWS TO USE

A new case for an apple a day: Recent research shows that this supermarket staple packs a powerful disease-fighting punch. Its pectin and polyphenols may help prevent colon cancer, suggests a study published in *Nutrition*. And Cornell University scientists discovered that feeding mice the equivalent of 1 apple daily reduced breast cancer tumor growth by 24 percent. Plus, apple-eating adults have a 27 percent lower risk of metabolic syndrome, finds research presented at Experimental Biology.

Rustic Plum-Walnut Tart

Crust

- 1 cup whole grain pastry flour
- ¼ teaspoon salt
- ¼ teaspoon ground cinnamon
- 2 tablespoons canola oil
- 4 tablespoons ice water

Filling

- ¼ cup Grape-Nuts or low-fat granola
- 2 tablespoons whole grain pastry flour
- 2 tablespoons chopped toasted walnuts
- ⅓ cup + 1 teaspoon sugar
- 6 plums, pitted and quartered
- 1 tablespoon fat-free milk
- 2 tablespoons red currant jelly

To make the crust:

PREHEAT the oven to 400°F. Line a baking sheet with foil and coat with cooking spray.

COMBINE the flour, salt, and cinnamon in a medium bowl. Stir the oil slowly into the flour mixture with a fork until coarse crumbs form. Stir in enough ice water to form a slightly sticky dough. Form into a ball and flatten into a disk. Cover and refrigerate for 15 minutes.

PLACE the dough between 2 pieces of waxed paper and roll into a 12" circle. Remove the top piece of paper and invert the dough onto the baking sheet. Peel off the top piece of paper.

To make the filling:

PULSE the cereal, flour, walnuts, and ⅓ cup of the sugar in a food processor until finely ground. Spread over the dough, leaving a 1½" border around the edge. Arrange the plums in concentric circles over the nut mixture. Fold the pastry border over the outside edge of the plums. Brush the milk over the dough and sprinkle with the remaining 1 teaspoon sugar.

BAKE for 30 to 40 minutes, or until the crust is golden and the juices are bubbling. With a long metal spatula, loosen the pastry bottom. Slide the tart onto a serving platter and let cool.

MELT the jelly in a small saucepan over low heat. Brush over the plums just before serving.

Total time: 1 hour 5 minutes ✳ Makes 8 servings

Per serving: 186 calories, 3 g protein, 34 g carbohydrates, 5 g fat, 0 g saturated fat, 96 mg sodium, 3 g fiber

This free-form tart makes a simple dessert that's casual enough for every day yet delicious enough for guests.

Chocolate-Walnut-Cherry Tart

1 sheet frozen puff pastry, thawed

1 egg

1 jar (12 ounces) hot fudge sauce

1 bag (2 ounces) chopped walnuts, finely chopped in a food processor

½ cup cherry preserves

1 tablespoon sugar

PREHEAT the oven to 375°F. Fit the puff pastry into a 9" pie pan. The edges will overlap. Set aside.

BEAT the egg with a fork in a medium bowl. Stir in the fudge sauce and beat until smooth. Stir in the walnuts.

POUR into the prepared crust. Dollop the preserves over the filling, swirling lightly. Fold the crust points over the filling (it will not be completely covered). Sprinkle the sugar over the crust. Bake for 25 minutes, or until the pastry is browned and puffed. Cool on a rack for 2 hours, or until just warm.

Total time: 2 hours 35 minutes ✳ Makes 12 servings

Per serving: 188 calories, 3 g protein, 29 g carbohydrates, 7 g fat, 2 g saturated fat, 121 mg sodium, 1 g fiber

Serve this rich confection within a few hours of baking so the flaky crust remains crispy. Don't worry about storing leftovers; there won't be any.

French Mixed-Fruit Galette

1 refrigerated pie crust
(9" diameter)

1 jar (12 ounces) peach
preserves

3 tablespoons cornstarch

1 bag (1 pound) frozen mixed
berries, thawed

PREHEAT the oven to 375°F. Coat a 9" cake or pie pan with cooking spray. Fit the crust into the pan, allowing the excess crust to flop over the sides.

WHISK together the preserves and cornstarch in a medium bowl until smooth. Stir in the berries until well blended. Pour into the crust. Fold the excess crust toward the center. (There will be an uncovered center portion of filling.) Bake for 1 hour, or until the filling bubbles in the center. Cool in the pan on a rack.

Total time: 1 hour 5 minutes ✳ Makes 8 servings

Per serving: 266 calories, 1 g protein, 50 g carbohydrates, 7 g fat, 3 g saturated fat, 100 mg sodium, 2 g fiber

This rustic tart is the kind that home cooks prepare in France. It requires no top crust, so it comes together very quickly. If mixed berries aren't available, replace them with halved frozen strawberries or frozen raspberries.

Pistachio Cream Tarts

6 **frozen puff pastry shells**

1 **box (3 ounces) instant pistachio pudding**

1 **cup half-and-half**

½ **cup shelled unsalted pistachio nuts, coarsely chopped**

2 **tablespoons confectioners' sugar (optional)**

PREHEAT the oven to 400°F. Place the shells on a baking sheet. Bake for 15 minutes, or until browned and puffed. Cool on a rack for at least 1 hour.

MEASURE ¼ cup of the pudding mix into a bowl. (Reserve the remainder for another recipe.) Add the half-and-half. Whisk until smooth. Set aside 2 tablespoons of the nuts. Stir the remaining nuts into the pudding. Cover with plastic wrap and chill.

REMOVE the tops from the pastry shells. Set aside. Place 1 shell bottom on a dessert plate. Divide the pudding mixture among the shells. Sprinkle the reserved nuts over the pudding and onto the plates. Place the reserved tops askew over the pudding. Dust the shells and plates with the sugar, if desired.

Total time: 1 hour 15 minutes ✳ Makes 6 servings

Per serving: 249 calories, 7 g protein, 39 g carbohydrates, 27 g fat, 8 g saturated fat, 338 mg sodium, 2 g fiber

Pale green and pretty, these individual desserts are just the thing for a tea or luncheon. The cooled shells can be stored in an airtight metal tin for up to 12 hours before serving.

Plum-Blueberry Cobbler

8 plums, quartered

1 pint fresh or frozen
   blueberries

½ cup + 4 teaspoons sugar

2 tablespoons + 1 cup
   unbleached flour

¾ teaspoon baking powder

⅛ teaspoon salt

½ cup buttermilk

1 egg white

1½ tablespoons vegetable oil

PREHEAT the oven to 375°F. Coat an 8" × 8" baking dish with nonstick spray.

COMBINE the plums, blueberries, ½ cup of the sugar, and 2 tablespoons of the flour in a large bowl. Pour into the baking dish.

WHISK together the baking powder, salt, 3 teaspoons of the remaining sugar, and the remaining 1 cup flour in a medium bowl. Stir in the buttermilk, egg white, and oil until well blended. Drop the batter in tablespoonfuls on top of the fruit. Sprinkle the remaining 1 teaspoon sugar over the batter.

BAKE for 35 to 40 minutes, or until golden and bubbling. Remove to a rack to cool. Serve warm or at room temperature.

Total time: 55 minutes ✳ Makes 8 servings

Per serving: 204 calories, 4 g protein, 42 g carbohydrates, 3 g fat, 0 g saturated fat, 75 mg sodium, 2 g fiber

You can change up this delicious recipe with any fruit combination you desire—try peaches and raspberries, apricots and blackberries, or pears and dried cranberries.

Pear and Cranberry Crisp

1 lemon

8 ripe pears, cored and cut into ½" chunks

1 cup dried cranberries

⅔ cup pear nectar or apple juice

⅓ cup granulated sugar

3 tablespoons + ¼ cup whole grain pastry flour

⅔ cup old-fashioned rolled oats

¼ cup packed light brown sugar

2 tablespoons butter, melted

1 teaspoon ground cinnamon

PREHEAT the oven to 375°F. Coat a 1½-quart baking dish with cooking spray.

GRATE 1 teaspoon of zest from the lemon into a large bowl. Halve the lemon and squeeze the juice into the bowl. Gently stir in the pears, cranberries, pear nectar or apple juice, granulated sugar, and 3 tablespoons of the flour until well blended. Place in the baking dish.

STIR together the oats, brown sugar, butter, cinnamon, and the remaining ¼ cup flour in a medium bowl. Sprinkle over the pear mixture. Bake for 40 to 50 minutes, or until the filling is bubbling and the top is browned. Cool on a rack for at least 10 minutes before serving.

Total time: 1 hour 15 minutes ✳ Makes 4 servings

Per serving: 293 calories, 3 g protein, 68 g carbohydrates, 4 g fat, 2 g saturated fat, 25 mg sodium, 8 g fiber

So simple yet so delicious. A fruit crisp is a classic comfort food—warm fruit bathed in sauce and topped with a sweet crumb topping that becomes crisp when baked.

Strawberry-Rhubarb Crisp

2 pints strawberries, hulled and quartered lengthwise

2 cups fresh or frozen and thawed rhubarb (cut into ½" pieces)

2 tablespoons quick-cooking tapioca

¼ teaspoon ground ginger

¾ cup sugar

1 teaspoon ground cinnamon

⅓ cup whole grain pastry flour

Pinch of salt

2 tablespoons butter

½ cup old-fashioned rolled oats

1½ tablespoons honey

COMBINE the strawberries, rhubarb, tapioca, ginger, ½ cup of the sugar, and ¼ teaspoon of the cinnamon in a 2-quart baking dish. Let stand for 20 minutes.

PREHEAT the oven to 400°F.

STIR together the flour, salt, and the remaining ¼ cup sugar and ¾ teaspoon cinnamon in a medium bowl. Cut in the butter into the mixture until fine crumbs form. Stir in the oats and honey until the mixture is crumbly. Sprinkle over the fruit.

BAKE for 35 to 40 minutes, or until the fruit is bubbling and the topping is golden brown. Serve warm or at room temperature.

Total time: 1 hour 20 minutes ✱ Makes 6 servings

Per serving: 239 calories, 3 g protein, 49 g carbohydrates, 5 g fat, 2 g saturated fat, 54 mg sodium, 4 g fiber

Rhubarb is an excellent source of fiber. When shopping, pick the redder stalks, which are less sour.

—Nina Zlotnik, LaSalle, Ontario

Fruit 'n' Dip

1 container (8 ounces) light frozen whipped topping, thawed

2 containers (8 ounces each) fat-free fruit-flavored yogurts, such as strawberry and blueberry

½ cup raspberry fruit spread

1 cantaloupe, cut into cubes

1 pound strawberries

2 kiwifruit, peeled and cut into slices

STIR together the whipped topping, yogurts, and fruit spread in a large bowl. Place the cantaloupe, strawberries, and kiwifruit on a plate and serve with the dip.

Total time: 20 minutes ❋ Makes 8 servings

Per serving: 191 calories, 4 g protein, 38 g carbohydrates, 3 g fat, 3 g saturated fat, 47 mg sodium, 2 g fiber

66

Anyone who prepares this easy recipe will be so thrilled with how simple, tasty, and guilt free it is that they will instantly say, 'I can't believe I can eat this—it's wonderful!' —Nina

99

Coffee Cup Soufflés

1 tablespoon butter, at room temperature

5 tablespoons granulated sugar

¼ cup cornstarch

3 tablespoons packed light brown sugar

3 tablespoons unsweetened cocoa powder

1½ teaspoons instant espresso powder

¼ teaspoon ground cinnamon

1¼ cups evaporated fat-free milk

2 teaspoons vanilla extract

6 egg whites, at room temperature

⅛ teaspoon salt

PREHEAT the oven to 400°F. Coat six 7-ounce ovenproof coffee cups, soufflé dishes, or custard cups with the butter. Dust evenly with 2 tablespoons of the granulated sugar. Place on a baking sheet.

WHISK together the cornstarch, brown sugar, cocoa powder, espresso powder, cinnamon, and 2 tablespoons of the remaining granulated sugar in a medium saucepan. Whisk in the milk. Cook over medium heat, whisking frequently, for 5 minutes, or until the mixture comes to a boil and thickens. Remove from the heat. Whisk in the vanilla extract. Pour into a bowl and place a sheet of plastic wrap directly onto the surface of the milk mixture to prevent a skin from forming.

BEAT the egg whites and salt in a large bowl with an electric mixer on high speed until foamy. Gradually beat in the remaining 1 tablespoon granulated sugar until stiff, glossy peaks form. Gently stir about one-third of the egg whites into the milk mixture to lighten it. Fold the remaining whites into the egg mixture until no white streaks remain.

DIVIDE evenly among the prepared cups. Bake for 13 to 15 minutes, or until puffed and firm to the touch. Serve immediately.

Total time: 45 minutes ❋ Makes 6 servings

Per serving: 172 calories, 8 g protein, 30 g carbohydrates, 2 g fat, 2 g saturated fat, 181 mg sodium, 1 g fiber

Espresso powder and cocoa powder give these soufflés a mocha flavor. For pure chocolate flavor, eliminate the espresso powder.

Caramel Crème Custard

1¾ **cups low-fat milk**

⅓ **cup sugar**

2 **teaspoons cornstarch**

¼ **teaspoon salt**

2 **eggs**

½ **teaspoon vanilla extract**

½ **teaspoon caramel flavoring**

WHISK together the milk, sugar, cornstarch, and salt in a medium saucepan. Bring to a simmer over medium-low heat. Simmer, whisking constantly, for 3 minutes, or until small bubbles form on the side.

WHISK the eggs lightly in a medium bowl. Whisk ½ cup of the hot milk mixture into the egg mixture until blended. Slowly whisk back into the milk mixture. Cook, stirring constantly, for 5 minutes, or until the mixture coats the back of a spoon.

POUR into a large bowl and chill for 30 minutes, or until cooled. Stir in the vanilla extract and caramel flavoring until smooth.

DIVIDE among 4 small bowls or cups. Serve warm, or chill for at least 8 hours to serve cold.

Total time: 1 hour ✱ Makes 4 servings

Per serving: 160 calories, 7 g protein, 23 g carbohydrates, 5 g fat, 2 g saturated fat, 224 mg sodium, 0 g fiber

293

Desserts

You can vary the taste of the custard by substituting different flavorings for the caramel—try coconut, almond, or rum for a nice change of pace.
                                                              —Marla

Spiced Kahlua Custards

2 cups unsweetened light soy milk

½ cup brewed coffee

¼ cup coffee liqueur (such as Kahlua)

1 tablespoon instant coffee powder

1 teaspoon ground cinnamon

½ teaspoon ground allspice

2 eggs

2 egg whites

¼ cup sugar

⅛ teaspoon salt

Chocolate-covered espresso beans (optional)

PREHEAT the oven to 350°F. Set six 6- or 8-ounce custard cups into a 13" × 9" baking dish.

WHISK together the soy milk, coffee, liqueur, coffee powder, cinnamon, and allspice in a medium saucepan. Cook over medium heat for 4 minutes, or just until bubbles form around the edge of the pan. Remove from the heat.

WHISK together the eggs, egg whites, sugar, and salt in a large bowl until well blended. Gradually stir in the milk mixture until blended. Divide the mixture into the custard cups. Add boiling water to the baking dish to come halfway up the sides of the custard cups.

BAKE for 40 to 45 minutes, or until a knife inserted in the center of a custard comes out clean. Carefully remove the cups from the water and cool on a rack. Cover with plastic wrap and chill for at least 4 hours. Garnish with the espresso beans, if using.

Total time: 5 hours   ✳   Makes 6 servings

Per serving: 166 calories, 5 g protein, 22 g carbohydrates, 2 g fat, 1 g saturated fat, 123 mg sodium, 1 g fiber

Turn a standard cup of joe into a satisfying treat. This puddinglike dessert is as creamy and delicious as traditional custards but without the usual fat and calories.

Tiramisu

½ cup hot tap water

2 tablespoons instant espresso powder

32 ladyfingers, split

3 large egg whites, at room temperature

1 cup sugar

3 tablespoons cold water

¼ teaspoon cream of tartar

4 ounces mascarpone cheese

4 ounces reduced-fat cream cheese, at room temperature

1 tablespoon semisweet chocolate shavings

STIR together the hot water and espresso powder in a small bowl. Lightly brush the flat side of each ladyfinger with the espresso mixture with a pastry brush.

BRING about 2" of water to a simmer in a large saucepan. Combine the egg whites, sugar, cold water, and cream of tartar in a medium heatproof bowl that will fit over the saucepan. Place the bowl over the saucepan. Beat the egg white mixture for 4 minutes with an electric mixer on low speed. Increase the speed to high and beat for 4 minutes, or until very thick. Remove the bowl from the saucepan. Beat for 4 minutes, or until the mixture is very light and fluffy.

PLACE the mascarpone and cream cheese in a large bowl. Using the same beaters, beat until creamy. Add 1 cup of the egg whites and beat until smooth. Gradually fold in the remaining egg whites.

LINE the bottom of a 3-quart baking dish with 16 of the ladyfingers. Top with one-quarter of the filling. Repeat 3 times to use all the ladyfingers and filling. Sprinkle with the chocolate. Cover and refrigerate for at least 4 hours and up to 3 days before serving.

Total time: 4 hours 30 minutes ✳ Makes 12 servings

Per serving: 244 calories, 6 g protein, 36 g carbohydrates, 9 g fat, 5 g saturated fat, 91 mg sodium, 0 g fiber

If you don't have instant espresso powder, substitute 3 tablespoons of instant coffee powder. Ladyfingers are delicate sponge cakes shaped like a wide finger and are available in most supermarkets. Mascarpone is a dense Italian triple cream cheese made from cow's milk and is available in Italian markets and some supermarkets.

—Jacqueline Longino, Grand Bay, Alabama

Sugar-Free Banana Pudding

2½ cups fat-free milk

1 package (0.9 ounce) fat-free, sugar-free instant banana cream pudding

1 package (1 ounce) fat-free, sugar-free instant cheesecake pudding

1 container (8 ounces) fat-free plain yogurt

1 container (1 pound) sugar-free frozen whipped topping, thawed

4 large ripe bananas, sliced

1 package (9 ounces) sugar-free vanilla wafers, such as Murray, chopped

WHISK together the milk and banana and cheesecake pudding mixes in a large bowl for 2 minutes, or until thickened. Fold in the yogurt and half of the topping.

LAYER half of the pudding, bananas, and wafers in a large bowl. Top with half of the remaining topping, spreading evenly over the top. Repeat the layering. Cover with plastic wrap and chill for at least 2 hours.

Total time: 2 hours 30 minutes ✳ Makes 112 servings

Per serving: 257 calories, 4 g protein, 45 g carbohydrates, 7 g fat, 1 g saturated fat, 224 mg sodium, 6 g fiber

You can make this lactose-free by using Lactaid skim milk instead of regular . . . that's what I did!

—Jacqueline

Amaretti Pudding

2½ cups low-fat milk

⅓ cup packed light brown sugar

¼ cup cornstarch

¼ teaspoon salt

1 teaspoon vanilla extract

5 large amaretti cookies, crumbled

HEAT 2 cups of the milk in a medium saucepan over medium heat for 5 minutes, or until small bubbles form around the edge. Remove from the heat.

COMBINE the sugar, cornstarch, and salt in a medium bowl. Gradually whisk in the remaining ½ cup milk until smooth. Whisk in the warm milk. Pour into the saucepan and bring to a boil over medium heat, stirring constantly. Cook, stirring, for 1 minute, or until thickened.

REMOVE from the heat and stir in the vanilla extract. Spoon into 4 dessert dishes, cover, and chill for 1½ hours, or until cold.

SPRINKLE with the amaretti crumbs to serve.

Total time: 2 hours ✳ Makes 4 servings

Per serving: 195 calories, 5 g protein, 36 g carbohydrates, 3 g fat, 2 g saturated fat, 231 mg sodium, 0 g fiber

Look for amaretti in gourmet shops, Italian grocery stores, and many supermarkets, often packed in brightly colored tins or bags. If you can't find them, try another crisp topping, such as crumbled chocolate or vanilla wafers, your favorite breakfast cereal, or a few spoonfuls of toasted coconut.

French Vanilla Pudding

2 **egg yolks**

½ **cup sugar**

2 **tablespoons cornstarch**

⅛ **teaspoon salt**

2 **cups milk**

½ **vanilla bean, split lengthwise in half**

2 **tablespoons butter, softened**

WHISK together the egg yolks in a medium bowl.

COMBINE the sugar, cornstarch, and salt in a medium saucepan. Whisk in the milk and add the vanilla bean. Bring to a boil and cook, stirring frequently, over medium heat for 10 minutes, or until the pudding has thickened. Remove the pan from the heat.

REMOVE the vanilla bean and scrape the seeds back into the pan. Discard the bean. Slowly whisk about 1 cup of the hot pudding mixture into the egg yolks. Whisk back into the pan and cook, whisking constantly, for 2 minutes, or until the pudding has thickened. Stir in the butter.

PLACE the pudding in a bowl and cover with a piece of waxed paper or plastic wrap on the surface of the pudding. Refrigerate for 1 hour, or until chilled.

Total time: 1 hour 20 minutes ✳ Makes 4 servings

Per serving: 220 calories, 5 g protein, 27 g carbohydrates, 10 g fat, 6 g saturated fat, 128 mg sodium, 0 g fiber

You may not think that a pudding can be decadent, but one taste of this fantastic flavor and you'll see that the proof is in the pudding! A simple vanilla bean is the magic in the mix.

Brown Rice Pudding

1¼ cups water

¼ teaspoon salt

1 tablespoon grated lemon zest

½ cup brown rice

3 cups low-fat milk

1 tablespoon vanilla extract

3 tablespoons packed brown sugar

¼ cup shredded sweetened coconut

Chopped mango or papaya (optional)

COMBINE the water, salt, and 1½ teaspoons of the lemon zest in a large saucepan. Bring to a boil and add the rice. Reduce the heat to low, cover, and simmer for 40 minutes, or until the rice is tender and most of the water is absorbed. Stir in the milk, vanilla extract, sugar, and the remaining 1½ teaspoons lemon zest. Bring to a boil.

REDUCE the heat to low and simmer, stirring frequently to prevent sticking, especially toward the end of the cooking time, for 40 to 45 minutes, or until the pudding thickens and the rice is very tender. (It will thicken more on standing.)

POUR the pudding into a bowl and let cool to room temperature, stirring occasionally. Cover with plastic wrap and chill for at least 4 hours.

SPOON the pudding into 6 individual serving dishes. Top with the coconut and mango or papaya, if using.

Total time: 5 hours ✽ Makes 6 servings

Per serving: 151 calories, 5 g protein, 25 g carbohydrates, 3 g fat, 2 g saturated fat, 154 mg sodium, 1 g fiber

You'll love this dessert's unique coupling of nutty and sweet flavors, and the brown rice adds nutritious fiber.

Cherry Tapioca Pudding

3 tablespoons quick-cooking
  tapioca

⅓ cup sugar

2 large eggs

¼ teaspoon ground cardamom

¼ teaspoon ground cinnamon

4 cups fat-free milk

¼ cup dried cherries

1 teaspoon vanilla extract

STIR together the tapioca, sugar, eggs, cardamom, and cinnamon in a medium saucepan until smooth. Stir in the milk. Bring to a boil over medium heat. Reduce the heat to low and simmer, stirring constantly, for 5 minutes.

REMOVE from the heat and stir in the cherries and vanilla extract. Pour into a serving bowl and cover the surface with plastic wrap. Chill for at least 2 hours.

Total time: 2 hours 15 minutes ✳ Makes 8 servings

Per serving: 123 calories, 6 g protein, 22 g carbohydrates, 2 g fat, 1 g saturated fat, 81 mg sodium, 1 g fiber

Sweet, tart cherries add dimension to classic tapioca pudding. Dried blueberries, cranberries, or raisins work well, too.

Banana-Berry Parfaits

24 chocolate wafers

4½ cups fat-free milk

3 packages (0.44 ounce each) fat-free, sugar-free instant cheesecake or white chocolate pudding

1 container (8 ounces) fat-free frozen whipped topping, thawed

1 container (8 ounces) fat-free sour cream

2 cups raspberries, blueberries, sliced strawberries, or a mix

2 bananas, sliced

RESERVE 4 cookies for garnish and halve. Place the remaining cookies in a resealable plastic bag and coarsely crush with a rolling pin or wooden spoon. Set aside.

WHISK together the milk and pudding mix in a large bowl for 2 minutes, or until thickened. Fold in the whipped topping and sour cream.

RESERVE ¼ cup of the berries for garnish. Layer one-third of the pudding and half of the wafers, berries, and bananas into 8 parfait glasses. Repeat the layering. Finish with the remaining pudding. Garnish with the reserved cookies and berries.

Total time: 20 minutes ✳ Makes 8 servings

Per serving: 282 calories, 8 g protein, 54 g carbohydrates, 3 g fat, 1 g saturated fat, 721 mg sodium, 3 g fiber

303

Desserts

My brother-in-law gave me this recipe several years ago, and I started using the fat-free, sugar-free ingredients so I could eat it on my Weight Watchers plan. I have shared this recipe a lot over the years, and it is always a big hit.
—**Sharon**

Dark Chocolate Pudding

¼ cup sugar

¼ cup malted milk powder

3 tablespoons unsweetened cocoa powder

2 tablespoons cornstarch

1 teaspoon instant coffee powder

2 cups low-fat milk

1 ounce unsweetened chocolate, finely chopped

1 teaspoon vanilla extract

WHISK together the sugar, malted milk powder, cocoa powder, cornstarch, and coffee powder in a medium saucepan until blended. Gradually whisk in the milk. Cook over medium heat, stirring constantly, for 10 minutes, or until the pudding thickens and comes to a boil. Reduce the heat to low and add the chocolate. Cook, stirring constantly, for 1 minute, or until the chocolate melts.

REMOVE from the heat and stir in the vanilla extract. Pour the pudding into 4 custard cups. Cover with plastic wrap and chill for at least 2 hours.

Total time: 2 hours 20 minutes ✳ Makes 8 servings

Per serving: 179 calories, 6 g protein, 28 g carbohydrates, 6 g fat, 4 g saturated fat, 70 mg sodium, 2 g fiber

Here is a healthier, more sophisticated version of the ultimate comfort food. The creamy and satisfying texture is all you need for finishing a perfect meal.

Tropical Fluff

- 1 can (20 ounces) crushed pineapple in its own juice
- 1 package (0.44 ounce) sugar-free instant orange gelatin
- 1 package (1.34 ounces) fat-free, sugar-free vanilla instant pudding
- 1 cup fresh raspberries
- ¼ cup flaked coconut
- 1 container (8 ounces) sugar-free frozen whipped topping, thawed

STIR together the pineapple (with juice), gelatin, and pudding mix in a large bowl until well blended.

STIR in the raspberries, coconut, and topping until blended. Chill for at least 2 hours.

Total time: 2 hours 10 minutes ✳ Makes 6 servings

Per serving: 199 calories, 2 g protein, 37 g carbohydrates, 1 g fat, 1 g saturated fat, 367 mg sodium, 2 g fiber

I love to cook, and my husband loves anything orange. This is a great low-calorie, low-sugar dessert.

—Lois

Pumpkin Mousse

1 cup fat-free milk

1 package (1.5 ounces) fat-free, sugar-free instant vanilla pudding

1 cup 100% pure pumpkin puree

1 teaspoon pumpkin pie spice

WHISK together the milk and pudding mix in a large bowl for 2 minutes, or until thickened. Stir in the pumpkin and spice until well blended.

SERVE immediately or chill to serve cold.

Total time: 5 minutes ❋ Makes 4 servings

Per serving: 77 calories, 3 g protein, 16 g carbohydrates, 0 g fat, 0 g saturated fat, 463 mg sodium, 2 g fiber

I like to serve this dish, a favorite of my dad's, in parfait glasses sprinkled with a few gingersnap crumbs.

—Angela

Fruited Bread Pudding

8 slices multigrain bread, cut
  into 1" cubes

2 cups 2% milk

¾ cup all-fruit peach preserves

2 teaspoons vanilla extract

¾ teaspoon ground cinnamon

⅛ teaspoon salt

5 large eggs

¼ cup dried cranberries,
  blueberries, or cherries

COAT a 9" × 9" baking dish with cooking spray. Add the bread.

WHISK together the milk, preserves, vanilla extract, cinnamon, and salt in a large saucepan. Cook over medium heat, stirring occasionally, for 5 minutes, or until small bubbles form around the edge. Remove from the heat.

WHISK together the eggs in a large bowl. Whisk in ½ cup of the hot milk mixture until blended. Whisk in the remaining milk mixture. Pour evenly over the bread, saturating the cubes. Sprinkle with the dried fruit. Cover with foil and let stand for 30 minutes.

PREHEAT the oven to 350°F. Remove the foil from the baking dish and bake for 45 to 50 minutes, or until a knife inserted in the center comes out clean. Cool on a rack for 15 minutes. Serve warm or at room temperature.

Total time: 1 hour 50 minutes   ✽   Makes 8 servings

Per serving: 234 calories, 9 g protein, 37 g carbohydrates, 6 g fat, 2 g saturated fat, 214 mg sodium, 2 g fiber

Peach adds the flavors of summer to this dish. For other seasonal recipes, change the preserves to strawberry in the spring, apple in the fall, and orange in the winter.

Old-Fashioned Bread Pudding

2 cups fat-free milk

½ cup maple syrup

2 eggs

2 egg whites

½ teaspoon vanilla extract

½ teaspoon ground cinnamon

¼ teaspoon ground nutmeg

¼ teaspoon salt

1½ cups cubed stale whole wheat bread (about 3 slices)

½ cup raisins

PREHEAT the oven to 350°F. Coat a 1-quart baking dish with cooking spray.

WHISK together the milk, syrup, eggs, egg whites, vanilla extract, cinnamon, nutmeg, and salt in a large bowl. Stir in the bread and raisins. Let stand for 5 minutes. Pour into the baking dish.

BAKE for 1 hour, or until a knife inserted in the center comes out clean. Cool on a rack for at least 15 minutes before serving.

Total time: 1 hour 30 minutes ✳ Makes 4 servings

Per serving: 298 calories, 12 g protein, 57 g carbohydrates, 4 g fat, 1 g saturated fat, 368 mg sodium, 2 g fiber

As a grandparent, I raised two grandchildren. Cooking for teenagers while making healthy changes in family recipes was a challenge, but they were helpful and tried almost anything. This recipe is now a favorite of my granddaughter—she loves its nutty flavor.

—Carol

Potluck Trifle

1 package (1.5 ounces) fat-free instant chocolate pudding

2 cups fat-free milk

1 package (10 ounces) fat-free pound cake, cut into ½" slices

1 jar (10 ounces) all-fruit raspberry preserves

¼ cup dry sherry or orange juice

1 pint strawberries, sliced

WHISK together the pudding mix and milk in a large bowl for 2 minutes, or until thickened. Arrange a single layer of the cake slices in the bottom of a deep glass bowl. Spread with one-third of the preserves and sprinkle with a generous tablespoon of the sherry or orange juice. Top with one-third of the strawberries and one-third of the pudding. Repeat the layering 2 more times, ending with the pudding. Cover with plastic wrap and refrigerate for at least 2 hours.

Total time: 2 hours 15 minutes ✳ Makes 8 servings

Per serving: 246 calories, 5 g protein, 55 g carbohydrates, 1 g fat, 0 g saturated fat, 304 mg sodium, 2 g fiber

Hailing from England, a trifle combines delicious custard with cake soaked in spirits. Traditional versions call for homemade custard and sponge cake, but this easy variation uses convenient pudding mix and pound cake.

[**QUICK TIP: WHAT YOUR SCALE SAYS ABOUT YOUR BRAIN**

If it registers a healthy weight, your mind is likely youthful, too. In a recent UCLA study, overweight people had 4 percent less brain tissue than normal-weight adults—the equivalent of their minds aging 8 years. One possible cause: a high-calorie or high-fat diet, which clogs arteries in the brain, restricts blood flow, and causes cells to shrink.]

Light Strawberry Trifle

½ cup cold water

1 package (0.44 ounce) sugar-free instant strawberry gelatin

⅔ cup boiling water

1 container (1 pound) frozen light whipped topping, thawed

2 cups fat-free milk

1 package (1.34 ounces) fat-free, sugar-free instant vanilla pudding

1 teaspoon vanilla extract

½ angel food cake, cut into 1"–2" squares (6 cups)

2 cups sliced strawberries

1 cup blueberries

COMBINE the cold water and ice cubes in a measuring cup to measure ¾ cup. Stir the gelatin and boiling water in a large bowl for 2 minutes, or until the gelatin is dissolved. Stir in the ice water until the mixture begins to thicken. Remove any remaining pieces of ice. Stir in half of the topping until smooth. Chill for 30 minutes.

WHISK together the milk and pudding mix in a large bowl for 2 minutes, or until thickened. Stir in the vanilla extract.

PLACE the gelatin mixture on the bottom of a large glass or trifle bowl. Layer with the cake and three-quarters of the berries. Cover with the pudding mixture and spread with the remaining topping. Arrange the remaining berries on top.

Total time: 45 minutes ✳ Makes 12 servings

Per serving: 166 calories, 3 g protein, 30 g carbohydrates, 4 g fat, 4 g saturated fat, 293 mg sodium, 1 g fiber

This recipe is perfect for parties. I created it for our annual family Christmas party, and it was a big hit. Try different fruits and berries for seasonal colors.

—Emily

Zuccotto

¼ cup slivered blanched almonds

1 package (13.6 ounces) fat-free pound cake

3 tablespoons orange juice

2 tablespoons sweet Marsala wine or orange juice

2 cups low-fat vanilla Greek-style yogurt

½ cup confectioners' sugar

1 ounce semisweet chocolate, finely chopped

1 package (0.25 ounce) unflavored gelatin

¼ cup cold water

Sliced strawberries (optional)

PREHEAT the oven to 350°F. Place the almonds in a baking pan and toast for about 8 minutes, or until lightly browned. Chop.

COAT a deep 2-quart bowl with cooking spray. Line the bowl with plastic wrap. Cut the cake into twenty ¼"-thick slices. Place 1 slice in the center of the bottom of the bowl. Cut the remaining slices in half diagonally to form triangles. Arrange enough triangles around the inside of the bowl to cover completely, overlapping to fit.

COMBINE the orange juice and wine or additional orange juice in a cup. Brush lightly over the cake.

STIR together the yogurt, sugar, chocolate, and toasted almonds in a large bowl. Sprinkle the gelatin over the cold water and let stand for 1 minute in a small saucepan. Cook over low heat, stirring, for 2 to 3 minutes, or until the gelatin dissolves. Gradually whisk into the yogurt mixture, whisking constantly until it is completely incorporated. Spoon the yogurt mixture into the bowl to cover the cake. Cover the yogurt mixture completely with the remaining cake slices. Brush the remaining orange juice mixture onto the cake slices.

COVER with plastic wrap and chill for at least 3 hours, or overnight. To serve, uncover and invert the zuccotto onto a platter. Remove the bowl and plastic wrap. Top with the sliced strawberries (if using).

Total time: 3 hours 30 minutes ✳ Makes 4 servings

Per serving: 212 calories, 7 g protein, 38 g carbohydrates, 4 g fat, 1 g saturated fat, 162 mg sodium, 1 g fiber

In Italian, *zuccotto* means "skullcap"—this impressive dessert was apparently named for its domed shape. Similar to a trifle, zuccotto is best if made the day before serving.

Classic Cannoli

16 square wonton skins

2 tablespoons butter, melted

1 teaspoon ground cinnamon

1 container (1 pound) whole milk ricotta cheese

½ cup confectioners' sugar

1 teaspoon vanilla extract

PREHEAT the oven to 400°F. Coat 2 large baking sheets with cooking spray.

BRUSH the wonton skins with the butter and sprinkle with a pinch of the cinnamon. Shape into a tube by curling opposite corners around a cannoli mold. Place seam side down on the prepared baking sheet. Repeat to make a total of 16 shells (work in batches, if necessary, according to how many molds you have).

BAKE for 7 minutes, or until lightly browned at the edges. Remove from the oven and cool on a rack for 3 minutes, or until the shells have cooled on the molds and are crisp. Gently slide the shells onto the rack to cool completely.

BEAT the ricotta, sugar, and vanilla extract in a large bowl with an electric mixer on medium speed until smooth. Cover and chill until ready to serve.

SPOON the ricotta mixture into a pastry bag fitted with a large tip. Pipe into the shells from both ends, just before serving.

Total time: 1 hour ✳ Makes 16 servings

Per serving: 101 calories, 4 g protein, 9 g carbohydrates, 5 g fat, 3 g saturated fat, 70 mg sodium, 0 g fiber

If you don't have cannoli molds, use the thick handle of a metal whisk or another ovenproof tube about ½" in diameter.

Mousse-Filled Cannoli

1 cup fat-free milk

½ cup fat-free ricotta cheese

½ cup reduced-fat sour cream

1 package (1.5 ounces) fat-free, sugar-free instant white chocolate pudding

1 cup sugar-free frozen whipped topping

¾ cup mini semisweet chocolate chips

1 teaspoon vanilla extract

1 package (3 ounces) cannoli shells (6 shells)

WHISK together the milk, ricotta, sour cream, and pudding mix in a large bowl for 2 minutes, or until thickened. Fold in the whipped topping, chocolate chips, and vanilla extract. Pipe into shells.

Total time: 10 minutes ✳ Makes 6 servings

Per serving: 316 calories, 7 g protein, 45 g carbohydrates, 9 g fat, 5 g saturated fat, 435 mg sodium, 2 g fiber

This is the perfect dessert when I'm craving real chocolate: something that tastes really bad for you—but isn't!
—Nicole

Ice Cream Jelly Roll

2 teaspoons + 1 cup whole grain pastry flour

1 teaspoon baking powder

¼ teaspoon salt

4 large egg whites, at room temperature

¾ cup granulated sugar

4 large egg yolks, at room temperature

1 teaspoon vanilla extract

1 tablespoon confectioners' sugar

1 quart fat-free chocolate ice cream, softened

PREHEAT the oven to 375°F. Coat a 15" × 11" jelly-roll pan with cooking spray. Dust with 2 teaspoons of the flour. Tap out the excess.

COMBINE the remaining 1 cup flour, the baking powder, and salt in a medium bowl. Beat the egg whites in a medium bowl with an electric mixer on medium speed until frothy. Slowly beat in ½ cup of the granulated sugar until stiff peaks form.

PLACE the egg yolks, vanilla extract, and remaining ¼ cup granulated sugar in a large bowl. Beat with the same beaters for 5 minutes, or until thick and lemon-colored. Fold in one-third of the flour mixture and one-half of the egg whites. Repeat, beginning and ending with the flour.

POUR the batter into the pan and smooth the top.

BAKE for 8 minutes, or just until the top springs back when lightly touched in the center. Place a clean dish towel on the kitchen counter and sprinkle evenly with the confectioners' sugar. Loosen the edges of the baked cake and immediately invert onto the towel. Starting from a short end, roll up the cake (and the towel). Cool completely on a rack.

UNROLL the cake and remove the towel. Spread the top of the cake with the ice cream. Roll up the cake. Wrap in plastic wrap or foil and freeze for at least 30 minutes.

Total time: 1 hour 40 minutes ✱ Makes 4 servings

Per serving: 166 calories, 5 g protein, 33 g carbohydrates, 3 g fat, 1 g saturated fat, 144 mg sodium, 3 g fiber

Light white cake is filled with chocolate ice cream and rolled into a log. Try the cake with any favorite fat-free ice cream or frozen yogurt, such as peach, strawberry, and even orange sherbet.

Chocolate Hazelnut Fondue

½ ounce unsweetened chocolate, chopped

1 can (14 ounces) fat-free sweetened condensed milk

2 tablespoons unsweetened cocoa powder

Pinch of salt

3 tablespoons chocolate-hazelnut spread

½ teaspoon vanilla extract

Assorted cubed or sliced fresh fruit and angel food cake cubes

COOK the chocolate and about half of the condensed milk in a small saucepan over medium heat, stirring, for 3 minutes, or until the chocolate is melted. Remove from the heat and stir in the remaining milk. Sift the cocoa powder and salt on top. Stir until blended.

RETURN to the heat and cook, stirring, for 3 minutes, or until the fondue just begins to simmer. Remove from the heat. Stir in the chocolate-hazelnut spread and vanilla extract until smooth. Serve warm with the fruit and cake cubes.

Total time: 20 minutes ✳ Makes 8 servings

Per serving: 165 calories, 4 g protein, 33 g carbohydrates, 2 g fat, 1 g saturated fat, 72 mg sodium, 1 g fiber

Indulge your chocolate cravings by taking a dip in this rich, creamy sauce. With the saturated fats and calories cut back, you won't have those "morning after" regrets.

Chocolate Mousse Sandwiches

1 container (6 ounces) low-fat vanilla yogurt

1 package (1.4 ounces) fat-free, sugar-free instant Swiss chocolate or chocolate fudge pudding

1 container (8 ounces) fat-free frozen whipped topping, thawed

8 chocolate graham crackers, each broken in half

WHISK together the yogurt and pudding mix in a large bowl for 2 minutes, or until thickened. Stir in the topping.

ARRANGE half of the graham crackers on a baking sheet with sides. Spread ¼ cup of the chocolate mixture on each cracker on the baking sheet. Top with the remaining crackers. Press slightly.

FREEZE for 1 hour and up to 4 days.

Total time: 1 hour 10 minutes ✱ Makes 4 servings

Per serving: 195 calories, 3 g protein, 23 g carbohydrates, 3 g fat, 1 g saturated fat, 221 mg sodium, 1 g fiber

You can vary this and make all kinds of different types of mousse. Try using vanilla pudding and strawberry yogurt—delicious!
—Melissa

Italian Parfaits

2 teaspoons instant espresso powder

½ cup boiling water

8 nonfat chocolate chip biscotti, crushed

2⅔ cups nonfat vanilla frozen yogurt

4 teaspoons grated semisweet chocolate

DISSOLVE the espresso powder in the boiling water in a coffee cup. Set aside to cool.

DIVIDE one-third of the biscotti crumbs among 4 parfait glasses. Layer ⅓ cup of the frozen yogurt, 1 tablespoon of the espresso, and ½ teaspoon of the chocolate into each glass. Repeat. Top with the remaining crumbs and chocolate. Serve immediately or freeze for up to 1 hour.

Total time: 20 minutes ✱ Makes 4 servings

Per serving: 334 calories, 11 g protein, 57 g carbohydrates, 8 g fat, 3 g saturated fat, 217 mg sodium, 0 g fiber

This tempting dessert is deceptively low in fat—and supereasy to prepare. Just layer crushed biscotti in goblets with frozen yogurt, shaved chocolate, and espresso.

GOTTA TRY IT! INSTANT MOTIVATOR

Frustrated by a stuck scale? The Fitbit ($99; www.fitbit.com) counts calories day and night to spur you to move more and burn extra fat. The pinkie-size device is so small that our tester wore it on her underwear for top-secret tracking. It picks up movements from standing to strolling to running. Seeing the numbers add up motivated our tester to melt 2,439 calories in 1 day—without doing an actual workout.

Ginger Frozen Yogurt
with Sweet Plum Sauce

- 1 pint fat-free vanilla frozen yogurt, slightly softened
- 4 tablespoons finely chopped crystallized ginger
- 1 pound ripe plums (4), pitted and sliced
- 3 tablespoons sugar-free grape jam
- 1 tablespoon sugar
- ¼ cup sliced almonds, toasted and chopped

STIR together the frozen yogurt and ginger in a medium bowl. Place in the freezer.

COOK the plums, jam, and sugar in a medium saucepan over medium heat for 3 minutes, or until simmering. Reduce the heat to low, cover, and simmer for 12 minutes, or until the plums soften and break down. Uncover and simmer for 5 minutes, or until the sauce thickens slightly.

POUR the sauce into a bowl and let cool. Cover with plastic wrap and chill for at least 2 hours, or until cold.

SPOON the sauce into 4 individual serving dishes. Top with scoops of the frozen yogurt and sprinkle with the almonds.

Total time: 45 minutes   ✳   Makes 4 servings

Per serving: 191 calories, 6 g protein, 38 g carbohydrates, 3 g fat, 0 g saturated fat, 71 mg sodium, 2 g fiber

Frozen yogurt typically has less fat and fewer calories than its full-fat cousin, ice cream. Adorn it with high-fiber plums and a sprinkling of almonds, and you've made your frozen yogurt even healthier and more satisfying.

[it worked for me]

142 lbs lost!

�֍ SHERI HARKNESS

Doing it her way, Sheri Harkness started cutting her portions in half and ended up losing half her body weight.

My Story

My weight troubles began when my parents divorced in my junior year of high school. From the age of 16 on, I continued to pack on pounds at a steady rate—and no amount of yo-yo dieting could stop it. I had my first son at 25; between then and the birth of his brother, 2 years later, I gained an additional 25 pounds. I was determined that my boys would eat healthy, balanced meals each day—but for myself, I chose greasy takeout and liters of soda. Within 10 years, I had ballooned to almost 300 pounds.

I'd tried all the weight-loss gimmicks before the birth of my sons: the no-carb diet, cabbage diet, starvation diet, and even Weight Watchers. My younger sister (and best friend!) Karen, a personal trainer, had also encouraged me repeatedly to get fit once and for all—but I wasn't ready to face my weight problem. It wasn't until I stepped on the scale for a routine physical and watched the number settle at 282 pounds that I realized I needed to change. I devised my own strategy: I'd eat

Pounds lost: 142

Age: 41

Height: 5'8"

Weight then: 282 pounds

Weight now: 140 pounds

the same foods but halve the portions. Next I gave up the 2 liters of soda that I was guzzling each day. I did the math and realized that I drank 260,000 calories—or 74 pounds' worth of empty calories—per year. That was a huge eye-opener! With these simple changes alone, I quickly dropped a size and kept on losing.

About 2 weeks after I cut my food intake, I decided to go to the gym just 3 afternoons a week and walk on the treadmill for 15 minutes. At first it was hard and embarrassing. Despite that, I pushed forward at 3.1 miles per hour, step by step. Soon I was walking 4 days a week—and then riding a stationary bike and, finally, using the elliptical to burn up to 750 calories in an hour! After 2 months of building up my stamina with cardio, I was ready to accept the help that Karen had been offering me for so long. She e-mailed me extensive weight-training workouts, right down to photos of which machines to use. She was, and continues to be, an amazing mentor and confidant. Under her guidance, weight training became something that clicked for me: Muscle mass burns fat (without bulking you up!). How cool is that?

In February 2009, I participated in the Empire State Run Up, a race in which thousands climb the 86 floors up to the observatory deck of the Empire State Building. It was so much fun—and I couldn't believe how far I had come, losing 142 pounds in just 18 months!

My Top Tips

* Find a mantra . . . Mine's "never give up"—and while it seems obvious, it helped keep me on track!

* Make it about your health . . . Karen taught me to focus on my overall fitness rather than just a number on the scale. She was right—when I learned to love exercise and set goals at the gym, the weight loss that followed was just an added bonus!

* Change habits in stages . . . I didn't want to overwhelm myself, so I tackled both my diet and exercise issues in smaller, more manageable stages until I felt comfortable.

* Be your own best friend . . . You will fail from time to time; you are human. When you do, be kind and tell yourself what you would tell your best friend. Then get back on the horse!

Menus for Special Times

Losing weight can feel like one big "NO!" No carbs, no fat, no fun. But it shouldn't mean the end of good eating. As a matter of fact, the more you enjoy your meals, the more likely you are to stick to your eating plan. And what's more enjoyable than gathering over a meal with family and friends? Whether it's a simple brunch or an elegant dinner party, spending time with loved ones should be stress free and fun. Being prepared is the key to a great time while sticking to your plan. Following are menus designed to offer inspiration for using many of the recipes in this book.

Each menu includes a one-serving nutritional analysis and sometimes recommended nonrecipe sides that you can easily factor into your daily eating plan. The portion size for all recipes listed is one serving. And because *Prevention* recommends that you limit saturated fat intake to 10 percent of total calories— about 17 grams per day for most women—and sodium intake to less than 2,300 milligrams, we've noted with an asterisk (*) which menus are slightly high in these nutrients so you can remember to be mindful of your choices for the rest of the day.

So gather your famiy, cook up a healthy meal, and enjoy life's special times!

Spring Brunch

Good Morning Sunshine, page 66

1 cup cubed cantaloupe or
honeydew melon

Coffee or tea

Per serving: 435 calories, 28 g protein,
33 g carbohydrates, 24 g fat,
9 g saturated fat*, 422 mg sodium,
5 g fiber

Breakfast with Friends

Crepes with Banana and Kiwifruit,
page 76

Fat-free latte

Per serving: 396 calories, 25 g protein,
59 g carbohydrates, 7 g fat,
3 g saturated fat, 455 mg sodium,
4 g fiber

Breakfast On-the-Go

Sweet Potato–Corn Muffins, page 86

6 ounces low-fat vanilla Greek-style yogurt

1 apple

Per serving: 348 calories, 19 g protein, 62 g carbohydrates, 3 g fat, 1 g saturated fat, 375 mg sodium, 5 g fiber

Relaxed Summer Lunch

Grilled Zucchini Sandwiches, page 120

1 ounce baked potato chips

1 cup cubed watermelon

Per serving: 506 calories, 14 g protein, 80 g carbohydrates, 17 g fat, 3 g saturated fat, 769 mg sodium*, 8 g fiber

Midday Fiesta

Black Bean Chimichangas, page 133

½ cup jicama sticks

½ cup fat-free coffee frozen yogurt

Per serving: 550 calories, 18 g protein,
96 g carbohydrates, 10 g fat,
1 g saturated fat, 641 mg sodium,
13 g fiber

Burgers in the Backyard

Italian-Style Beef Burgers, page 105

1 cup salad greens with 1 tablespoon
light Italian dressing

Chocolate Mousse Sandwiches,
page 318

Per serving: 479 calories, 40 g protein,
43 g carbohydrates, 17 g fat,
6 g saturated fat*, 643 mg sodium,
3 g fiber

Easy Appetizer Party

½ serving Chicken "Not" Wings, page 148

½ serving Ham and Grissini Roll-Ups, page 150

1 serving Mustard-Glazed Snack Mix, page 152

½ serving Roasted Red Pepper Hummus with Cilantro, page 153

Per serving: 438 calories; 32 g protein; 44 g carbohydrates; 16 g fat; 5 g saturated fat; 1,054 mg sodium*; 8 g fiber

Christmas Dinner

4 ounces roasted turkey breast

1 small roasted red pepper

Christmas Ribbon Salad, page 244

Light Strawberry Trifle, page 311

Per serving: 549 calories, 34 g protein, 66 g carbohydrate, 8 g fat, 8 g saturated fat, 560 mg sodium*, 5 g fiber

Fall Harvest Dinner Party

4 ounces roasted pork tenderloin

Sweet Potato Casserole, page 237

1 cup steamed green beans

Sugar-Free Pumpkin Pie, page 278

Per serving: 564 calories, 34 g protein,
70 g carbohydrates, 18 g fat,
5 g saturated fat, 349 mg sodium,
12 g fiber

Casual Birthday Party

Chicken Tetrazzini, page 205

1 wedge (⅙ head) iceberg lettuce
with 1 tablespoon light Thousand
Island dressing

Rich Chocolate Layer Cake, page 262

Per serving: 518 calories, 23 g protein,
71 g carbohydrates, 17 g fat,
10 g saturated fat*, 398 mg sodium,
5 g fiber

Salad for Supper

Mandarin-Basil Shrimp Salad, page 214

Strawberry-Rhubarb Crisp, page 289

Per serving: 533 calories, 18 g protein,
87 g carbohydrates, 14 fat,
4 g saturated fat, 700 mg sodium*,
11 fiber

Make-Ahead Italian

Pasta-Ratatouille Casserole, page 224

1 cup romaine with
1 tablespoon light Caesar dressing

Amaretti Pudding, page 298

Per serving: 505 calories, 20 g protein,
77 g carbohydrates, 14 g fat,
5 g saturated fat, 942 mg sodium*,
6 g fiber

Simple Springtime Supper

Orange Chicken and Broccoli,
page 206

½ cup steamed brown rice

Strawberry Yogurt Pie, page 274

Per serving: 627 calories, 40 g protein,
30 g carbohydrates, 11 g fat,
2 g saturated fat, 609 mg sodium,
8 g fiber

Entertain with Ease

Herbed Butterflied Leg of Lamb,
page 182

1 baked potato

1 cup steamed broccoli with lemon

Fruit 'n' Dip, page 291

Per serving: 513 calories, 35 g protein,
73 g carbohydrates, 11 g fat,
5 g saturated fat, 378 mg sodium,
9 g fiber

Calorie & Nutrient Counter

There's no better way to upset your weight-loss goals than to not have the right foods to eat on hand. But with the sheer number of foods available in the average market, making the best choices isn't always as easy as it would seem. That's why we've gathered all the nutrition facts you need to consider in the following list of common foods. Use this handy chart as your guide to determine which of your favorite fresh fruits and vegetables offer the most fiber, learn which cuts of meat are leaner than others, and make sure you're not overloading on too much sodium or saturated fat in your cheese choices.

You can also use this chart to get a grasp on exactly what you're eating so you can find out where the bulk of your calories comes from. Then you can make simple substitutions that shave off calories without sacrificing taste or satisfaction. For example, consider trading a handful of pretzels for 3 cups of air-popped popcorn sprinkled with 1 tablespoon of grated Parmesan cheese—you'll save about 115 calories and enjoy loads more flavor while tripling your portion size. Need some more motivation? Just remember that when you're guessing how many calories you can eat, being off by just 100 calories a day can keep you 6 to 10 pounds overweight.

❋ BEANS AND LEGUMES

FOOD ITEM	SERVING SIZE	CALORIES	PROTEIN (G)
Baked beans	⅓ cup	126	5
Baked beans, vegetarian	⅓ cup	79	4
Bean sprouts (mung beans)	½ cup	13	1
Black beans, cooked with salt	½ cup	114	8
Black-eyed peas (cowpeas), cooked with salt	½ cup	99	7
Butter beans (lima), cooked with salt	½ cup	105	6
Cannellini beans, cooked without salt	½ cup	100	6
Chickpeas (garbanzo beans), cooked with salt	½ cup	134	7
Edamame (immature green soybeans), frozen, prepared	½ cup	95	8
Edamame, out of shell, cooked without salt	½ cup	100	10
Falafel, cooked	2¼" patty	57	2
French beans, cooked with salt	½ cup	114	6
Hummus	⅛ cup	54	1
Kidney beans, red, cooked with salt	½ cup	112	8
Lentils, brown, cooked with salt	½ cup	115	9
Navy beans, cooked with salt	½ cup	127	7
Pinto beans, cooked with salt	½ cup	122	8
Refried beans, canned	½ cup	118	7
Refried beans, fat-free	½ cup	130	6
Refried beans, vegetarian	½ cup	100	6
Soybeans, dry-roasted, salted	¼ cup	194	17
White beans, small, cooked with salt	½ cup	127	8

CARB (G)	FIBER (G)	SUGAR (G)	FAT (G)	SAT FAT (G)	SODIUM (MG)
18	5	0	4	2	352
18	3	7	1	0	288
3	1	2	0	0	6
20	8	0	1	0	204
18	6	3	0.5	0	205
20	5	1	0	0	215
17	5	1	1	0	40
22	6	4	2	0	199
8	4	2	4	0	5
9	1	2	2.5	0	70
5	0	0	3	0	50
21	8	0	1	0	214
6	1	0	3	0	74
20	7	0	0	0	211
20	8	2	0	0	236
24	10	0	1	0	216
22	8	0	1	0	203
20	7	0	2	1	379
18	6	1	0	0	580
17	6	2	1	0	560
14	4	0	9	1	70
23	9	0	1	0	213

(continued)

 CHEESE

FOOD ITEM	SERVING SIZE	CALORIES	PROTEIN (G)
American, pasteurized process, fat-free	1" cube	24	4
American, pasteurized process, low-fat	1" cube	32	4
American cheese food	1 oz	93	6
American cheese food, low-fat	1" cube	32	4
Blue, crumbled	1 Tbsp	30	2
Brie	1" cube	57	4
Cheddar	1" cube	69	4
Cheddar, fat-free	1" cube	40	8
Cheddar, low-fat	1" cube	30	4
Cottage cheese, low-fat 1%	4 oz	81	14
Cottage cheese, fat-free, large-curd, dry	½ cup	96	20
Cottage cheese, low-fat 2%	¼ cup	51	8
Cream cheese	2 Tbsp	101	2
Cream cheese, fat-free	2 Tbsp	28	4
Cream cheese, low-fat	2 Tbsp	69	3
Feta	1" cube	45	2
Monterey Jack, fat-free	1" cube	40	8
Monterey Jack, low-fat	1" cube	53	5
Mozzarella, fat-free, shredded	¼ oz	42	9
Mozzarella, low-sodium	1" cube	50	5
Mozzarella, part-skim, low-moisture	1 oz	86	7
Mozzarella, string	1 (1 oz)	80	8
Muenster	1" cube	66	4
Muenster, low-fat	1" cube	49	4
Parmesan, grated	2 Tbsp	43	4
Parmesan, hard	1" cube	40	4

CARB (G)	FIBER (G)	SUGAR (G)	FAT (G)	SAT FAT (G)	SODIUM (MG)
2	0	2	0	0	244
1	0	0	1	1	257
2	0	2	7	4	452
1	0	0	1	1	257
0	0	0	2.5	1.5	118
0	0	0	5	3	107
0	0	0	6	4	106
1	0	1	0	0	220
0	0	0	1	1	106
3	0	3	1	1	459
2	0	2	0	0	15
2	0	0	1	1	229
1	0	0	10	6	86
2	0	0	0	0	158
2	0	0	5	3	89
1	0	1	4	3	190
1	0	1	0	0	220
0	0	0	4	2	96
1	1	0	0	0	210
1	0	0	3	2	3
1	0	0	6	4	150
1	0	0	6	3	240
0	0	0	5	3	113
1	0	1	3	2	108
0	0	0	3	2	153
0	0	0	3	2	165

(continued)

❋ CHEESE *(cont.)*

FOOD ITEM	SERVING SIZE	CALORIES	PROTEIN (G)
Provolone	1" cube	60	4
Ricotta	¼ cup	107	7
Ricotta, low-fat	¼ cup	85	7
Swiss	1" cube	57	4
Swiss, low-fat	1" cube	27	4
Swiss, low-fat, singles	1 slice	50	8

❋ OTHER DAIRY

FOOD ITEM	SERVING SIZE	CALORIES	PROTEIN (G)
Sour cream	1 Tbsp	31	0
Yogurt, banana, low-fat	4 oz	120	5
Yogurt, blueberry–French vanilla, low-fat	4 oz	120	5
Yogurt, coffee, fat-free	4 oz	103	6
Yogurt, plain, fat-free	4 oz	63	6
Yogurt, plain, low-fat	4 oz	71	6
Yogurt, plain, whole-milk	4 oz	69	4
Yogurt, strawberry, fat-free, Breyer's	4 oz	62	4
Yogurt, strawberry, low-fat, Breyer's	4 oz	109	4
Yogurt, vanilla, low-fat	4 oz	96	6

CARB (G)	FIBER (G)	SUGAR (G)	FAT (G)	SAT FAT (G)	SODIUM (MG)
0	0	0	5	3	149
2	0	0	8	5	52
3	0	0	5	3	77
1	0	0	4	3	29
1	0	0	1	1	39
1	0	0	1	1	73

CARB (G)	FIBER (G)	SUGAR (G)	FAT (G)	SAT FAT (G)	SODIUM (MG)
1	0	0	3	2	8
21	0	18	2	2	60
24	0	21	1	0	70
20	0	20	0	0	78
9	0	9	0	0	87
8	0	8	2	1	79
5	0	5	4	2	52
11	0	9	0	0	51
21	0	20	1	1	59
16	0	16	1	1	75

(continued)

EGGS

FOOD ITEM	SERVING SIZE	CALORIES	PROTEIN (G)
Egg, hard-cooked	1 large	78	6
Egg, poached	1 large	71	6
Egg, scrambled	1 large	102	7
Egg white, cooked	1 large	17	4
Egg white, Egg Beaters	¼ cup	30	6

✳ FATS AND OILS

FOOD ITEM	SERVING SIZE	CALORIES	PROTEIN (G)
Butter, with salt	1 tsp	34	0
Butter, without salt	1 tsp	34	0
Butter-margarine blend, stick, without salt	1 tsp	33	0
Flaxseed oil	1 tsp	40	0
Margarine, hard, corn and soybean oils	1 tsp	33	0
Margarine, hard, corn oil	1 tsp	34	0
Margarine, hard, soybean oil	1 tsp	34	0
Margarine, regular, with salt	1 tsp	34	0
Margarine, regular, without salt	1 tsp	34	0
Oil, canola	1 tsp	40	0
Oil, olive	1 tsp	40	0
Oil, safflower	1 tsp	40	0
Oil, sesame	1 tsp	40	0
Oil, walnut	1 tsp	40	0

CARB (G)	FIBER (G)	SUGAR (G)	FAT (G)	SAT FAT (G)	SODIUM (MG)
1	0	1	5	2	62
0	0	0	5	2	147
1	0	1	7	2	171
0	0	0	0	0	55
1	0	0	0	0	115

CARB (G)	FIBER (G)	SUGAR (G)	FAT (G)	SAT FAT (G)	SODIUM (MG)
0	0	0	4	2	27
0	0	0	4	2	1
0	0	0	4	1	1
0	0	0	5	0	0
0	0	0	4	1	30
0	0	0	4	1	44
0	0	0	4	1	44
0	0	0	4	1	44
0	0	0	4	1	0
0	0	0	5	0	0
0	0	0	5	1	0
0	0	0	5	0	0
0	0	0	5	1	0
0	0	0	5	0	0

(continued)

FISH

FOOD ITEM	SERVING SIZE	CALORIES	PROTEIN (G)
Cod, Atlantic, baked	3 oz	89	19
Flounder, baked	3 oz	99	21
Grouper, baked	3 oz	100	21
Halibut, Atlantic and Pacific, baked	3 oz	119	23
Mahi mahi, baked	3 oz	93	20
Salmon, Coho, wild, baked	3 oz	118	20
Salmon, pink, canned, drained	3 oz	116	20
Swordfish, baked	3 oz	132	22
Tilapia, baked or broiled	3 oz	109	22
Tuna, bluefin, baked	3 oz	156	25
Tuna, StarKist Chunk Light, canned in water, drained	2 oz	70	15
Tuna, white, canned in water, drained	3 oz	109	20
Tuna, yellowfin, baked	3 oz	118	25

 # FRUIT

FOOD ITEM	SERVING SIZE	CALORIES	PROTEIN (G)
Apple	1 medium (2¾")	72	0
Apricot	1	17	0
Avocado	¼ cup	58	1
Banana	1 large (8")	121	1
Blackberries	1 cup	62	2
Blueberries	½ cup	42	1
Cantaloupe, wedged	⅛ medium	23	1
Cranberries	1 cup	44	0
Grapefruit, pink, red, white	½ medium	41	1

CARB (G)	FIBER (G)	SUGAR (G)	FAT (G)	SAT FAT (G)	SODIUM (MG)
0	0	0	1	0	66
0	0	0	1	0	89
0	0	0	1	0	45
0	0	0	3	0	59
0	0	0	1	0	96
0	0	0	4	1	49
0	0	0	4	1	339
0	0	0	4	1	98
0	0	0	2	1	48
0	0	0	5	1	42
0	0	0	0	0	230
0	0	0	3	1	320
0	0	0	1	0	40

CARB (G)	FIBER (G)	SUGAR (G)	FAT (G)	SAT FAT (G)	SODIUM (MG)
19	3	14	0	0	1
4	1	3	0	0	0
3	2	0	5	1	3
31	4	17	0	0	1
14	8	7	1	0	1
11	2	7	0	0	1
6	1	5	0	0	11
12	4	4	0	0	2
10	1	9	0	0	0

(continued)

FRUIT *(cont.)*

FOOD ITEM	SERVING SIZE	CALORIES	PROTEIN (G)
Grapes, green or red	½ cup	52	1
Lemon	1 medium (2⅛")	17	1
Nectarine	1 medium (2¾")	69	2
Orange	1 large (3¹⁄₁₆")	86	2
Peach	1 medium	58	1
Pear	½ medium	52	0
Pineapple	¼	57	1
Plum	1 (2⅛")	30	0
Raspberries, red	¾ cup	48	1
Strawberry	1 medium	4	0
Watermelon, sliced	1 wedge (¹⁄₁₆ melon)	86	2

GRAINS AND RICE

FOOD ITEM	SERVING SIZE	CALORIES	PROTEIN (G)
Couscous, cooked	⅓ cup	59	2
Oat bran, cooked	⅓ cup	29	2
Oats, rolled, dry	2 Tbsp	37	1
Quinoa, dry	2 Tbsp	79	3
Rice, brown, long-grain, cooked	¼ cup	54	1
Rice, brown, medium-grain, cooked	¼ cup	55	1
Rice, brown, short-grain, dry	1½ Tbsp	66	1
Rice, whole grain, brown, Uncle Ben's 10-minute, dry	¼ cup	170	1

CARB (G)	FIBER (G)	SUGAR (G)	FAT (G)	SAT FAT (G)	SODIUM (MG)
14	1	12	0	0	2
5	2	1	0	0	1
16	3	12	1	0	0
22	4	17	0	0	0
14	2	13	0	0	0
14	3	9	0	0	1
15	2	11	0	0	1
8	1	7	0	0	0
11	6	4	1	0	1
1	0	1	0	0	2
22	1	18	0	0	3

CARB (G)	FIBER (G)	SUGAR (G)	FAT (G)	SAT FAT (G)	SODIUM (MG)
12	1	0	0	0	3
8	2	n/a	1	0	1
7	1	0	1	0	0
15	1	n/a	1	0	4
11	1	0	0	0	2
11	1	n/a	0	0	0
15	1	0	1	0	2
35	2	0	1.5	0	0

(continued)

❋ GRAINS AND RICE *(cont.)*

FOOD ITEM	SERVING SIZE	CALORIES	PROTEIN (G)
Rice, white, long-grain, cooked	¼ cup	51	1
Rice, wild, cooked	⅓ cup	55	2

❋ MEATS

FOOD ITEM	SERVING SIZE	CALORIES	PROTEIN (G)
BEEF			
Bottom round, all lean, roasted, boneless	3 oz	144	24
Filet mignon, lean, broiled	3 oz	164	24
Flank steak, lean, braised	3 oz	201	24
Ground patty, 10% fat, raw	4 oz	199	23
Ground, extra lean, raw (5% fat)	4 oz	155	24
Hot dog, beef, fat-free	1 frank	62	7
Roast beef, lunchmeat, medium-rare	1 oz	30	6
Steak, top sirloin, lean, broiled	3 oz	160	26
PORK			
Bacon, medium slice, cooked	1 slice	43	3
Canadian bacon, grilled	1 slice	43	6
Chop, center lean, with bone, braised	3 oz	172	25
Chop, sirloin, lean, with bone, braised	1 chop	142	19
Ground, cooked	3 oz	252	22
Ham, low-sodium, 96% fat-free, roasted, boneless	1 oz	47	6
Hot dog, pork	1 frank	204	10
Ribs, country-style, lean, braised	3 oz	199	22

CARB (G)	FIBER (G)	SUGAR (G)	FAT (G)	SAT FAT (G)	SODIUM (MG)
11	0	0	0	0	0
12	1	0	0	0	2

CARB (G)	FIBER (G)	SUGAR (G)	FAT (G)	SAT FAT (G)	SODIUM (MG)
0	0	0	5	2	32
0	0	0	7	3	50
0	0	0	11	5	61
0	0	0	11	5	75
0	0	0	6	3	75
3	0	0	1	0	455
1	0	1	1	1	235
0	0	0	6	2	54
0	0	0	3	1	185
0	0	0	2	1	363
0	0	0	7	3	53
0	0	0	6	2	38
0	0	0	18	7	62
0	0	0	2	1	275
0	0	0	18	7	620
0	0	0	12	4	54

Calorie &
Nutrient Counter

(continued)

✳ MEATS *(cont.)*

FOOD ITEM	SERVING SIZE	CALORIES	PROTEIN (G)
Sausage, pork, cooked	1 oz (1 each)	82	4
Tenderloin, roasted, lean	3 oz	139	24
VEAL			
Breast, braised, boneless, lean	3 oz	185	26
Ground, broiled	3 oz	146	21
Loin, roasted, lean	3 oz	149	22

✳ NUTS, SEEDS, AND BUTTERS

FOOD ITEM	SERVING SIZE	CALORIES	PROTEIN (G)
Almond butter, plain, with salt	1 Tbsp	101	2
Almonds, dry-roasted, with salt	½ oz (11 nuts)	85	3
Almonds, natural, sliced	½ oz	82	3
Brazil nuts, dried	1 nut	33	1
Brazil nuts, dried	½ oz (3 nuts)	93	2
Cashew butter, plain, with salt	1 Tbsp	94	3
Cashew nuts, dry-roasted, with salt	½ oz	81	2
Cashew nuts, raw	½ oz	78	3
Flaxseed, ground	1 Tbsp	37	1
Macadamia nuts, dry-roasted, with salt	½ oz (5–6 nuts)	101	1
Mixed nuts, dry-roasted, with peanuts, with salt	½ oz	84	2
Peanut butter, creamy, with salt	1 Tbsp	94	4
Peanut butter, with salt, reduced-fat	1 Tbsp	83	4
Peanut butter, crunchy, with salt	1 Tbsp	95	4
Peanut butter, natural	1 Tbsp	100	4

Calorie &
Nutrient Counter

CARB (G)	FIBER (G)	SUGAR (G)	FAT (G)	SAT FAT (G)	SODIUM (MG)
0	0	0	7.5	3	200
0	0	0	4	1	48
0	0	0	8	3	58
0	0	0	6	3	71
0	0	0	6	2	82

CARB (G)	FIBER (G)	SUGAR (G)	FAT (G)	SAT FAT (G)	SODIUM (MG)
3	1	1	9	1	72
3	2	1	7	1	48
3	2	1	7	1	0
1	0	0	3	1	0
2	1	0	9	2	0
4	0	1	8	2	98
5	0	1	7	1	91
4	1	1	6	1	2
2	2	0	3	0	2
2	1	1	11	2	38
4	1	1	7	1	95
3	1	1	8	2	73
6	1	1	5	1	86
3	1	1	8	1	78
4	1	1	8	1	60

(continued)

❋ NUTS, SEEDS, AND BUTTERS *(cont.)*

FOOD ITEM	SERVING SIZE	CALORIES	PROTEIN (G)
Peanuts, dry-roasted, with salt	½ oz	83	3
Peanuts, shelled, cooked, with salt	1 Tbsp	36	2
Pecans, dried, chopped	⅛ cup	94	1
Pecans, dried, halved	⅛ cup	86	1
Pecans, dry-roasted, with salt	½ oz	101	1
Pistachios, dry-roasted, with salt	½ oz	81	3
Walnuts, dried, black	1 Tbsp	48	2
Walnuts, dried, halved	½ oz	93	2
Walnuts, English, ground	⅛ cup	65	2

❋ PASTA

FOOD ITEM	SERVING SIZE	CALORIES	PROTEIN (G)
Angel hair, whole wheat, dry	1 oz	106	4
Bow ties, semolina, dry	1 oz	103	4
Fettuccine (tagliatelle), semolina, dry	1 oz	102	4
Fettuccine (tagliatelle), spinach, dry	1 oz	98	4
Lasagna, semolina, dry	1 oz	102	4
Linguine, semolina, dry	1 oz	102	4

CARB (G)	FIBER (G)	SUGAR (G)	FAT (G)	SAT FAT (G)	SODIUM (MG)
3	1	1	7	1	115
2	1	0	2.5	0.5	84
2	1	1	10	0	0
2	1	1	9	1	0
2	1	1	11	1	54
4	2	1	7	1	57
1	1	0	5	0	0
2	1	0	9	0	0
1	1	0	7	1	0

CARB (G)	FIBER (G)	SUGAR (G)	FAT (G)	SAT FAT (G)	SODIUM (MG)
21	3	1	1	0	5
21	1	1	0	0	1
21	1	1	1	0	2
20	1	1	1	0	9
21	1	1	1	0	1
21	1	1	1	0	2

(continued)

✱ PASTA *(cont.)*

FOOD ITEM	SERVING SIZE	CALORIES	PROTEIN (G)
Penne, semolina, dry	1 oz	106	4
Penne, whole wheat, dry	1 oz	106	4
Spaghetti, whole wheat, dry	1 oz	99	4

Note: For most pasta shapes, 1 ounce of dry pasta makes approximately ½ cup cooked.

✱ POULTRY

FOOD ITEM	SERVING SIZE	CALORIES	PROTEIN (G)
CHICKEN			
Chicken, breast, boneless, without skin, roasted	½ breast	143	27
Chicken, drumstick, without skin, roasted	1 drumstick	181	26
Chicken, thigh, boneless, without skin, roasted	1 thigh	109	13
Chicken frankfurter	1 frank	116	6
Chicken lunchmeat, deli	1 oz	23	5
TURKEY			
Turkey, breast, without skin, roasted	3 oz	133	25
Turkey, dark meat, without skin, roasted	3 oz	135	25
Turkey, dark meat, with skin, roasted	3 oz	144	24
Turkey, ground, breast, 99% fat-free, cooked	3 oz	120	28
Turkey, light meat, with skin, roasted	1 lb	134	19
Turkey frankfurter	1	102	6
Turkey sausage, smoked, hot	1 oz	44	4

CARB (G)	FIBER (G)	SUGAR (G)	FAT (G)	SAT FAT (G)	SODIUM (MG)
22	1	1	0.5	0	3
21	3	1	1	0	5
21	4	1	0.5	0	2

CARB (G)	FIBER (G)	SUGAR (G)	FAT (G)	SAT FAT (G)	SODIUM (MG)
0	0	0	3	1	77
0	0	0	8	2	86
0	0	0	6	2	46
3	0	0	9	2	616
0	0	0	0	0	210
0	0	0	3	1	54
0	0	0	3	1	69
0	0	0	5	1	68
0	0	0	2	0	65
0	0	0	6	2	43
1	0	0	8	3	642
1	0	1	2	1	260

SEAFOOD

FOOD ITEM	SERVING SIZE	CALORIES	PROTEIN (G)
Crab, Alaskan, king crab, steamed	3 oz	82	16
Crab, baked or broiled	3 oz	117	16
Crab, imitation (surimi)	3 oz	81	6
Crab, sautéed	3 oz	117	16
Lobster, Northern steamed	3 oz	83	17
Shrimp, cooked	3 oz	84	17
Shrimp, steamed	1 large	5	1

VEGETABLES

FOOD ITEM	SERVING SIZE	CALORIES	PROTEIN (G)
Alfalfa sprouts	½ cup	4	1
Artichoke	1 medium	60	4
Asparagus, cooked	8 spears	26	3
Bell pepper, chopped	1 cup	30	1
Bell pepper, boiled	1 cup	38	1
Broccoli, chopped, boiled	1 cup	55	4
Broccoli, florets, fresh	1 cup	20	2
Brussels sprouts, raw	1 cup	38	3
Cabbage, raw	1 medium leaf	6	0
Carrot	1 medium	25	1
Carrot, baby	1 medium	4	0
Cauliflower	¼ medium head	36	3
Celery	1 medium stalk	6	0
Celery, chopped	1 cup	16	1

CARB (G)	FIBER (G)	SUGAR (G)	FAT (G)	SAT FAT (G)	SODIUM (MG)
0	0	0	1	0	911
0	0	0	5.5	1	270
13	0	5	0	0	715
0	0	0	5	1	270
1	0	0	1	0	323
0	0	0	1	0	190
0	0	0	0	0	12

CARB (G)	FIBER (G)	SUGAR (G)	FAT (G)	SAT FAT (G)	SODIUM (MG)
0	0	0	0	0	1
13	7	1	0	0	397
5	2	2	0	0	17
7	3	4	0	0	4
9	2	3	0	0	3
11	5	2	1	0	64
4	2	0	0	0	19
8	3	2	0	0	22
1	1	1	0	0	4
6	2	3	0	0	42
1	0	0	0	0	8
8	4	4	0	0	43
1	1	1	0	0	32
3	2	2	0	0	81

(continued)

✳ VEGETABLES *(cont.)*

FOOD ITEM	SERVING SIZE	CALORIES	PROTEIN (G)
Cherry tomatoes, red	1 cup	27	1
Corn, sweet white or yellow	½ cup	66	2
Corn, sweet white or yellow	1 large ear	123	5
Cucumber with peel, raw	1 (8¼")	45	2
Garlic	1 clove	4	0
Green beans, snap, raw	1 cup	34	2
Green beans, with almonds, frozen, Green Giant	1 cup	91	3
Lettuce, iceberg	5 large leaves	10	1
Lettuce, romaine	4 leaves	19	1
Mushrooms, brown Italian	5	27	3
Onion, green (scallions), tops and bulbs, chopped	½ cup	16	1
Onion, red or yellow	1 medium	44	1
Peas, green, raw	½ cup	59	4
Peas, snow, whole, raw	½ cup	13	1
Potato, baked, with skin, without salt	1 medium	161	4
Sauerkraut, canned, low-sodium	1 cup	31	1
Spinach	3 oz	20	2
Spinach, cooked, with salt	1 cup	41	5
Spinach, cooked, without salt	1 cup	41	5
Squash, summer	1 medium	31	2
Sweet potato, baked, with skin, without salt	1 small	54	1
Tomato, red	1 medium	22	1
Zucchini, with skin, raw	1 medium	31	2

CARB (G)	FIBER (G)	SUGAR (G)	FAT (G)	SAT FAT (G)	SODIUM (MG)
6	2	4	0	0	7
15	2	2	1	0	12
27	4	5	2	0	21
11	2	5	0	0	6
1	0	0	0	0	1
8	4	2	0	0	7
8	3	3	4.5	0	144
2	1	1	0	0	8
4	2	1	0	0	9
4	1	2	0	0	6
4	1	1	0	0	8
10	2	5	0	0	4
10	4	4	0	0	4
2	1	1	0	0	1
37	4	2	0	0	17
6	4	3	0	0	437
3	2	0	0	0	67
7	4	1	0	0	551
7	4	1	0	0	126
7	2	4	0	0	4
12	2	4	0	0	22
5	1	3	0	0	0
7	2	3	0	0	20

Photo Credits

Cover photography: © Mitch Mandel

Recipe photography: © Mitch Mandel; food styling by Christine Langfeld; prop styling by Paige Hicks

All other photography © Mitch Mandel, with the following exceptions:

© Getty Images: Pages 3 (far left & far right), 5 (top center & bottom right), 6, 9, 14 (bottom left & right), 22, 26, 30, 33, 34, 38, 47

© Robert Gerheart: Page 5 (center right)

© Thomas MacDonald: Pages 12 (far left), 49 (bottom center)

© Kurt Wilson: Page 12 (2nd from right)

© Maren Caruso: Page 13

© Image Source: Pages 14 (left, 2nd from top), 49 (top right)

© Photodisc: Pages 14 (right, 2nd from top), 49 (bottom right)

© Stockbyte: Page 18

© Veer: Page 35

© Dirk Anschütz: Page 36

© Photo Alto: Page 43

© Alamy: Page 48 (left)

© Alex Martinez: Page 100

© Melanie Grizzel: Page 142

© Anna Knott: Page 178

© Taghi Naderzad: Page 246

© Karen Pearson: Page 322

Courtesy photos: Pages 101, 143, 179, 247, 323

Index

Underscored page references indicate boxed text. **Boldfaced** page references indicate photographs.

Conversion Chart

These equivalents have been slightly rounded to make measuring easier.

VOLUME MEASUREMENTS		
U.S.	IMPERIAL	METRIC
¼ tsp	–	1 ml
½ tsp	–	2 ml
1 tsp	–	5 ml
1 Tbsp	–	15 ml
2 Tbsp (1 oz)	1 fl oz	30 ml
¼ cup (2 oz)	2 fl oz	60 ml
⅓ cup (3 oz)	3 fl oz	80 ml
½ cup (4 oz)	4 fl oz	120 ml
⅔ cup (5 oz)	5 fl oz	160 ml
¾ cup (6 oz)	6 fl oz	180 ml
1 cup (8 oz)	8 fl oz	240 ml

WEIGHT MEASUREMENTS	
U.S.	METRIC
1 oz	30 g
2 oz	60 g
4 oz (¼ lb)	115 g
5 oz (⅓ lb)	145 g
6 oz	170 g
7 oz	200 g
8 oz (½ lb)	230 g
10 oz	285 g
12 oz (¾ lb)	340 g
14 oz	400 g
16 oz (1 lb)	455 g
2.2 lb	1 kg

LENGTH MEASUREMENTS	
U.S.	METRIC
¼"	0.6 cm
½"	1.25 cm
1"	2.5 cm
2"	5 cm
4"	11 cm
6"	15 cm
8"	20 cm
10"	25 cm
12" (1')	30 cm
2.2 lb	1 kg

PAN SIZES	
U.S.	METRIC
8" cake pan	20 × 4 cm sandwich or cake tin
9" cake pan	23 × 3.5 cm sandwich or cake tin
11" × 7" baking pan	28 × 18 cm baking tin
13" × 9" baking pan	32.5 × 23 cm baking tin
15" × 10" baking pan	38 × 25.5 cm baking tin
	(Swiss roll tin)
1½ qt baking dish	1.5 liter baking dish
2 qt baking dish	2 liter baking dish
2 qt rectangular baking dish	30 × 19 cm baking dish
9" pie plate	22 × 4 or 23 × 4 cm pie plate
7" or 8" springform pan	18 or 20 cm springform or
	loose-bottom cake tin
9" × 5" loaf pan	23 × 13 cm or 2 lb narrow
	loaf tin or pâté tin

TEMPERATURES		
FAHRENHEIT	CENTIGRADE	GAS
140°	60°	–
160°	70°	–
180°	80°	–
225°	105°	¼
250°	120°	½
275°	135°	1
300°	150°	2
325°	160°	3
350°	180°	4
375°	190°	5
400°	200°	6
425°	220°	7
450°	230°	8
475°	245°	9
500°	260°	–